Population
Opposing Viewpoints®

Other Books of Related Interest in the Opposing
Viewpoints Series:

Population
Opposing Viewpoints ®

David Bender & Bruno Leone, *Series Editors*

Charles F. Hohm, Department of Sociology,
 San Diego State University, *Book Editor*
Lori Justine Jones, San Diego State University,
 Assistant Editor

OPPOSING
VIEWPOINTS
SERIES®

Greenhaven Press, Inc., San Diego, CA

Greenhaven Press, Inc.
PO Box 289009
San Diego, CA 92198-9009

Cover photo: Owen McGoldrick/ Wideworld

Library of Congress Cataloging-in-Publication Data

Population : opposing viewpoints / Charles F. Hohm, book editor,
  Lori J. Jones, assistant editor.
     p.   cm. — (Opposing viewpoints series)
  Includes bibliographical references and index.
  Summary: Considers opposing opinions on various issues concerning world population including problems of rapid growth, the effects of population on the environment, and ways of decreasing human fertility.
  ISBN 1-56510-215-0 (lib. : acid-free paper) — ISBN 1-56510-214-2 (pbk. : acid-free paper).
  1. Population. [1. Population.] I. Hohm, Charles F., 1947–   .
II. Jones, Lori J., 1961–   . III. Series: Opposing viewpoints series (Unnumbered)
HB883.P67   1995
304.6—dc20   94-41042
                                                                    CIP
                                                                     AC

"Congress shall make no law . . . abridging the freedom of speech, or of the press."

First Amendment to the U.S. Constitution

The basic foundation of our democracy is the First Amendment guarantee of freedom of expression. The Opposing Viewpoints Series is dedicated to the concept of this basic freedom and the idea that it is more important to practice it than to enshrine it.

Contents

Why Consider Opposing Viewpoints?

> *"The only way in which a human being can make some approach to knowing the whole of a subject is by hearing what can be said about it by persons of every variety of opinion and studying all modes in which it can be looked at by every character of mind. No wise man ever acquired his wisdom in any mode but this."*
>
> John Stuart Mill

In our media-intensive culture it is not difficult to find differing opinions. Thousands of newspapers and magazines and dozens of radio and television talk shows resound with differing points of view. The difficulty lies in deciding which opinion to agree with and which "experts" seem the most credible. The more inundated we become with differing opinions and claims, the more essential it is to hone critical reading and thinking skills to evaluate these ideas. Opposing Viewpoints books address this problem directly by presenting stimulating debates that can be used to enhance and teach these skills. The varied opinions contained in each book examine many different aspects of a single issue. While examining these conveniently edited opposing views, readers can develop critical thinking skills such as the ability to compare and contrast authors' credibility, facts, argumentation styles, use of persuasive techniques, and other stylistic tools. In short, the Opposing Viewpoints Series is an ideal way to attain the higher-level thinking and reading skills so essential in a culture of diverse and contradictory opinions.

In addition to providing a tool for critical thinking, Opposing Viewpoints books challenge readers to question their own strongly held opinions and assumptions. Most people form their opinions on the basis of upbringing, peer pressure, and personal, cultural, or professional bias. By reading carefully balanced opposing views, readers must directly confront new ideas as well as the opinions of those with whom they disagree. This is not to simplistically argue that everyone who reads opposing views will—or should—change his or her opinion. Instead, the series enhances readers' depth of understanding of their own views by encouraging confrontation with opposing ideas. Careful examination of others' views can lead to the readers' understanding of the logical inconsistencies in their own opinions, perspective on why they hold an opinion, and the consideration of the possibility that their opinion requires further evaluation.

Evaluating Other Opinions

To ensure that this type of examination occurs, Opposing Viewpoints books present all types of opinions. Prominent spokespeople on different sides of each issue as well as well-known professionals from many disciplines challenge the reader. An additional goal of the series is to provide a forum for other, less known, or even unpopular viewpoints. The opinion of an ordinary person who has had to make the decision to cut off life support from a terminally ill relative, for example, may be just as valuable and provide just as much insight as a medical ethicist's professional opinion. The editors have two additional purposes in including these less known views. One, the editors encourage readers to respect others' opinions—even when not enhanced by professional credibility. It is only by reading or listening to and objectively evaluating others' ideas that one can determine whether they are worthy of consideration. Two, the inclusion of such viewpoints encourages the important critical thinking skill of objectively evaluating an author's credentials and bias. This evaluation will illuminate an author's reasons for taking a particular stance on an issue and will aid in readers' evaluation of the author's ideas.

As series editors of the Opposing Viewpoints Series, it is our hope that these books will give readers a deeper understanding of the issues debated and an appreciation of the complexity of even seemingly simple issues when good and honest people disagree. This awareness is particularly important in a democratic society such as ours in which people enter into public debate to determine the common good. Those with whom one disagrees should not be regarded as enemies but rather as people whose views deserve careful examination and may shed light on one's own.

Thomas Jefferson once said that "difference of opinion leads to inquiry, and inquiry to truth." Jefferson, a broadly educated man, argued that "if a nation expects to be ignorant and free . . . it expects what never was and never will be." As individuals and as a nation, it is imperative that we consider the opinions of others and examine them with skill and discernment. The Opposing Viewpoints Series is intended to help readers achieve this goal.

David L. Bender & Bruno Leone,
Series Editors

Introduction

*"The survival of mankind and of the earth . . .
are in serious jeopardy. . . . Continued growth in
the number of people . . . will inevitably increase
the substantial damage . . . already suffered."*

"A Call to Reason," signed by eighty-eight Nobel
laureates, The New York Times, *August 30, 1994*

*"By most serious measures, the world has done
pretty well while the population 'exploded.'"*

Ben Wattenberg, The Washington Times, *August 18, 1994*

"Population" is a topic that engenders much passion and debate. For centuries, scholars and authorities have argued whether population growth and density are necessary for economic prosperity—or whether population growth and density are responsible for such problems as hunger and poverty.

There are several major points of contention in the current debate on population. One is whether world population is growing too rapidly. No one disagrees that the population of *homo sapiens* on planet Earth has been increasing at a geometric rate. There is, however, varying opinion on whether this growth represents a problem; many agree with Julian Simon, who believes "the more, the merrier"—more people are an asset, not a liability. And even among those who view population growth as a problem, there is widespread variance in opinions on how to deal with it.

Convictions on both of these questions—whether population increase is a problem and, if so, how it should be dealt with—are often deeply rooted in a sense of affiliation with either the more developed or the less developed nations. Many of the developed nations are currently experiencing negative rates of population growth—their births are not sufficient to offset their deaths. While many of the less developed countries have also lowered their rates of growth, "about 90 percent [of the increase in world population] is taking place in the developing countries," according to Amartya Sen, economics and philosophy professor at Harvard University and president of the American Economic Association. Sen discerns a "self-regarding worry [that] causes panic in the richer countries of the world and has much to do with the current anxiety in the West about the 'world population problem.'. . . Many Northerners fear being engulfed by people from Asia and Africa, whose share of the world population . . . is expected . . . to rise to 78.5 percent by 2050 AD."

Others who see a problem in population growth focus on reduced living standards in less developed countries. Pat M. Holt, former chief of staff of the Senate Foreign Relations Committee, notes that while the world's population did not reach one billion until about 1800, now "another billion are being added every twelve years. This rate of growth cannot be sustained. The pressure of people on resources is already reducing living standards in much of the world and is causing environmental degradation that will lead to further declines."

Clearly, such different definitions of the "problem" will require different solutions. Proposed solutions to "the population problem" are widely diverse and often contradictory. Paradoxically, both those who see no overpopulation problem and many of those in the less developed nations who do see a problem call for an emphasis on "development." Those who see more people as an asset maintain that the asset cannot be realized until it is developed: To be productive citizens, people need food, education, and health care that many in poor countries do not receive. Many "Southerners"—those in less developed countries—also see in development a cure for overpopulation. When people feel secure economically and when they have faith that most of their children will survive childhood, these advocates say, they will feel less need to have many children.

On the other hand, many "Northerners"—those in more developed countries—call for Southern nations to adopt strong birth control policies first. Reduce fertility now, they urge; then, when there are fewer people, there will be more resources available for each person. The Programme of Action of the United Nations International Conference on Population and Development held in Cairo, Egypt, in September 1994, contained many suggestions for "family planning" options to be made available to everyone, including adolescents. Such suggestions, strongly supported by many of the developed nations, are often violently opposed by their supposed beneficiaries. They represent one aspect of a war, as *Christian Science Monitor* writer Howard LaFranchi put it, that "the wealthy North [is] waging against the ever-growing populations of the South." LaFranchi quotes Manuel Gómez Granados, spokesman for the Mexican

13

Institute for Social Christian Doctrine: "This is a form of war, like the cold war, only now the rich countries want to impose their concepts of family and what they consider a modern style of living on the poor countries. We must tell them we are not interested in their model."

The issue is not too many people in the South, according to Sylvia Marcos, a Mexican women's rights advocate; it is a question of distribution and consumption of resources. "A U.S. child will spend and consume so much more than a child born in Mexico. There's no comparison in the impact on the environment," she charges. Her conviction is echoed by Betsy Hartmann, director of the Hampshire College Population and Development Program in Amherst, Massachusetts. LaFranchi, quoting Hartmann, notes that "'even the UN blames the developing world's poor for most deforestation, which conveniently ignores reality.' If Southeast Asia's forests are disappearing, [Hartmann] says, it is largely to satisfy wealthy countries' desires for tropical woods."

That the controversies regarding population are deep-seated and heartfelt is obvious. Other population issues that raise similar passions include immigration, the status and rights of women, and AIDS. All of these issues and others are framed by the five major questions addressed in *Population: Opposing Viewpoints*: Historical Debate: Is There a Population Problem? Is the World's Population Growing Too Fast? Is Overpopulation Responsible for Hunger, Poverty, and Environmental Problems? What Are the Effects of Immigration into the United States? What Population Policies Should Be Pursued? The viewpoints presented in this volume provide a wide range of opinions on important aspects of population.

Historical Debate: Is There a Population Problem?

Population

Chapter Preface

In 1798 an English clergyman, Thomas Robert Malthus, wrote *An Essay on the Principle of Population*, postulating that population tends to grow much faster than the food supply and concluding that human misery will always result from this natural law. A pious scholar who had studied philosophy and economics as well as theology, Malthus wrote to refute the views of such contemporaries as William Godwin and the marquis de Condorcet, who promoted a rosier view of mankind's development. While his more optimistic colleagues tended to agree with Johann Peter Süssmilch ("the father of German demography") that population growth was a necessary precondition to economic and social prosperity, Malthus drew on the work of another English clergyman/scholar, Joseph Townsend, who felt that discouraging population growth was a necessary function of the state.

In a sense, the debate was between those who considered more people an asset and those who considered them a liability, or at least a burden. That debate took a political twist half a century after Malthus published his *Essay*, when Frederick Engels (best known as coauthor, with Karl Marx, of *The Communist Manifesto*) entered the fray. Engels argued that Malthus's theory of population had been contrived by capitalists to explain and rationalize poverty. Charging that the whole concept of overpopulation was a myth, Engels contended that reorganizing society on communist lines would end poverty.

A new element entered the debate in the mid-twentieth century, ushered in on a wave of extreme optimism about the ability of science to solve nearly every problem. J.H. Fremlin expresses this faith that science will come up with new food production and building techniques, as well as innovations not yet imagined, that will enable a sustainable population to expand almost indefinitely. "Neo-Malthusian" Garrett Hardin examines a representative argument of this faith—that mankind will, through science, be able to find space to continue to expand by migrating to other planets—and finds it lacking in logic.

The debates on population often are based on predictions—dire or rosy—about the effects of having more or fewer people on earth. The viewpoints in this chapter provide a historical perspective of the opening salvos of that debate.

> *"The Almighty will bless, protect, and maintain a people that obeys His command to multiply and populate the earth."*

The State Should Encourage Population Growth: Four Rules

Johann Peter Süssmilch

The work of German statistician/demographer Johann Peter Süssmilch (1707-67) is not well known to the English-speaking world, primarily because none of his books have been translated into English. Süssmilch was a first-rate thinker, however, and his major contribution to population studies was his extensive work on demography (the study of population)—the first such attempt in any language. The first edition of his book *The Divine Order in the Transformation of the Human Race as Demonstrated Through Birth, Death, and the Multiplication of the Same* was published in 1741. Süssmilch was very pro-natalist and thought that one of the primary duties of the state was to promote marriage and childbearing, following the rules he sets forth in this viewpoint.

As you read, consider the following questions:

1. What obstacles does Süssmilch say the state should try to remove so that citizens can marry at an early age?
2. What should the state do to enhance childbearing within marriage, according to the author?
3. Why does the author believe the state should try to keep its citizens from emigrating to other countries?

Excerpted from "Removing Obstacles to Population Growth" by Johann Peter Süssmilch, translated by Eileen Hennessy. Reprinted, with the permission of the Population Council, from *Population and Development Review*, vol. 9, no. 3, September 1983, pp. 521-29.

Rule 1: The State Should Remove
Obstacles Delaying or Preventing Marriage

A [State] must first combat all forcible hindrances to marriage and reproduction, insofar as it lies within [its] power, and to the extent permitted by Providence and the relations among empires in the world. A State must therefore not keep any person from marrying, be he minister, layman, or soldier. War is a fearful destroyer of marriages and the population. Can the [State] then sufficiently abominate it according to its deserts? The fight against the plague often rewards prudence with a successful outcome. Can any expense and effort then be spared in keeping this grave enemy and waster of countries from its borders? As plague and war can quickly plunder the fruits of many previous years and the increase of humankind, so on the contrary sound and peaceful ages are most advantageous to the population, if the sources are not obstructed by other causes. From the annual surplus of births in the Prussian lands, which in an average year amounts to 24,000, it is clearly evident that every year of peace is a new conquest.

We must then distinguish two mainstays in the performance of the great duty to replenish the population, which same must be brought to the greatest possible perfection. They are, the plough and the loom. Many people perhaps hear these two words with contempt, but they are the principal supports of the State and the sources of power and wealth. By the plough I mean the science of using the land and soil of a State in such manner that is most beneficial to the populace and, consequently, to power and wealth. It can easily be adjudged that much intelligence, experience, and effort are part of such science. By the loom I understand all types of labor usually included under the terms manufactures and works. Both things together occupy the hands and diligence of a Nation, and no country can exist and flourish without well-ordered diligence. The cultivation of the land takes precedence over all other things. It is and must be the basis for manufactures and commerce, because it provides the raw materials for processing, and hands must therefore serve it. It is thus a grave error if preference is given to manufactures over agriculture and if the former are operated to the prejudice of the latter. . . .

Rule 2: The State Should Eliminate
All Impediments to Marital Fertility

The fertility of marriages varies, being in some places seven or sometimes eight children for every two marriages, in some places and at some periods nine children. This difference is of great importance, and warrants full attention on the part of the State, since the extent and the speed of replenishment of the population are dependent thereon. . . .

The first and most important cause [of this difference] resides in the fact that in a heavily populated country most males marry late, and the women, including rural folk, also marry almost too late, often not before the age of 30, and many still later. The years most appropriate for procreation slip by, and instead of ten or more children such marriages produce barely four or five, particularly since peasant women nurse their infants for a long time. If more people can be enabled to marry, they will also marry sooner. When in a province five births per marriage can be counted, this is a sign that there are more, and earlier, marriages in that province than in one in which four or even three children are produced by each marriage. If more people are to enter into matrimony, at an earlier age, then sufficient encouragement and adequate maintenance must be provided. . . . Improvements in agriculture, manufactures, and commerce are also involved herein.

The Biblical Injunction

God said: "Let us make mankind in our image and likeness; and let them have dominion over the fish of the sea, the birds of the air, the cattle, over all the wild animals and every creature that crawls on the earth.". . . Then God blessed them and said to them: "Be fruitful and multiply; fill the earth and subdue it."

Holy Bible, King James Version, Genesis 1:26-29.

Fear of the dangers of childbirth has a great influence on marital fertility. The State should therefore seek to alleviate this fear, insofar as is possible, by good means of assistance. It would be wise to have a good and inexpensive school for the training of midwives in every State.

The unequal marriages between young men and women over 40, and between young maidens and decrepit elderly men, are against the intention of the Creator of Nature and against the primary goal of matrimony, and they represent a disadvantage for the State; so they should be forbidden, and not permitted without dispensation and payment of a contribution, in proportion to means, to the widows' or marriage fund.

Parents who have many children must be given substantial financial support by the State, particularly those parents who live in large cities and are in the employ of the State, and who are devoid of means because in the city sustenance and upbringing are more costly, a certain general outlay of money is unavoidable, the children cannot be clothed and brought up in the same way as farm children; impecunious civil servants are seldom able to set anything aside, those who have some money must expend their wealth when they have many children, and, lastly, the functionaries whom the State will continue to need will for the most part also be drawn from among the children of the citizens and inhabitants of the large cities. . . .

Luxury is an impediment to marital fertility and fertility in general, as well as to marriage. . . .

The long nursing of children is a great impediment to marital fertility, particularly in the countryside, as we have already noted. But can it be limited by law, especially when it is done out of fear of the danger of childbirth, and when adequate means of assistance for diminishing that danger have not been set up? Here again, the best remedy would be to extend the assistance given to parents of many children also in the countryside. A peasant who has six, eight, and more children increases not only the security of the State but also its revenues, certainly in proportion, more than the farmer who has few or no children. Beer and brandy must be obtained for baptisms and marriages, from cities that pay excise taxes; the more children there are, the more fabric, shoes, books, hats and so on will be needed. Such a father therefore contributes more to the treasury of the State, and hence he is more deserving of certain advantages than is another. The same sort of encouragements can easily be discovered for the peasant as well. . . .

Rule 3: The State Should Help Preserve the Lives of Its Citizens

Many, if not most, of [the lives of] people [who die prematurely] could be saved if the State were sufficiently watchful, if it controlled evil practices, if it allocated the necessary funds for medical science. . . . I should like to note my inability to understand why more heed is not paid to the science that has as its object the precious thing that is human life. Quite good and almost adequate institutions exist almost everywhere for the very necessary instruction and the development of the human spirit through truth. The necessary attention has also been paid to the practice of law in civil society. Individuals are maintained in both fields at the expense of the State. Only the maintenance of human life seems to me everywhere to have been ignored. Some steps are undertaken, but insufficiently and inadequately. Physicians are maintained for the poor in the cities, but only in the large cities. But what is one physician for a place that has 50,000 or 100,000 or more inhabitants? Physicians are appointed for entire districts, to which, however, they attend only when dangerous diseases appear among men or animals, or when a murder occurs and they must investigate the case and the causes of a death and give their opinion thereon. But how poorly are they compensated? And how can a renowned practitioner in a city attend to illnesses in villages that are often six and more miles away? Everything I have observed in establishments connected with human life is in question. Yet better provisions appear to be simple. Hitherto medical science and the physician appear to have devoted themselves almost exclusively to the wealthy, who are able to pay them for their effort. There are preachers everywhere. How easy and how inexpensive it would be to establish, in good locations at two-mile intervals, a preacher who also has some knowledge of medical science, with reasonable compensation! The best minds could be sought out for the purpose, and with slight effort they could be enabled to devote three years to medicine, with somewhat less attention paid to the learning of oriental languages and Greek, if these have not already been learned in school. . . .

Rule 4: The State Must Endeavour to Keep Its Subjects at Home and Attract Foreigners, If Necessary

Devising ways to keep people [from leaving for other countries] is an obligation. A native-born subject is in most cases and respects better than two colonists. He is habituated to the customs and the way of life, and during time of war the fatherland can command greater loyalty from him. The first thing, then, is indeed to reflect whether sustenance for more families might not be created through improvements in agriculture, manufactures, and commerce? Whether there are not defects in the existing distribution of farmland, and whether same could not be redressed? Whether the domains of the princes and the extensive holdings of the large landowners, nobles, monasteries, convents, and cities should not be divided and broken up and populated with more peasants? . . . When manufactures fail, the worker leaves the country for places where he hopes to find sustenance; when they recover, he returns, or foreigners come in. Thus great intelligence and undiminished reflection and study are needed in order to determine whether everything that could and should be done is in fact being done? Whether the needs of a country can be met by its own subjects, or whether families are being induced, through negligence, to seek their sustenance in foreign countries, with consequent support and promotion of the power and riches of those countries? The history of the kingdoms of the world provides us with remarkable examples of this. . . . Seville and Spain as a whole have lost through the collapse of the wool and silk manufactures and are still losing because of the continuing neglect, since they are obliged to purchase their primary needs and fabrics from England, Holland, France, and Italy, and even from the Germans, although the country has the raw materials and they are moreover of the best quality. . . .

When there is reasonable freedom, security, and justice in a country, where good morals and fashions prevail, where the arts and sciences flourish, where the government pays heed to increasing the means of subsistence and to creating various sources of food, the people can be secured against emigration and foreigners will certainly be moved to enter the country. And, what is at all times the most important thing, the Almighty will bless, protect, and maintain a people that obeys His command to multiply and populate the earth; all such a people does will be successful.

"Speculation apart, it is a fact, that in England, we have more than we can feed, and many more than we can profitably employ under the present system of our laws."

The State Should Discourage Population Growth

Joseph Townsend

The English Poor Laws that provided the public relief from the end of the 1500s well into the 1800s generated heated debate among intellectuals of the time, among them Joseph Townsend (1739-1816). Townsend was a man of many talents—physician, geologist, Methodist clergyman. His *Dissertation on the Poor Laws, By a Well-Wisher to Mankind* was published in 1786, twelve years before Thomas Malthus's famous *Essay on the Principle of Population*. Though Townsend's work is void of the moralizing that appears in Malthus's later work, it makes many of the same points. A principal point, which he makes in the following viewpoint, is that welfare destroys the motivation to succeed and leads to excess population and misery.

As you read, consider the following questions:

1. How are population levels dependent on the quality of the land, according to the author?
2. What three remedies does Townsend list for countries where population is pressing on the land's ability to produce? Which two does he call "natural" remedies?
3. How does giving resources to the poor encourage overpopulation, in Townsend's view?

Excerpted from Section 9 of Joseph Townsend's *Dissertation on the Poor Laws*, 1786. Reprinted, with the permission of the Population Council, from *Population and Development Review*, vol. 8, no. 3, September 1982, pp. 608-11.

On the subject of population we have had warm disputes, whilst some have lamented that our numbers are decreasing, and others with confidence have boasted that our population has rapidly advanced; all seeming to be agreed, that the wealth of a country consists in the number of its inhabitants. When industry and frugality keep pace with population, or rather when population is only the consequence of these, the strength and riches of a nation will bear proportion to the number of its citizens: but when the increase of people is unnatural and forced, when it arises only from a community of goods, it tends to poverty and weakness. In respect to population, some countries will reach their ne plus ultra [highest possible point] sooner, and some later, according as they surmount the obstacles which impede their progress. This period can be retarded by improvements in agriculture, by living harder or by working more, by extensive conquests or by increasing commerce.

People Are Dependent on the Land

The cultivation of rice in China enabled them to feed some millions of people, more than could have been maintained by any other grain; whereas in the highlands of Scotland, where neither rice nor yet wheat will grow, the inhabitants soon became a burthen to the soil. Their chief dependence for supporting the present population is on frugality, and constant, steady, unremitted labour, without any hope of being able to advance their numbers. Oatmeal and water, with a little milk, is their common food, and to procure this they work as long as they can see. They till the soil; they watch their cattle; and, at their leisure hours, they spin all the linen and the woollen which their families consume.

The Romans, even when they had lost their domestic industry and habits of economy, were able to feed their increasing citizens by tribute from the distant provinces, as the Spaniards do by purchasing provisions with the gold and silver of Peru. The Dutch have no other refuge but in good government, industry, and commerce, for which their situation is most favourable. Their pastures are rich, but not sufficient to maintain half the number of their inhabitants, who are employed and fed by every nation upon earth, but reside in Holland for the convenience of the water-carriage, the security of their persons, and the protection of their property.

Remedies for Excess Population

When a country is so far advanced in population as to be distressed for food; and when the forementioned resources have been exhausted, it has then reached its utmost limits; and in such a case, against increasing want there can be two remedies

Reprinted by permission of Chuck Asay and Creators Syndicate.

only which are natural, and one unnatural: for either none must marry, but they who can maintain a family, or else all who are in distress must emigrate. If these natural remedies are rejected, it can remain only for the poor to expose their children the moment they are born, which is the horrid practice adopted in the richest country upon earth [England] to preserve the community from famine. With regard to celibacy, we may observe, that where things are left to a course of nature, one passion regulates another, and the stronger appetite restrains the weaker. There is an appetite, which is and should be urgent, but which, if left to operate without restraint, would multiply the human species before provision could be made for their support. Some check, some balance is therefore absolutely needful, and hunger is the proper balance; hunger, not as directly felt, or feared by the individual for himself, but as foreseen and feared for his immediate offspring. Were it not for this the equilibrium would not be preserved so near as it is at present in the world, between the numbers of people and the quantity of food. Various are the circumstances to be observed in different nations, which tend to blunt the shafts of Cupid, or at least to quench the torch of Hymen. In many parts of Europe, we see multitudes of both sexes, not from policy, but from superstition and religious prejudice, bound by irrevocable vows of chastity. In other parts we hear of numbers who are compelled to spend their days in a seraglio, where it is not to be expected that all should be prolific; whilst in consequence of this unjustifiable practice, a corresponding number must pass through the world without leaving a representative behind them. But in every country, at least on this side of the Atlantic Ocean, we find a similar effect from prudence; and without the assistance of either a seraglio, or a convent, the younger branches of the best families have been left to wither. In every country, multitudes would marry, if they had a comfortable prospect for themselves, and for their children; but if all should listen to this call of nature, deaf to a louder call, the whole world in a few years would be distressed with famine. Yet, even in such a case, when it is impolitic that all should marry, this should be wholly left to every man's discretion, and to that balance of the appetites which nature has established. But if, notwithstanding the restraints of distress and poverty, they who are not able to maintain a family will yet marry, there can be no resource but in emigration. In the highlands of Scotland, when the inhabitants became a burthen to the soil, they tried every possible expedient; and, when all others failed, their young men with reluctance turned their back upon a country which was not able to support them. It is well known that their emigrations are considerable. They do not issue forth in assembled multitudes, like swarms from the northern hives of old; nor do they, like a torrent, overflow and desolate the adjacent countries; but, like the silent dew, they drop upon the richest pastures, and wandering to the remotest corners of the earth in quest of food, with the industry of bees they collect their honey from the most luxuriant flowers. These active, hardy, and laborious people, are to be found in the temperate, in the torrid, and in the frigid zones, in every island, and on every habitable mountain of Europe, Asia, Africa, and America. Yet in their native country, the numbers never fail: the supply is constant. Now, if, instead of collecting for themselves, wherever food is to be found, these wanderers had been equally supported on their barren mountains by contributions from the more fertile vallies of the South, can we imagine that the births in Scotland would be fewer than they are at present? The overflowings of their population might have been accelerated, but could not thereby have been retarded. Having no contributions from the South, they have quitted their country, and made room for others. We are told, upon the best authority, that in the highlands of Scotland, a woman will bring twenty children into the world, and rear only two. Had she sufficient food for more, more would live. The women there, like the women in all countries which are come to their utmost height of population, are more prolific than the soil. To provide more food on their bleak and barren mountains, is beyond a question. But if now, to rear these twenty children, a poor's rate were to be collected in more fertile countries, yet in countries which are fully peopled in proportion to their labour, and to the produce of the soil, is it not evident, that the scarcity and distress would only be transferred, and that the children of the South must die, that the children of the North might live? But, supposing these should live; yet at best they could only take the place of those that died, and more women in the North would increase and multiply, till they felt the same degree of pressure which they feel at present. Neither Switzerland nor the coast of Africa, are depopulated by emigrations, because the quantity of food in each remains unaltered. It is with the human species as with all other articles of trade without a premium; the demand will regulate the market.

Giving Resources to the Poor Encourages Overpopulation

By establishing a community of goods, rather by giving to the idle and to the vicious, the *first* claim upon the produce of the earth, many of the more prudent, careful, and industrious citizens are straitened in their circumstances, and restrained from marriage. The farmer breeds only from the best of all his cattle; but our laws choose rather to preserve the worst, and seem to be anxious lest the breed should fail! The cry is, Population, population! population, at all events! But is there any reasonable fear of depopulation? We have seen that corn upon an average has been considerably cheaper since the commencement of the present [eighteenth] century, than it was for an equal term before; yet wages have been raised in the proportion of six to four, and the rent of land is doubled. May we not infer from hence, that the produce of the soil must have increased nearly in the same proportions. If we consider the improvements which have been made in agriculture, by clearing woods, inclosing wastes, draining morasses, laying the common fields in severalty, and making roads; by the introduction of clover, saintfoin [an herb grown for forage], turneps, and potatoes; by the breaking up of extensive downs; and by the superior skill of the present race in the management of all sorts of land, with respect to stocking, manuring, cropping, not forgetting their superior weight of capital to work with; we shall cease to wonder at this vast increase of produce. But is it possible that the produce should be thus increased, and not the people also who consume it? We need not desire any man to visit London, Norwich, Bath, Bristol, Hull, Liverpool, Leeds, Wakefield, Manchester, and Birmingham: we need not call upon him to view our mines of coal, copper, lead, iron, and tin, with all the new manufactures which depend on these; but let him, at least, count our flocks, and calculate the quantity of corn produced by recent improvements in our tillage; then let him ask himself if our population is increased.

Whilst food is to be had, there is no fear of wanting people. But should the population of a country get beyond the produce of the soil, and of the capital engaged in trade, how shall these people find employment? Whenever this shall be the case, the evil will increase, and the capital will go on constantly diminishing; like as in private life, when a gentleman breaks in upon his principal to pay the ordinary expences of his family. When a trading nation is obliged to spend more than the revenue which is derived from commerce, and not from accident, but as the effect of some abiding cause, exceeds continually the profit of its trade, without some substantial reformation, the ruin of that nation will be inevitable. Should the capital itself accumulate, the interest of money would be lowered, the demand for labour would increase, and the superlucration [excessive profit] on this increase of trade would continue to enlarge the capital. Speculation apart, it is a fact, that in England, we have more than we can feed, and many more than we can profitably employ under the present system of our laws.

"The power of population is indefinitely greater than the power in the earth to produce subsistence for man."

Overpopulation Is a Serious Problem

Thomas Robert Malthus

In the most famous work on population ever written, *An Essay on the Principle of Population* (1798), Thomas Robert Malthus (1766-1834) attacked the English Poor Laws as an ill-thought-out way to reduce poverty in England. In fact, he argued, public relief only results in stimulating population growth and making the situation worse. In the following viewpoint, Malthus states that two kinds of checks, positive and preventive, work to keep population from growing indefinitely. Late marriage was one of Malthus's preventive checks. It is interesting to note that Malthus practiced what he preached: This one-time country parson waited to get married until he was 39 (when he became a professor of history and political economy), and he limited himself to three children, only one of whom lived to maturity.

As you read, consider the following questions:

1. What are the mathematical growth rates of population and of food production, according to Malthus? What problems does he infer from these rates?
2. What "positive" checks to population growth does the author describe?
3. According to the author, what are the "preventive" checks to population growth?

Excerpted from Thomas Robert Malthus, "An Essay on the Principle of Population" (1798).

I have read some of the speculations on the perfectibility of man and of society with great pleasure. I have been warmed and delighted with the enchanting picture which they hold forth. I ardently wish for such happy improvements. But I see great, and, to my understanding, unconquerable difficulties in the way to them. These difficulties it is my present purpose to state, declaring, at the same time, that so far from exulting in them, as a cause of triumph over the friends of innovation, nothing would give me greater pleasure than to see them completely removed.

A New View of an Old Argument

The most important argument that I shall adduce is certainly not new. The principles on which it depends have been explained in part by David Hume, and more at large by Dr. Adam Smith. It has been advanced and applied to the present subject, though not with its proper weight, or in the most forcible point of view, by Mr. Alfred Russel Wallace, and it may probably have been stated by many writers that I have never met with. I should certainly therefore not think of advancing it again, though I mean to place it in a point of view in some degree different from any that I have hitherto seen, if it had ever been fairly and satisfactorily answered.

The cause of this neglect on the part of the advocates for the perfectibility of mankind is not easily accounted for. I cannot doubt the talents of such men as William Godwin and the marquis de Condorcet. I am unwilling to doubt their candour. To my understanding, and probably to that of most others, the difficulty appears insurmountable. Yet these men of acknowledged ability and penetration, scarcely deign to notice it, and hold on their course in such speculations, with unabated ardour and undiminished confidence. I have certainly no right to say that they purposely shut their eyes to such arguments. I ought rather to doubt the validity of them, when neglected by such men, however forcibly their truth may strike my own mind. Yet in this respect it must be acknowledged that we are all of us too prone to err. If I saw a glass of wine repeatedly presented to a man, and he took no notice of it, I should be apt to think that he was blind or uncivil. A juster philosophy might teach me rather to think that my eyes deceived me and that the offer was not really what I conceived it to be.

In entering upon the argument I must premise that I put out of the question, at present, all mere conjectures, that is, all suppositions, the probable realization of which cannot be inferred upon any just philosophical grounds. A writer may tell me that he thinks man will ultimately become an ostrich. I cannot properly contradict him. But before he can expect to bring any reasonable person over to his opinion, he ought to shew, that the necks of mankind have been gradually elongating, that the lips have grown harder and more prominent, that the legs and feet are daily altering their shape, and that the hair is beginning to change into stubs of feathers. And till the probability of so wonderful a conversion can be shewn, it is surely lost time and lost eloquence to expatiate on the happiness of man in such a state; to describe his powers, both of running and flying, to paint him in a condition where all narrow luxuries would be contemned, where he would be employed only in collecting the necessaries of life, and where, consequently, each man's share of labour would be light, and his portion of leisure ample.

Domestic Virtue and Happiness for All

A more simple-minded virtuous man, full of domestic affections, than Mr. Malthus could not be found in all England. . . . The desire of his heart and the aim of his work were that domestic virtue and happiness should be placed within the reach of all, as nature intended. He found, in his day, that a portion of the people were underfed; and that one consequence of this was a fearful mortality among infants; and another consequence, the growth of a recklessness among the destitute which caused infanticide, corruption of morals, and, at best, marriage between pauper boys and girls, while multitudes of respectable men and women, who paid rates instead of consuming them, were unmarried at forty, or never married at all. Prudence as to the time of marriage, and making due provision for it, was, one would think, a harmless enough recommendation under the circumstances.

Harriet Martineau (1831), quoted by D.V. Glass, ed., *Introduction to Malthus*, 1953.

I think I may fairly make two postulata.

First, That food is necessary to the existence of man.

Secondly, That the passion between the sexes is necessary and will remain nearly in its present state.

These two laws, ever since we have had any knowledge of mankind, appear to have been fixed laws of our nature, and, as we have not hitherto seen any alteration in them, we have no right to conclude that they will ever cease to be what they now are, without an immediate act of power in that Being who first arranged the system of the universe, and for the advantage of his creatures, still executes, according to fixed laws, all its various operations.

I do not know that any writer has supposed that on this earth man will ultimately be able to live without food. But Mr. Godwin has conjectured that the passion between the sexes may in time be extinguished. As, however, he calls this part of his work a deviation into the land of conjecture, I will not dwell longer upon it at present than to say that the best arguments for the perfectibility of man are drawn from a contemplation of the great progress that he has already made from the savage state and the difficulty of saying where he is to stop. But towards the extinction of the passion between the sexes, no progress whatever has hitherto been made. It appears to exist in as much force at present as it did two thousand or four thousand years ago. There are individual exceptions now as there always have been. But, as these exceptions do not appear to increase in number, it would surely be a very unphilosophical mode of arguing, to infer merely from the existence of an exception, that the exception would, in time, become the rule, and the rule the exception.

Assuming then, my postulata as granted, I say, that the power of population is indefinitely greater than the power in the earth to produce subsistence for man.

Population Growth Geometric; Food Supply, Arithmetic

Population, when unchecked, increases in a geometrical ratio. Subsistence increases only in an arithmetical ratio. A slight acquaintance with numbers will shew the immensity of the first power in comparison of the second.

By that law of our nature which makes food necessary to the life of man, the effects of these two unequal powers must be kept equal.

This implies a strong and constantly operating check on population from the difficulty of subsistence. This difficulty must fall some where and must necessarily be severely felt by a large portion of mankind.

Through the animal and vegetable kingdoms, nature has scattered the seeds of life abroad with the most profuse and liberal hand. She has been comparatively sparing in the room and the nourishment necessary to rear them. The germs of existence contained in this spot of earth, with ample food, and ample room to expand in, would fill millions of worlds in the course of a few thousand years. Necessity, that imperious all pervading law of nature, restrains them within the prescribed bounds. The race of plants, and the race of animals shrink under this great restrictive law. And the race of man cannot, by any efforts of reason, escape from it. Among plants and animals its effects are waste of seed, sickness, and premature death. Among mankind, misery and vice. . . .

Preventive and Positive Checks to Population Growth

A foresight of the difficulties attending the rearing of a family acts as a preventive check, and the actual distresses of some of the lower classes, by which they are disabled from giving the proper food and attention to their children, acts as a positive check to the natural increase of population.

England, as one of the most flourishing states of Europe, may be fairly taken for an example, and the observations made will apply with but little variation to any other country where the population increases slowly.

Preventive Checks in England

The preventive check appears to operate in some degree through all the ranks of society in England. There are some men, even in the highest rank, who are prevented from marrying by the idea of the expenses that they must retrench, and the fancied pleasures that they must deprive themselves of, on the supposition of having a family. These considerations are certainly trivial, but a preventive foresight of this kind has objects of much greater weight for its contemplation as we go lower.

A man of liberal education, but with an income only just sufficient to enable him to associate in the rank of gentlemen, must feel absolutely certain that if he marries and has a family he shall be obliged, if he mixes at all in society, to rank himself with moderate farmers and the lower class of tradesmen. The woman that a man of education would naturally make the object of his choice would be one brought up in the same tastes and sentiments with himself and used to the familiar intercourse of a society totally different from that to which she must be reduced by marriage. Can a man consent to place the object of his affection in a situation so discordant, probably, to her tastes and inclinations? Two or three steps of descent in society, particularly at this round of the ladder, where education ends and ignorance begins, will not be considered by the generality of people as a fancied and chimerical, but a real and essential evil. If society be held desirable, it surely must be free, equal, and reciprocal society, where benefits are conferred as well as received, and not such as the dependent finds with his patron or the poor with the rich.

These considerations undoubtedly prevent a great number in this rank of life from following the bent of their inclinations in an early attachment. Others, guided either by a stronger passion, or a weaker judgment, break through these restraints, and it would be hard indeed, if the gratification of so delightful a passion as virtuous love, did not, sometimes, more than counterbalance all its attendant evils. But I fear it must be owned, that the more general consequences of such marriages, are rather calculated to justify than to repress the forebodings of the prudent.

The sons of tradesmen and farmers are exhorted not to marry, and generally find it necessary to pursue this advice till they are settled in some business, or farm that may enable them to support a family. These events may not, perhaps, occur till they are far advanced in life. The scarcity of farms is a very general complaint in England. And the competition in every kind of business is so great that it is not possible that all should be successful.

The labourer who earns eighteen pence a day and lives with some degree of comfort as a single man, will hesitate a little before he divides that pittance among four or five, which seems to be but just sufficient for one. Harder fare and harder labour he would submit to for the sake of living with the woman that he loves, but he must feel conscious, if he thinks at all, that should he have a large family, and any ill luck whatever, no degree of frugality, no possible exertion of his manual strength could preserve him from the heart rending sensation of seeing his children starve, or of forfeiting his independence, and being obliged to the parish for their support. The love of independence is a sentiment that surely none would wish to be erased from the breast of man, though the parish law of England, it must be confessed, is a system of all others the most calculated gradually to weaken this sentiment, and in the end, may eradicate it completely.

The servants who live in gentlemen's families, have restraints that are yet stronger to break through in venturing upon marriage. They possess the necessaries, and even the comforts of life, almost in as great plenty as their masters. Their work is easy and their food luxurious compared with the class of labourers. And their sense of dependence is weakened by the conscious power of changing their masters, if they feel themselves offended. Thus comfortably situated at present, what are their prospects in marrying? Without knowledge or capital, either for business, or farming, and unused, and therefore unable to earn a subsistence by daily labour, their only refuge seems to be a miserable alehouse, which certainly offers no very enchanting prospect of a happy evening to their lives. By much the greater part, therefore, deterred by this uninviting view of their future situation, content themselves with remaining single where they are.

If this sketch of the state of society in England be near the truth, and I do not conceive that it is exaggerated, it will be allowed, that the preventive check to population in this country operates, though with varied force, through all the classes of the community. The same observation will hold true with regard to all old states. The effects, indeed, of these restraints upon marriage are but too conspicuous in the consequent vices that are produced in almost every part of the world, vices, that are continually involving both sexes in inextricable unhappiness.

Positive Checks in England

The positive check to population by which I mean the check that represses an increase which is already begun, is confined chiefly, though not perhaps solely, to the lowest orders of society. This check is not so obvious to common view as the other I have mentioned, and, to prove distinctly the force and extent of its operation would require, perhaps, more data than we are in possession of. But I believe it has been very generally remarked by those who have attended to bills of mortality that of the number of children who die annually, much too great a proportion belongs to those who may be supposed unable to give their offspring proper food and attention, exposed as they are occasionally to severe distress and confined, perhaps, to unwholesome habitations and hard labour. This mortality among the children of the poor has been constantly taken notice of in all towns. It certainly does not prevail in an equal degree in the country, but the subject has not hitherto received sufficient attention to enable any one to say that there are not more deaths in proportion among the children of the poor, even in the country, than among those of the middling and higher classes. Indeed, it seems difficult to suppose that a labourer's wife who has six children, and who is sometimes in absolute want of bread, should be able always to give them the food and attention necessary to support life.

"Is it necessary for me to give any more details of this vile and infamous doctrine [Malthus's population theory], this repulsive blasphemy against man and nature . . . ?"

Overpopulation Is a Myth

Frederick Engels

The work of Thomas Malthus generated a tremendous reaction, both positive and negative. Frederick Engels (1820-1895) responded to Malthus with as much force as anyone, and his conclusion was that Malthusian theory was very misguided. The following viewpoint is from Engels's *Outline of a Critique of Political Economy*, which was published in 1844. Engels asserts that Malthusian theory confuses means of subsistence with means of employment.

Engels was born in Prussia, the son of a textile manufacturer. Because of his revolutionary activities, he was forced to flee Prussia and settle in England. While in England, Engels wrote many books with Karl Marx, the most famous being *The Communist Manifesto*. Engels managed one of his father's factories in England, earning enough to support himself, Marx, and Marx's family.

As you read, consider the following questions:

1. Engels points out that Malthus's theory blames the poor for surplus population. What problem does Engels have with this?
2. What does Engels have to say about the way Malthus handled the concepts of "means of subsistence" and "means of employment"?
3. What are the author's views on the potential for improvements in food production?

Excerpted from Frederick Engels, "Outlines of a Critique of Political Economy" (1844), translated by Ronald L. Meek in *Marx and Engels on the Population Bomb*. New York: International Publishers, 1954.

Malthus, the originator of [the theory of population], asserts that population constantly exerts pressure on the means of subsistence; that as production is increased, population increases in the same proportion; and that the inherent tendency of population to multiply beyond the available means of subsistence is the cause of all poverty and all vice. For if there are too many people, then in one way or another they must be eliminated; they must die, either by violence or through starvation. When this has happened, however, a gap appears once more, and this is immediately filled by other propagators of population, so that the old poverty begins anew. Moreover, this is the case under all conditions—not only in the civilized but also in the natural state of man. The savages of New Holland, who live *one* to the square mile, suffer just as much from overpopulation as England. In short, if we want to be logical, we have to recognize *that the earth was already overpopulated when only one man existed.* Now the consequence of this theory is that since it is precisely the poor who constitute this surplus population, nothing ought to be done for them, except to make it as easy as possible for them to starve to death; to convince them that this state of affairs cannot be altered and that there is no salvation for their entire class other than that they should propagate as little as possible; or that if this is not practicable, it is at any rate better that a State institution for the painless killing of the children of the poor should be set up—as suggested by "Marcus," [pseudonym of an English author who published in 1858 a pamphlet entitled *On the Possibility of Limiting Populousness,* in which Malthus's theory was carried to an absurdity]—each working-class family being allowed two-and-a-half children, and the excess being painlessly destroyed. The giving of alms would be a crime, since it would encourage the growth of surplus population; but it would be very advantageous to make poverty a crime and the workhouse a corrective institution, as has already happened in England under the new "liberal" Poor Law. It is true, of course, that this theory does not accord at all well with the biblical teaching of the perfection of God and of his creation, but "it is a bad refutation which puts forward the Bible against the facts."

Means of Subsistence vs. Means of Employment

Is it necessary for me to give any more details of this vile and infamous doctrine, this repulsive blasphemy against man and nature, or to follow up its consequences any further? Here, brought before us at last, is the immorality of the economists in its highest form. What were all the wars and horrors of the monopoly system when compared with this theory? And it is precisely this theory which is the cornerstone of the liberal system of free trade, whose fall will bring the whole edifice down with it. For once competition has here been proved to be the cause of misery, poverty and crime, who will still dare to say a word in its defense? . . .

If Malthus had not taken such a one-sided view of the matter, he could not have missed seeing that surplus population or labor power is always bound up with surplus wealth, surplus capital and surplus landed property. Population is too great only when productive power in general is too great. The state of affairs in every overpopulated country, in particular England, from the time when Malthus wrote onwards, demonstrates this quite unmistakably. These were the facts which Malthus ought to have examined in their entirety, and whose examination ought to have led to the correct conclusion; instead, he picked out one of these facts, neglecting the others, and thus arrived at his own crazy conclusion. His second mistake was to confuse means of subsistence with means of employment. That population always presses against the means of employment, that the number of people who are propagated corresponds to the number who can be employed, in short, that the propagation of labor power has up to now been regulated by the law of competition and has therefore also been subject to periodical crises and fluctuations—all these are facts, the establishment of which stands to the credit of Malthus. But means of employment are not means of subsistence. The means of employment increase only as the final result of an increase of machine power and capital; whereas the means of subsistence increase as soon as there is any increase at all in productive power. Here a new contradiction in political economy comes to light. The demand of the economists is not a real demand, their consumption is an artificial consumption. For the economists, only those who can offer an equivalent for what they receive are real demanders, real consumers. If, however, it is a fact that every adult produces more than he can himself consume, that children are like trees, returning abundantly the expenditure laid out on them—and surely these are facts?—one would imagine that every worker ought to be able to produce far more than he needs, and that the community ought therefore to be glad to furnish him with everything that he requires; one would imagine that a large family would be a most desirable gift to the community. But the economists, with their crude outlook, know no other equivalent apart from that which is paid over to them in tangible hard cash. They are so firmly entangled in their contradictions that they are just as little concerned with the most striking facts as they are with the most scientific principles.

A Resolution of Malthus's Contradiction

We shall destroy the contradiction simply by resolving it. With the fusion of those interests which now conflict with one another, there will disappear the antithesis between surplus population in one place and surplus wealth in another, and also the wonderful phenomenon—more wonderful than all the wonders of all the religions put together—that a nation must starve to death from sheer wealth and abundance; and there will disappear too the crazy assertion that the earth does not possess the power to feed mankind. This assertion is the highest wisdom of Christian economics—and that our economics is essentially Christian I could have demonstrated from its every statement, from its every category, and shall in due time so demonstrate. The Malthusian theory is merely the economic expression of the religious dogma of the contradiction between spirit and nature, and of the corruption of both resulting from it. I hope I have shown the futility of this contradiction—which has long been resolved for religion and together with it—in the economic sphere also; moreover, I will not accept any defense of the Malthusian theory as competent which does not begin by explaining to me, on the basis of the theory itself, how a people can die of hunger from sheer abundance, and which does not bring this explanation into harmony with reason and the facts.

Marx on the Laws of Population

The laboring population therefore produces, along with the accumulation of capital produced by it, the means by which itself is made relatively superfluous, is turned into a relative surplus-population; and it does this to an always increasing extent. This is a law of population peculiar to the capitalist mode of production; and in fact every specific historic mode of production has its own special laws of population, historically valid within its limits alone. An abstract law of population exists for plants and animals only, and only insofar as man has not interfered with them.

Karl Marx, *Capital*, vol. 1, 1867.

The Malthusian theory, however, was an absolutely necessary transitional stage, which has taken us infinitely further forward. Thanks to this theory, as also thanks to economics in general, our attention has been drawn to the productive power of the soil and of humanity, so that now, having triumphed over this economic despair, we are forever secure from the fear of overpopulation. From this theory we derive the most powerful economic arguments in favor of a social reorganization; for even if Malthus were altogether right, it would still be necessary to carry out this reorganization immediately, since only this reorganization, only the enlightenment of the masses which it can bring with it, can make possible that moral restraint upon the instinct for reproduction which Malthus himself puts forward as the easiest and most effective countermeasure against overpopulation. Thanks to this theory we have come to recognize in the dependence of man upon competitive conditions his most complete degradation. It has shown us that in the last analysis private property has turned man into a commodity, whose production and consumption also depend only on demand; that the system of competition has thereby slaughtered, and is still slaughtering today, millions of people—all this we have seen, and all this impels us to do away with this degradation of humanity by doing away with private property, competition and conflicting interests.

Vast Improvements in Food Production Are Possible

However, in order to deprive the general fear of overpopulation of all foundation, let us return once again to the question of the relation of productive power to population. Malthus puts forward a calculation upon which his whole system is based. Population increases in geometrical progression—$1 + 2 + 4 + 8 + 16 + 32$, etc. The productive power of the land increases in arithmetical progression—$1 + 2 + 3 + 4 + 5 + 6$. The difference is obvious and horrifying—but is it correct? Where has it been proved that the productivity of the land increases in arithmetical progression? The area of land is limited—that is perfectly true. But the labor power to be employed on this area increases together with the population; and even if we assume that the increase of output associated with this increase of labor is not always proportionate to the latter, there still remains a third element—which the economists, however, never consider as important—namely, science, the progress of which is just as limitless and at least as rapid as that of population. For what great advances is the agriculture of this century obliged to chemistry alone—and indeed to two men alone, Sir Humphry Davy and Justus Liebig? But science increases at least as fast as population; the latter increases in proportion to the size of the previous generation, and science advances in proportion to the body of knowledge passed down to it by the previous generation, that is, in the most normal conditions it also grows in geometrical progression—and what is impossible for science? But it is ridiculous to speak of overpopulation while the valley of the Mississippi alone contains enough waste land to accommodate the whole population of Europe, while altogether only one-third of the earth can be described as cultivated, and while the productivity of this third could be increased sixfold and more merely by applying improvements which are already known.

"Though it is difficult to be quite certain, one could expect most people to be able to live and reproduce in the conditions considered."

Scientific Progress Will Solve the Population Problem

John H. Fremlin

John H. Fremlin is professor emeritus of applied radioactivity at the University of Birmingham, England. Fremlin's major research emphasis has been on the relative health risks of different energy sources. His book *Power Production: What Are the Risks?* deals with these concerns. In the following viewpoint, Fremlin postulates a series of stages in adapting the earth to population growth that would eventually allow the planet to sustain up to 10 quintillion (10^{18}) people.

As you read, consider the following questions:

1. What lifestyle changes would people have to make to accommodate the ever-increasing population densities envisioned in Fremlin's scenario?
2. Why doesn't Fremlin believe that food production for an ever-increasing world population is a problem?
3. What one factor does the author believe could force a limit on the absolute size of the world's population? How?

Abridged from J.H. Fremlin, "How Many People Can the World Support?" *New Scientist* 415 (1964):285-87. Reprinted with permission.

The world population is now about 3 billion and is increasing at a rate corresponding to a doubling in 37 years. In view of the increasing importance attached to the immediate effects of the rapid growth in human numbers, it is of interest to examine ultimate technical limits to this growth. Traditionally, these limits have usually been regarded as fixed by possible food supplies although, in practice, at least in historical times, the actual limiting factor has more often been disease.

Diseases are now nearly, and will soon be entirely, eliminated as effective controllers of population growth but it is not at all clear that difficulties in food production will take their place. It is true that there is a limit to the improvement of agricultural output by application of existing scientific knowledge, but by the time this limit is reached other methods of food-production will have been devised. I shall explore the possibility that the real limits are physical rather than biological.

I shall assume throughout an effective degree of world cooperation in the application of food technology, etc. This is quite evidently essential if the maximum world population is to be reached. There are of course many ways of *not* reaching the maximum, but none of these will be discussed here.

In order to give a time scale, it is supposed that the rate of increase of population remains constant at the present value—that is to say, doubling every 37 years. In fact the rate is itself accelerating, so that, in the absence of limitations, this time scale will be too long.

Stage 1: Up to 400 Billion in 260 Years

Using existing crop plants and methods it may not be practicable to produce adequate food for more than four doublings of the world population, though the complete elimination of all land wild-life, the agricultural use of roofs over cities and roads, the elimination of meat-eating and the efficient harvesting of sea food might allow two or three further doublings—say seven in all. That would give us, with the present doubling time of 37 years, 260 years to develop less conventional methods, and would allow the population of the world to increase to about 130 times its present size, or about 400 billion.

Stage 2: Up to 3 Trillion in 370 Years

The area of ice-free sea is some three times that of land. Photosynthesis by single-celled marine organisms may be more efficient than that of the best land plants. If organisms could be found capable of the theoretical maximum efficiency (8 percent of total solar radiation, according to A. A. Niciporovic), we should gain a factor of three in yield. We could then double our numbers a further three more times if all the wild-life in the sea, too, was removed and replaced by the most useful organisms growing under controlled conditions, with the optimum concentration of carbonates, nitrates and minerals. (Of course a reserve of specimens of potentially useful species could be preserved, perhaps in a dormant state.) Again, for maximum efficiency we must harvest and consume directly the primary photosynthesising organisms, rather than allow the loss of efficiency involved in the food-chains leading to such secondary organisms as zooplankton or fish.

By this stage, we should have had ten doublings, which at the present rate would take some 370 years, with a final world population of 3 trillion. Since the world's surface (land and sea) is 500 trillion square metres, each person would have a little over 160 square metres for his maintenance—about a thirtieth of an acre—which does not seem unreasonable by more than a factor of two, so long as no important human activity other than food production takes place on the surface.

No serious shortages of important elements need be envisaged so far, though extensive mining operations for phosphates might be needed, and we have not yet approached any real limit.

Stage 3: Up to 15 Trillion in 450 Years

At first sight, it seems that a very big leap forward could be taken if we use sources of power other than sunlight for photosynthesis. The solar power received at the Earth's surface is only about 1 kilowatt per square metre at the equator at midday, and the average value over the day and night sides of the globe is a quarter of this. Over half of it is in the regions of the spectrum of no use for photosynthesis.

About 1 kilowatt-year per square metre could be produced by the complete fission of the uranium and thorium in about 3 cm depth of the Earth's crust or by fusion of the deuterium in about 3 mm depth of seawater, so that adequate power should be available for some time. It is, however, difficult to see how the overall thermal efficiency from fuel to the light actually used for photosynthesis could be even as good as the ratio of useful to non-useful solar radiation (about 40 percent).

It would, therefore, be better to use large satellite reflectors in orbit to give extra sunlight to the poles and to the night side of the Earth. A large number of mirrors could be maintained in quasi-stable orbits about 1½ million kilometres outside the Earth's orbit, any deviations being controlled by movable "sails" using the pressure of sunlight. To double our total radiation income would require a total area of about 100 million square kilometres of mirror which, in aluminium a tenth of a micron thick, would weigh about 30 million tons. With plenty of people to design and make the equipment it should not be difficult by the time it would be required, and it would bring the whole Earth to equatorial conditions, melting the polar ice and allowing one further doubling of population.

A second doubling of radiation income would give the whole Earth midday equatorial conditions round the clock, which would be exceedingly difficult to cope with without serious overheating. The overall efficiency of local power sources for photosynthesis is likely to be less than that of sunlight, so that no real gain in ultimate population size can be expected from their use, without an even more serious overheating of the entire globe.

Quality vs. Quantity of Life

If we were willing to be crowded together closely enough, to eat foods which would bear little resemblance to the foods we eat today, and to be deprived of simple but satisfying luxuries such as fireplaces, gardens and lawns, a world population of 50 billion persons would not be out of the question. And if we really put our minds to the problem we could construct floating islands where people might live and where algae farms could function, and perhaps 100 billion persons could be provided for. If we set strict limits to physical activities so that caloric requirements could be kept at very low levels, perhaps we could provide for 200 billion persons.

Harrison Brown in Garrett Hardin, ed., *Population, Evolution, and Birth Control: A Collage of Controversial Ideas*, 2nd ed., 1969.

If, however, the mirrors outside the Earth's orbit were made of selectively reflecting material, reflecting only the most useful part of the spectrum, and if a further satellite filter were used, inside the Earth's orbit, to deflect the useless 60 percent of direct solar radiation, a further gain of a factor of 2½ should easily be possible without creating thermally impossible conditions, at the cost only of perhaps a 10-100 times increase of weight of mirror plus filter—not difficult for the larger population with an extra 50 years of technical development. We should then have attained a world population of 15 trillion about 450 years from now.

Stage 4: Up to 1 Quadrillion in 680 Years

A considerably larger gain is in principle obtainable if the essential bulk foods: fats, carbohydrates, amino acids and so on, could be directly synthesised. Biological methods might still be permitted for a few special trace compounds. The direct rate of energy production resulting from the conversion of our food into our waste products is only about 100 watts per person and, if high-temperature energy from nuclear fuel (or sunlight) could be efficiently used, waste products could in principle be changed back into food compounds with the absorption of little more energy. Cadavers could be homogenised and would not, at least for physical reasons, need to be chemically treated at all. The fresh mineral material which would have to be processed to allow for population growth would be much less than 1 percent of the turnover, and its energy requirements can be neglected.

If we suppose that the overall efficiency could not be increased beyond 50 percent, a further 100 watts per person would be dissipated as heat in the process of feeding him. We have some hundreds of years to work up the efficiency to this value, so at least this ought to be possible. Some further power would be needed for light, operation of circulation machinery, communications etc., but 50 watts per person should suffice.

As we have seen, the long-term average heat income of the Earth's surface is at present about 250 watts per square metre, and this could be doubled without raising the temperature above the normal equatorial value. (The initial rate of rise would be low till the polar ice had gone, which might take 100 years.) We thus have 500 watts per head, could support 1 quadrillion people altogether. The population density would be 2 per square metre, averaged over the entire land and sea surface of the Earth.

Stage 4a: Up to 12 Quadrillion in 800 Years: Dead End

Above 2 people per square metre, severe refrigeration problems occur. If the oceans were used as a heat sink, their mean temperature would have to rise about 1°C per year to absorb 500 watts per square metre. This would be all right for the doubling time of 37 years, at the end of which we should have 4 people per square metre. Half another doubling time could be gained if efficient heat pumps (which, for reasons of thermal efficiency, would require primary energy sources of very high temperature) could be used to bring the ocean to the boil.

Two more doublings would be permitted if the oceans were converted into steam, though that would create an atmospheric pressure comparable with the mean ocean bottom pressure at present. Since the resulting steam blanket would also be effectively opaque to all radiation, no further heat sink could be organised and this procedure would therefore seem to lead to a dead end.

Stage 5: Up to 60 Quadrillion in 890 Years

A preferable scheme would be the opposite one of roofing in the ocean to stop evaporation (this would, in any case, probably have been done long before, for housing) and hermetically sealing the outer surface of the planet. All of the atmosphere not required for ventilation of the living spaces could then be pumped into compression tanks, for which no great strength would be needed if they were located on ocean bottoms. Heat pumps could then be used to transfer heat to the solid outer skin, from which, in the absence of air, it would be radiated directly into space. The energy radiated from a black body goes up as T^4, where T is the absolute temperature (°K), but for a *fixed rate* of heat extraction from the living space, at a fixed temperature (say, 30°C or 303°K), the heat-power *radiated* must for thermodynamic reasons be proportional to T even if the refrigeration equipment is perfectly efficient (see any good textbook on the principles of refrigeration). Hence the rate of heat extraction will go up no faster than T^3 where T is the outer surface temperature.

Other Possible Limitations

All the same, this gives more promising results than would the use of the ocean as a temporary heat sink. An outer skin temperature of 300°C would give a heat extraction of 3 kW per square metre and 1,000°C would give an extraction ten times greater. If heat removal were the sole limitation, then we could manage about 120 persons per square metre for an outer skin temperature of 1,000°C—which represents nearly six further doublings of population after the end of Stage 4, with a world population of 60 quadrillion in 890 years' time. 1,000°C may be a rather modest figure for the technology of A.D. 2854 and the population could, as far as heat is concerned, be able to double again for each rise of absolute skin temperature of $\sqrt[3]{2}$ or 26 percent. The difficulties in raising it much further while keeping all thermodynamic efficiencies high would, however, seem to be formidable. A rise to 2,000°C would give us less than three further doublings.

We seem, therefore, to have found one possible absolute limit to human population, due to the heat problem, which at the present rate would be reached 800-1,000 years from now, with a world population of 10^{16}-10^{18}. . . .

Other possible limitations than heat will doubtless have occurred to readers, but these do not seem to be absolute. The most obvious is perhaps the housing problem for 120 persons per square metre. We can safely assume, however, that in 900 years' time the construction of continuous 2,000-storey buildings over land and sea alike should be quite easy. That would give 7½ square metres of floor space for each person in 1,000 storeys (though wiring, piping, ducting and lifts [elevators] would take up to half of that) and leave the other 1,000 storeys for the food-producing and refrigerating machinery. It is clear that, even at much lower population densities, very little horizontal circulation of persons, heat or supplies could be tolerated and each area of a few kilometres square, with a population about equal to the present world population, would have to be nearly self-sufficient. Food would all be piped in liquid form and, of course, clothes would be unnecessary.

Raw materials should not be a problem. The whole of the oceans and at least the top 10 kilometres of the Earth's crust would be available, giving a wide choice of building, plumbing and machine-building materials. Even with 8 tons of people per square metre (reckoning 15 people to the ton) all the necessary elements of life could be obtained; some from air and sea (C, H, O, N, Na, Cl, Ca, K and some trace elements) and some from the top 100 metres of solid crust (Fe, S, P, I and remaining trace elements). Only after a further hundredfold increase in population would it be needful to go below the top 10 km of crust for some elements (N, S, P, I). Such an increase would need an outer skin temperature of 5,000°C (comparable with the surface of the Sun) to radiate away the body heat, which would seem to be well beyond the possible limits.

A question of obvious importance which is not easy to answer is whether people could in fact live the nearly sessile [permanently attached to a base] lives, with food and air piped in and wastes piped out, which would be essential. Occasional vertical and random horizontal low speed vehicular or moving-belt travel over a few hundred metres would be permissible, however, so that each individual could choose his friends out of some ten million people, giving adequate social variety, and of course communication by video-phone would be possible with anyone on the planet. One could expect some ten million Shakespeares and rather more Beatles to be alive at any one time, so that a good range of television entertainment should be available. Little heat-producing exercise could be tolerated. The extrapolation from the present life of a car-owning, flat-dwelling office-worker to such an existence might well be less than from that of the neolithic hunter to that of the aforesaid office-worker. Much more should be known about social conditioning in a few hundred years' time and, though it is difficult to be quite certain, one could expect most people to be able to live and reproduce in the conditions considered.

"Those who seriously propose interstellar migration as a solution to overpopulation . . . are unwilling to accept the necessity of consciously controlling population numbers. "

Scientific Progress Will Not Solve the Population Problem: The Case of Interstellar Migration

Garrett Hardin

Garrett Hardin is professor emeritus of human ecology at the University of California, Santa Barbara. During the last three decades, he has been one of the most productive and influential scholars calling for Zero Population Growth (births equaling deaths) on planet Earth. In the following viewpoint, Hardin argues that those who rely on scientific progress to solve the problems of overpopulation are simply unwilling to face facts. To illustrate, he projects the costs of interstellar migration as a solution to overpopulation, and finds the equations unworkable.

As you read, consider the following questions:

1. How much does Hardin estimate it would cost to send one person to a habitable planet 4.3 light-years away?
2. Hardin points out that it would take at least 350 years for humans to reach another habitable planet and that births would have to equal deaths during this 10-generation voyage. What paradoxes does he say that this represents?

Garrett Hardin, "Interstellar Migration and the Population Problem," *The Journal of Heredity* 50 (1959):68-70. Reprinted by permission of Oxford University Press.

Anyone who discusses population problems with lay audiences is, sooner or later, confronted with questions of this sort: "But why worry about overpopulation? Won't we soon be able to send our surplus population to other planets?" It is not only the audience that adopts this point of view; sometimes the lecturer does, as appears from an Associated Press dispatch of 6 June 1958. Monsignor Irving A. DeBlanc, director of the National Catholic Welfare Conference's Family Life Bureau, is reported as favoring such mass migration, "deploring an often expressed idea that birth control is the only answer to problems created by a fast-growing world population."

Neither physicists nor professional demographers have, so far as I know, recommended extra-terrestrial migration as a solution to the population problem, but the idea appears to be gaining ground among the laity even without scientific support. The psychological reasons for embracing this idea are two. On the one hand, some Roman Catholics welcome it because it appears to offer an escape from the dilemma created by the Church's stand against "artificial" methods of birth control. On the other hand, citizens of all churches worship the new religion called Progress, of which Jules Verne is the prophet. In this religion all things are possible (except acceptance of the impossible). Who is to set limits to Science (with a capital S)? Yesterday, the telephone and the radio; today television and ICBM's; and tomorrow,—Space!— which will solve all our earthly problems, of course.

This is heady stuff. Strictly speaking, since it springs from an essentially religious feeling and is non-rational, it cannot be answered by a rational argument. Nevertheless, for the sake of those bystanders whose minds are still open to a rational analysis it is worthwhile reviewing the facts and principles involved in the proposal to solve the population problem by interplanetary travel.

The Cost of Space Travel

It now [1959] seems possible that, before the century is out, manned landings may be made on Venus or Mars, with the establishment of temporary quarters thereon. But all evidence points to the unsuitability of these, or any other planets of our sun, as abodes for *Homo sapiens*. We must, therefore, look beyond the solar system, to other stars for possible planets for colonization.

The nearest star is Alpha Centauri, which is 4.3 light-years away. How long would it take us to get there? The rockets that we are now planning to send to the moon will have a maximum velocity in the neighborhood of 10 kilometers per second, or about 19,000 miles per hour. This may sound fast. But a body traveling at such a speed towards Alpha Centauri (which is 4.07×10^{13} kilometers distant) would require 129,000 years to reach its destination. Surely no one believes that a fleet of

**"... An Atmosphere That Could
Support Life ..."**

From *Herblock on All Fronts* (New American Library, 1980). Reprinted with permission.

spaceships with so long a transit time would solve our explosive population problem. The question is, then, what is the probability of improvements in space travel that would significantly cut down the time required to make such an interstellar journey? In trying to answer this question I have relied on an analysis by L. R. Shepherd [in L.J. Carter, ed., *Realities of Space Travel*, 1957], to which the interested reader is referred for technical details.

Shepherd presumes a technology in the release and utilization of nuclear energy that may take several centuries to achieve. To give the worshippers of Progress the maximum advantage we will assume that such an advanced technology is available *now*, and see how long it would take to travel to the nearest star. Using fantastically optimistic assumptions, Shepherd calculates that it might be possible to make the transit in a mere 350 years. The average speed of the trip would be about 7,000,000 m.p.h., though the maximum speed would be somewhat more, since 50 years would be required for acceleration at the beginning of the trip and another 50 years for deceleration at the end. (In passing, it should be noted that acceleration is more of a limiting factor than is velocity.)

The Economics of Interstellar Migration

To evaluate interstellar migration as a population control measure we must examine its economics. Here the unknowns are obviously great, but from data assembled by A. V. Cleaver [also in Carter, *Realities of Space Travel*] it appears that the foreseeable cost of a rocket ship could hardly be as little as $50 a pound, assuming economies of mass production and allowing nothing for research and development costs. How many pounds of ship would be required per man? Since we have no data on such a spaceship, let us borrow from our knowledge of atomic submarines, which are perhaps not too dissimilar. A spaceship designed to be self-maintaining for 350 years could hardly be less complicated or less bulky than an underwater craft capable of operating away from its depots for only a month or two. According to a news release the submarine *Seawolf* weighs 3,000 tons and carries 100 men, a burden of 60,000 lbs. per man. A spaceship of a similar design, at $50 a pound, would cost $3,000,000 per man travelling in it. Would this be a reasonable cost for solving the population problem? Those who propose such a solution presume, or even recommend, that we do not alter our present reproductive habits. What would it cost to keep the population of the United States fixed at its present level by shipping off the surplus in spaceships?

According to a recent estimate of the U. S. Bureau of the Census our population is increasing by about 3,000,000 people per year. To ship this increase off to other planets would, on the above conservative assumptions, cost about $9 trillion per year. The Gross National Product is now nearly $450 billion per year. In other words, to solve our national population problem by this means we would, then, have to spend 20 times as much as our entire income on this purpose alone, allowing nothing for any other use, not even for food. It would surely be unrealistic to suppose that we shall do this in the near future.

Another aspect of the population problem is worth commenting on. Many philanthropically minded citizens feel that it is an obligation of the United States to solve the population problems of the entire world, believing that we should use the riches produced by our technology to make up for the deficiencies in luck or foresight of other peoples. Let's examine the economics of so doing. According to a recent estimate the population of the world is increasing at a rate of 123,000 per day. To remove one day's increment by the postulated spaceship would cost about $369 billion. In other words, we Americans, by cutting our standard of living down to 18 percent of its present level, could in *one year's time* set aside enough capital to finance the exportation of *one day's increase* in the population of the entire world. Such a philanthropic desire to share the wealth may be judged noble in intent, but hardly in effect.

In passing, it should be noted that we have so far made no mention of certain assumptions that are of critical importance in the whole picture. We have assumed that our nearest star has planets; that at least one of these planets is suitable for human habitation; that this suitable planet is uninhabited—or, if inhabited, that the humanoids thereon will gracefully commit suicide when they find we need their planet for our *Lebensraum* [term used esp. by Nazis to denote territory required for political and economic expansion]. (The tender feelings that would make impossible the control of reproduction on earth would presumably not interfere with the destruction of life on other planets.) Should Alpha Centauri have no planet available for migratory earthlings, our expedition would presumably set out for an even more distant star, perhaps eventually becoming a latterday interstellar Flying Dutchman.

Paradoxes of Space Emigration

Cogent as the economic analysis of the problem is, it does not touch on issues that are of even greater importance. Consider the human situation on board this astronautical *Mayflower*. For 350 years the population would have to live under conditions of complete sociological stasis, the like of which has never been known before. No births would be permitted, except to replace the dead (whose substance would, of course, have to be returned to the common stores). Marriages would certainly have to be controlled, as would all other social interactions, and with an iron hand. In the spaceship, Progress would be unendurable. The social organization would have to persist unchanged for 10 generations' time, otherwise there would be the risk that some of the descendants of the original crew might wish to change the plans. It would be as though the spaceship had to set sail, so to speak, under Captain John Smith and arrive at its goal under

President Eisenhower, without the slightest change in ideas or ideals. Can we who have so recently seen how fragile and mutable a flower Education is suppose that we could set up so stable a system of indoctrination? Paradoxically, only a people who worship Progress would propose to launch such a craft, but such worshippers would be the worst possible passengers for it.

Those who seriously propose interstellar migration as a solution to overpopulation do so because they are unwilling to accept the necessity of consciously controlling population numbers by means already at hand. They are unwilling to live, or to admit living, in a closed universe. Yet—and here is the second paradox—that is precisely the sort of universe the interstellar migrants would be confined to, for some 10 generations. Since the present annual rate of growth of the world's population is about 1.7 percent, by the time the first ship arrived at its destination, the whole fleet of spaceships en route would enclose a total population six times as large as that still present on the earth. That is, in attempting to escape the necessities of living in a closed universe, we would confine to the closed universes of spaceships a population six times as great as that of the earth.

Moreover, there would be a differential element in the emigration from the mother planet. The proposal to emigrate is made by those who, for religious or other reasons, are unwilling to curb the reproductive proclivities of mankind. But not for such as these is the kingdom of a spaceship. They must stay behind while the ship is manned by those whose temperament creates no need for emigration. The reproductively prudent would be exiled from a world made unbearably crowded by the imprudent—who would stay home to perpetuate the problem into the next generation. Whether the difference between the two groups is basically biological, or merely sociological, would not matter. In either case, natural selection would enter in. The end result of this selective emigration would be to create an earth peopled only by men and women unwilling to control their breeding, and unwilling, therefore, to make use of the very means they propose to escape the consequences.

A Return to the Vision of Malthus

The proposal to eliminate overpopulation by resort to interstellar migration is thus seen to yield not a rational solution at all. The proposal is favored only by men who have more faith in gadgetry than they do in rationality. Should men of this temper prevail, and should the gadgetry prove equal to the quantitative demands put upon it, the result would nevertheless be the ultimate production of a world in which the only remaining controls of population would be the "misery and vice" foreseen by Malthus 161 years ago.

Periodical Bibliography

The following articles have been selected to supplement the diverse views presented in this chapter. They are available from the Population Council, One Dag Hammarskjöld Plaza, New York, NY 10017.

Giovanni Botero

"Giovanni Botero on the Forces Governing Population," *Population and Development Review*, vol. 11, no. 2, 1985.

Denis Diderot

"Diderot's Encyclopedia on Population," *Population and Development Review*, vol. 15, no. 1, 1989.

E. Dupreel

"Dupreel on Population and Progress," *Population and Development Review*, vol. 8, no. 4, 1982.

Benjamin Franklin

"Benjamin Franklin on the Causes and Consequences of Population Growth," *Population and Development Review*, vol. 11, no. 1, 1985.

Henry George

"Henry George on Disproof of the Malthusian Theory," *Population and Development Review*, vol. 13, no. 2, 1987.

Thomas Jefferson

"Thomas Jefferson on Population," *Population and Development Review*, vol. 19, no. 1, 1993.

A.J. Lotka

"Lotka on Population Study, Ecology, and Evolution," *Population and Development Review*, vol. 15, no. 3, 1989.

Ludwig von Mises

"Ludwig von Mises on the Limitation of Offspring," *Population and Development Review*, vol. 10, no. 3, 1984.

Frank Notestein

"Frank Notestein on Population Growth and Economic Development," *Population and Development Review*, vol. 9, no. 2, 1983.

E.G. Ravenstein

"Ravenstein on Global Carrying Capacity," *Population and Development Review*, vol. 16, no. 1, 1990.

Alfred Sauvy

"Alfred Sauvy on the World Population Problem: A View in 1949," *Population and Development Review*, vol. 16, no. 4, 1990.

George Bernard Shaw

"Bernard Shaw on 'the Population Question,'" *Population and Development Review*, vol. 9, no. 1, 1983.

Is the World's Population Growing Too Fast?

Population

Chapter Preface

Very few topics produce as much passion as does population growth. The work and ideas of Thomas Malthus, who postulated that population grows at a geometric rate while food supplies grow only arithmetically, will be recognizable in some of the viewpoints in this chapter, as will the ideas of opponents of Malthusian theory.

There is no debate on whether the species *homo sapiens* has been growing on planet Earth. That is a fact. Human population on earth grew from less than 400 million at the time of Christ, to 1 billion at the beginning of the 19th century, to 2 billion in 1930, to 3 billion in 1960, to 4 billion in 1975, to 5 billion in 1987, and to 5.5 billion in 1993. Clearly, the number of people has been growing geometrically—and most of the growth is extremely recent, in terms of our history.

The debate on population, instead of centering on whether growth has occurred, centers on a number of other issues: whether this growth is too rapid; whether the "carrying capacity" of the earth has already been exceeded; whether "overpopulation" is the main, causal variable responsible for most of the globe's problems; and whether population growth needs to be controlled.

In a 1994 article entitled "People Aren't the Problem," Jacqueline P. Kasun contends that the idea of "overpopulation" is a myth. She maintains that "if all of the people in the world moved to Texas, each person could be given the space available in the typical American home and all the rest of the world would be empty." Kasun figures that the population density of this great "city" would be 20,000 persons per square mile, as compared to San Francisco's 16,000 persons per square mile and the 30,000 persons per square mile in Brooklyn, New York. She further states that the rate of world population growth is rapidly declining, that today's farmers are using a mere fraction of available cropland, that "global deforestation" is a myth, that the "warming of the globe" is not a certainty, and that the elimination of environmental pollution will entail a change in our behavior (not just a reduction in our numbers).

Kasun's views on population issues represent one end of the "opinion continuum" on population. Four of the viewpoints in this chapter tend to oppose Kasun's views and four tend to support her. Is the world's population growing too fast? The viewpoints in the following chapter debate this question.

"That Earth's life-support systems are strained to the bursting point by the runaway growth of humanity's numbers is apparent to anyone with eyes to see."

Overpopulation Is the Root of Most of the World's Problems

Frank Graham Jr.

Frank Graham Jr. is a freelance writer specializing in nature and conservation, and has written numerous books, among them *Since Silent Spring* (1970), *Where the Place Called Morning Lies* (1973), *Potomac: The Nation's River* (1976), and *The Audubon Ark* (1990). Since 1958, he has been a field editor for *Audubon Magazine*. According to Graham, overpopulation is the primary cause of the planet's social, economic, and environmental problems. He is also of the opinion that pro-life organizations unfairly attack environmentalists concerned with reducing the rate of population growth.

As you read, consider the following questions:

1. According to Graham, why is overpopulation the root cause of almost all the earth's social, economic, and environmental problems?
2. What do you think the author meant when he said, "Abortion is not an environmental issue, but population control is very much one"?

From Frank Graham Jr., "Talk of the Trail," *Audubon*, January 1990, © 1990 National Audubon Society. Reprinted with permission.

A profound nastiness has crept into the opposition to environmental organizations in recent years. Attributing this new malevolence to the movement's growing impact on national affairs doesn't entirely explain the phenomenon.

Campaigners for sound wildlife management, energy conservation, or forest protection inevitably collide with special interests, and sometimes rub them the wrong way. Sparks will fly, but a little goodwill often helps to bring the animosity back down to a reasonable level. (Some of us even gave James Watt [Secretary of the Interior during the Ronald Reagan Administration] the benefit of the doubt as a pious if wrong-headed bloke until he was caught with his hand out in the sleaze line at HUD [lobbying for a grant from the Department of Housing and Urban Development for a Maryland developer].) But close encounters with the creepy-crawlies are another matter.

Fanatics Against Population Control

The present nastiness is the offspring of fanaticism. Nowhere does fanaticism (fueled by religion, cultural customs, racism, or xenophobia) intrude itself into public debate more stridently today than over the question of population control. That Earth's life-support systems are strained to the bursting point by the runaway growth of humanity's numbers is apparent to anyone with eyes to see. Overpopulation is the root cause of almost all of the globe's social, economic and environmental problems.

There are those perverse souls who brand any expression of this well-documented danger as misanthropy, or describe it as an attempt to hold down the numbers of some "inferior race." Yet the human misery and environmental blight that are brought on by too many people struggling for finite resources grow worse almost daily. World population increases by the equivalent of a new United States every three years. In 1900 the total stood at 1.5 billion, rose to 5.2 billion in 1990, and will swell to 6.2 billion in another decade.

For some years the U.S. government held to a rational population policy by supporting (if not very liberally) various United Nations programs for education and family-planning programs that promised to help developing countries deal with their most onerous problems. The Reagan Administration, in a move that was (and remains) a national embarrassment, cut off all aid to the United Nations Population Fund and the International Planned Parenthood Federation. Although United States law explicitly prohibits government funding for abortion programs overseas, some right-to-life groups raised the specter of "killing babies" as a prime reason for opposing family-planning aid to nations that desperately need it.

Abortion is not an environmental issue, but population control is very much one. Thus, National Audubon Society supports voluntary family planning and provides information to its members about the relationship between population growth and environmental quality. Audubon's director of population programs, Patricia Baldi, points out that spacing children and avoiding unwanted pregnancies are, indeed, among the ways to decrease the incidence of abortion.

Reprinted by permission: Tribune Media Services.

But in the summer of 1989, this moderate stand on population control brought the most irrational of the pro-lifers out in full cry. Several leading environmental organizations, including the National Wildlife Federation, Trout Unlimited, and National Audubon Society, became the targets of an orchestrated letter-writing campaign that can be described only as contemptible. Pat Baldi, for instance, received letters addressed to "Baldi the Baby Killer." One correspondent asked, "Are you only pro-life for four-legged animals and birds, etc?" Another, losing control of the mother tongue, fumed, "I will join my voice to spread the word that the Audubon Society is no longer a good place to help, since they urge the killing of our babies." And the magazine of the American Life League published a cartoon that showed a stork dropping a baby, presumably to its death, to illustrate an article calling Audubon a "pro-abortion organization." This coven of pro-lifers reserved its true comic talent for an old bugbear. According to *The Washington Post*, among the hate mail sent to Faye Wattleton of Planned Parenthood Federation of America was a cartoon "portraying her with big lips and kinky hair and calling her 'the black butcher.'"

As George Santayana long ago observed, "Fanaticism consists in redoubling your efforts when you have forgotten your aim."

"Other things being equal, countries with large populations enjoy higher and more rapidly growing output per worker."

Overpopulation Is Not a Problem: The More, the Merrier

Ed Rubenstein

Ed Rubenstein, *National Review* magazine's economic consultant since 1988, does not see overpopulation as a problem. Rather, he says, societies with large populations have more robust economies and standards of living. Rubenstein's essays have also appeared in the *Wall Street Journal*, the *New York Times*, the *Harvard Business Review*, and *Newsday*. Before moving to *National Review* he was a senior economist at W.R. Grace & Co., and a member of the Grace Commission.

As you read, consider the following questions:

1. What kind of relationship does the author see between population density and economic well-being?
2. How, in the author's opinion, does population growth spur economic growth?
3. According to Rubenstein, what role is immigration playing in the makeup of the United States' population?

A population time bomb hangs over the world, threatening humanity with overcrowding, starvation, and conflict. So argued the World Bank and most other international development agencies—until recently. But the stellar economic success of many "overcrowded" countries has led some economists to revise their thinking on the role of population:

Population Matters

	Population Per Square Mile	GNP Per Capita	
		Dollars, 1988	Average Annual Percentage Growth, 1965–1988
Singapore	11,910	9,070	7.2
Hong Kong	9,744	9,220	6.3
South Korea	1,189	3,600	6.8
Japan	844	21,020	4.3
India	658	340	1.8
China	288	330	5.4
Argentina	30	2,520	0.0

The population of capitalist Hong Kong grew from 700,000 in 1945 to 5.6 million in 1987, yet earnings rose at unprecedented rates. Singapore also flourished, and is now forced to import labor to alleviate a labor shortage. Of course these are small city-states, but does anyone think that a large hinterland attached to them would be as poor as Mainland China?

At the other extreme, sparsely populated, statist Argentina has stagnated for at least 25 years.

Population Growth Does Not Decrease Economic Growth

In the short run Malthus is right: another baby or another immigrant invariably lowers living standards for those around him. Over periods measured in decades, however, economists (including Nobel laureate Simon Kuznets, perhaps the greatest economic historian of modern times) have found no evidence that population growth decreases economic growth. Since World War II, per-person income in less-developed countries has grown faster than that of developed countries despite far faster population growth in the developing world.

Population Growth Spurs Economic Growth

How does population growth spur economic growth? In *Population Matters* (1990), Julian Simon notes that American fathers work the equivalent of two to five weeks a year extra for each additional child, more than offsetting the mother's withdrawal from the workforce. Population growth increases the demand for investment and reduces the risk of overbuilding in housing and other highly cyclical industries. Other things being equal, countries with large populations enjoy higher and more rapidly growing output per worker.

Largely unnoticed amidst the current economic gloom, the United States seems to be pulling out of a long demographic slump. The nation's fertility rate climbed to an estimated 2.1 lifetime births per woman in the first half of 1990, the highest figure since 1971. Based on the earlier rates, the Census Bureau had forecast a declining U.S. population by the year 2038.

Further, the 1990 immigration law provides for a 30 per cent annual increase in slots, from 640,000 to 700,000, with the number of those admitted because of specific skills increasing proportionately more. But we are in no danger of becoming a nation of immigrants: there were 800,000 immigrants in 1980, and at the turn of the century immigration topped one million for six consecutive years. Only 6 per cent of the U.S. population today is foreign born—less than in Britain, France, and Germany; far less than in Canada and Australia.

---

*"[At current rates,] by 2150 there would be
694,213,000,000 of us, a little over 125 times
our present population."*

There Are Too Many
People on the Planet

Joel E. Cohen

Joel E. Cohen, a professor of population at Rockefeller University, has published widely in population studies. Cohen is a
trustee for the Russell Sage Foundation, was a MacArthur
Foundation Prize fellow (1981-86), and was the 1992 winner of
the Mindel Sheps award for mathematical demography from the
Population Association of America. Cohen, like many demographers, sees zero population growth (where births on the planet
equal deaths) as inevitable. The only questions are (1) when will
it arrive and (2) how will it be achieved—with death rates rising
to match current birth rates or with birth rates decreasing to
match current death rates.

As you read, consider the following questions:

1. The author points out that various studies by economists
   show that population size and growth are positively
   correlated with economic growth. What does he say these
   studies ignore?
2. According to Cohen, what factors must be considered when
   looking at population size and the ability to produce
   sufficient food to feed a given population?

From Joel E. Cohen, "How Many People Can Earth Hold?" *Discover*, November 1992.
Copyright ©1992 The Walt Disney Co. Reprinted with permission of *Discover* magazine.

According to the United Nations, which follows these things closely, some 5.3 billion people enlivened our planet in 1990. By November 1992, that number will have increased to 5.5 billion, an addition nearly equal to the population of the United States. Of course no one, including the UN, has a reliable crystal ball that reveals precisely how human numbers will change. Still, people have to plan for the future, and so the UN's analysts and computers have been busy figuring what might happen. One possibility they consider is that future world fertility rates will remain what they were in 1990. The consequences of this, with accompanying small declines in death rates, are startling. By 2025, when my now-16-year-old daughter will have finished having whatever children she will have, the world would have 11 billion people, double its number today. Another doubling would take only a bit more than 25 years, as the faster-growing segments of the population become a larger proportion of the total. At my daughter's centennial, in 2076, the human population would have more than doubled again, passing 46 billion. By 2150 there would be 694,213,000,000 of us, a little over 125 times our present population.

There, in 2150, the projections of the United Nations Population Division stop. Perhaps they stop because the numbers were growing too long to print in their allotted column widths. Perhaps they stop because the computers grew weary of the thought of so many births to celebrate, so many marriages to consummate, so many dead to bury. At any rate, there, in 2150, the computers—and an unchanging urge to go forth and multiply—leave us with a hypothetical 12,100 people for every square mile of land, or 3,500 people for every square mile of Earth's surface, oceans included. At this rate of growth the population would, before 2250, surpass 30 *trillion*, more than 200 people for every *acre* of the planet's surface, wet or dry.

Surely the United States, though, with its wide-open spaces and its much more leisurely population growth, could never suffer such a crowded fate, right? Wrong. Back in 1970 Ansley Coale, a demographer at Princeton, observed that the population of the United States had increased by half since 1940. At that growth rate, he calculated, the U.S. population would

> reach a billion shortly before the year 2100. Within six or seven more centuries we would reach one person per square foot of land area in the United States, and after about 1,500 years our descendants would outweigh the Earth if they continued to increase by 50 percent every 30 years. We can even calculate that, at that rate of increase, our descendants would, in a few thousand years, form a sphere of flesh whose radius would, neglecting relativity, expand at the velocity of light.

Here is what Coale concluded: "Every demographer knows

that we cannot continue a positive rate of increase indefinitely. The inexorable arithmetic of compound interest leads us to absurd conditions within a calculable period of time. Logically we must, and in fact we will, have a rate of growth very close to zero in the long run."

I know of no qualified scientist who disagrees: The human population must ultimately approach a long-term average growth rate of zero. That is a law from which no country or region is exempt. According to every plausible calculation that's ever been done, Earth could not feed even the 694 billion people that the UN projected for 2150 if present fertility rates were to continue. Though there is tremendous uncertainty about the details of when, where, and how, the long-term constraint of an average population growth of zero is likely to come into play within the next century and a half.

Problems Increase with Population Increase

We are constantly being reminded of the plight of the poor, the hungry, the homeless and the diseased. What does not make the headlines is that even if the proportion of those unfortunate people remains the same in relation to the total population, their number is bound to increase as the size of the population as a whole increases. . . . The best hope of limiting the increase in the number of such people would be if the world population could be stabilized.

Prince Philip of Great Britain, *The Washington Post*, March 30, 1990.

Theories regarding the limitations on population growth have come and gone over the years. In an essay published in 1798, the English clergyman Thomas Robert Malthus argued that human numbers always increase more rapidly than food supplies and that humans are condemned always to breed to the point of misery and the edge of starvation. The two centuries since his famous essay have not been kind to Malthus's theory. In that time human numbers have increased from fewer than 1 billion to today's 5.5 billion. In many parts of the world, food production has grown faster than the population, thanks to the opening of new lands, mechanization, fertilizers, pesticides, better water control, improved breeds of plants and animals, and better farmer know-how. Though many of today's bottom billion people live in misery on the edge of starvation, Malthus would be astonished at the relative well-being of most of a vastly enlarged population.

That Malthus's theory failed widely during the past two centuries does not prove that it will remain wrong for the next two.

66

Some observers see a coming vindication of Malthus in the recent faltering of growth rates of per capita food production in some regions. Many scientists have adopted Malthus's general strategy of supposing that limiting factors constrain populations, and in fact the theory has gained some scientific support from agricultural experiments. For example, if the yield of a crop field is limited by the paucity of nitrogen in the soil, then when nitrogen is added, the yield jumps until it is again limited by the shortage of another essential nutrient, such as phosphorus. When phosphorus is added to the nitrogen supplement, yield jumps again until, say, the crop becomes water-limited. In this way, crop yields are limited by the most constraining factor in a whole series of limiting factors. By analogy, human populations may be limited by land (for farming, living, and recreation), food (from marine as well as terrestrial sources), fresh water, energy, or biological diversity (to provide ecosystem services such as decomposition of organic wastes, the regeneration of oxygen, and natural enemies for pest species). . . .

The World Hunger Program at Brown University estimates that, with present levels of food production and an equal distribution of food, the world could sustain either 5.5 billion vegetarians, 3.7 billion people who get 15 percent of their calories from animal products (as in much of South America), or 2.8 billion people who derive 25 percent of their calories from animal products (as in the wealthiest countries).

The Capacity to Support *Homo Sapiens*—and Nothing Else?

Globally, food supply is limited physically by the plant energy available for consumption by animals and decomposers. Ecologists call this quantity the net primary production (NPP). It is the total amount of solar energy annually converted into living matter, minus the amount of energy the plants themselves use for respiration. NPP is equivalent to about 225 billion metric tons of organic matter a year, an amount that contains enough calories to feed about 1,000 billion [1 trillion] people. But that's only if every other consumer of green plants on Earth (including bacteria) were eliminated and at the same time people learned how to enjoy eating wood.

In 1986 Stanford biologists Peter Vitousek, Paul Ehrlich, and Anne Ehrlich and National Aeronautics and Space Administration ecologist Pamela Matson estimated that the 5 billion people then on Earth and their domestic animals directly consumed— that is, ate—about 3 percent of NPP in the form of vegetables and other plants. But they also estimated that humans actually "co-opted" about 19 percent of NPP, a figure arrived at by adding to what was directly consumed the material indirectly consumed in such activities as clearing land or converting it for human use.

This aggregate figure of 19 percent, or roughly one-fifth, of NPP does not mean the planet can support about five times as many people as the 5 billion it had in 1986. That's because the 19 percent itself is an average of 31 percent of *terrestrial* NPP and 2 percent of *aquatic* NPP. Since people already consume nearly one-third of terrestrial NPP, Earth could support five times as many people only if we either exploited the oceans much more than at present or greatly increased the NPP of the land. The present terrestrial NPP and present human consumption patterns would permit little more than a tripling of the human population, perhaps to 16 billion people, to the practical exclusion of most other terrestrial species. . . .

There are large uncertainties in the estimates of global agricultural carrying capacities [the number of individuals of a species that an environment can support for some period]. Still, agricultural and ecological calculations confirm the demographers' expectations that human population growth rates must drop near or below zero, at most within a century or so. The nondemographic calculations are silent on whether growth will stop because of fewer births or more deaths.

"One hears that 'we' have more people than 'we' have 'need' of, though 'we' inevitably goes undefined. What amazing arrogance and self-centeredness!"

There Is an Impending Shortage of People

Julian L. Simon

Julian L. Simon is a professor of management at the University of Maryland at College Park. Simon has published scores of articles and books in the area of economic demography. His books include *The Economics of Population and Economic Growth* (1977), *The Ultimate Resource* (1981), and *Population Matters: People, Resources, Environment and Immigration* (1990). Simon has served as editor of the journal *Research in Population Economics* and is the best known anti-neo-Malthusian scholar in the world today. In the following viewpoint he argues that expanding populations are not the cause of all our ills. Instead, Simon says, human beings are a resource to be cherished and utilized to better our overall standard of living.

As you read, consider the following questions:

1. Why, in Simon's opinion, is there an impending shortage of people?
2. What, according to the author, is the trend in the cost of raw materials? Why does he say this is the case?
3. In the author's opinion, what impact might the increased value placed on people have on the fertility rate in the United States? Why?

Excerpted from Julian Simon, *Population Matters*. New Brunswick, NJ: Transaction, 1990. Copyright ©1990 by Transaction Publishers. Reprinted with permission.

The population of the world is much greater now than it has been in the past. This observation usually evokes the knee-jerk reaction that "we" are therefore facing increased social problems. One hears that "we" have more people than "we" have "need" of, though "we" inevitably goes undefined. What amazing arrogance and self-centeredness!

Though there has been an increase in absolute numbers of humans on earth, the "need" for people has grown even faster. This makes sense when we measure the trend in the need for people the same way we measure the need for all economic goods—that is, by price. The increasing price of the services of people indicates that, along with the growth in total population, people have indeed been becoming more scarce.

The Decreasing Supply of Labor

Irving (Duke) Johnson, 66, has polished shoes on U Street in Washington, D.C. for 27 years. He "remembers when more than 25 'bootblacks' were working along the street." Now Johnson is the only one, according to the newspaper story.

The decline in the number of shoe polishers could in theory be due to a decline in either the demands for shoe polishing or in the supply of workers. But Booker T. Carrington, the "dean of the shoe-shine professionals" who has "more than half a century of experience," asserts that the explanation is a decline in the labor supply. The young boys "all are looking for the big money," he says. In other words, the pay necessary to attract shoe polishers has increased over the years.

So there has been an increasing shortage of shoe polishers in the nation's capital. By the same reasoning, there has been a decreasing supply of all labor in the United States and in the world. This is shown by the higher price that one must pay to obtain almost any type of help, from journalists in Washington to drivers in Delhi. And one can just as well say that there has been a growing shortage of people in the world.

Though paradoxical, this sounds quite unlike the conventional doomsday warnings, which point to the world's growing population. It is economic fact: We have been experiencing an increasing shortage of people even though there are more people on earth with each passing year. And we ought to start planning to make the necessary adjustments. Ben Wattenberg laments the "birth dearth" in the United States mainly for other reasons, but his call for more Americans complements the argument here.

The Increase in Availability of Natural Resources

To compound the paradox, the past centuries also reveal an amazing increase in natural resources. Yes, you read correctly. And this needs explaining. How can it be that we use some of our stock of a raw material, and yet we have even more available to us than we started with?

First we must be clear about the economic meaning of scarcity. As consumers, we complain that a good has become more scarce when we have to pay more for the services than we want from the resource. Conversely, we say a good has become less scarce when the price goes down. Current and future prices are all that matter economically with respect to resources. Discussion about how much of a good "really exists" is quite beside the point for economic purposes.

By now, "pure" economists and "practical" marketers agree that all raw material prices have been trending downward as far back as the data go. The most important price to consumers is the amount of labor time that one must trade to get a pound of, say, copper or iron. The U.S. prices of these and all other metals, relative to wages, have fallen by an astonishing factor of perhaps twenty since the founding of the country. And in U.S. terms, they have fallen by a factor of perhaps a thousand over the last few millenia. The prices of raw materials relative to consumer goods—the "terms of trade"—have also been falling over the years.

The doomsayers somehow remain unaware or unconvinced of this astonishing trend toward greater availability of natural resources relative to manufactured goods and services. The basis of their unbelief can only be theological or mystical or emotional, because there is no doubt about the statistical evidence.

The explanation lies in the increasing stock of knowledge about resources. A resource does not really exist until we understand what it will do for us, discover where to find it, and learn how to make it ready for our use. Finding new lodes of old resources, figuring out how to mine and refine them more efficiently, and discovering how to substitute new resources for the old ones all push the price down. The process usually begins with an expected or actual shortage caused by increased population or income. And the process usually ends with our having more resources and being better off than if the shortage had not threatened.

People Are Becoming Scarce

Now about people. World population has been growing rapidly. But does this imply "overpopulation"? Too many people? People becoming less scarce? The proper answer to all is "no."

Using normal economic procedure, let us compare the present state of scarcity to past scarcity by examining changes in the price of obtaining the services of people. The two appropriate price measures—wages and income—both clearly show that the average price of people has recently been going up everywhere

71

in the world, except in a few exceptional situations. The logic is inescapable: Despite the rising numbers of people, human beings have been getting more scarce.

'You mean you're it?'

Determining the long-run price of labor is trickier. The most meaningful index is the proportion of the labor force occupied in producing basic foodstuffs—that is, grain. To make arithmetic easy, let's assume a starting point of everyone working in subsistence agriculture, although even in the least-developed society perhaps 5 or 10 percent of the working population occupy themselves being priests or chiefs. (The actual figures both for China in 1949, and for the United States in 1800, were about 80 percent working in agriculture.) And let each working man stand for an entire household, neglecting the fact that in many places women do most of the farming work.

From Agricultural to Nonagricultural Societies

Think of a society that progresses from the entire labor force working in agriculture to only half working in agriculture. This shift means that each working person can support his own family plus that of another working person. And the other working person can now spend all his time producing other goods to trade for half of the agricultural output. Now both the agricultural and the nonagricultural workers have an income composed of as much food as in the original state, plus other goods that are of equal value, if both workers are of equal efficiency. Hence, each worker has an income equal to twice what it was in the original state.

Now compare the situation of the United States today, where each farmer provides food for about fifty other working persons. This implies that the farmer's production provides him about fifty times as much income as it did in the original state of subsistence agriculture. This squares with the fact that income per worker might be about $400 in the poorest country in the world and perhaps $20,000 in the United States.

We can dramatize this history by projecting it into the future. Another such multiplication of U.S. income would imply an average worker earning today's equivalent of $1,000,000 every year instead of, say, $20,000. And it is not beyond possibility that there should be another forty-fold increase in fewer years than passed between 1800 and now, given the speedup in the rate of productivity increase over the years.

Another dramatization: Poor countries now embarking on economic development may reach a level of income comparable to that of the United States now in perhaps half a century, or considerably less than a century.

The implication of this historical shift for a person's lifetime welfare is even more amazing. In addition to wages per hour and income per year rising, the number of years that a person lives to produce and enjoy this material welfare has increased greatly. The wage alone tells us how much it costs to purchase another person's services for an hour. But lifetime income tells us how much an entire human life is worth. (This was the way the market valued a slave, but that does not disqualify the concept. It is the appropriate concept when one thinks about the value of one's own human capital created with education.) This increase in length of life implies yet another doubling or tripling of a person's lifetime income, compared to the original state of subsistence agriculture.

The economic changes that lead to an increased shortage of people, and to increased economic value of life, have a variety of practical implications. The most obvious implication for business activity is that the poor countries will become much like today's rich countries in their purchasing and consumption patterns, as well as in their production patterns. Businesses in today's poor countries, and those that deal with countries that are now poor, will have to alter both what they produce and how they produce.

Production will have to adjust by giving up the idea that "life is cheap." This implies providing better protection against safety hazards. More costly will be the shift to technologies that use physical capital more intensively, along with less unskilled labor. This continues trends that began more than a century ago in such places as Great Britain and the United States.

The most important implication of the increased value of people is that it may reverse the trend toward a declining birth rate—if parents can find a way to recover their "investment" in their children. At present, parents in rich countries do not expect to be repaid for sending their children to expensive universities where the children acquire skills that will produce a high income return on the investment. Therefore, the high cost of education to the parents currently works to reduce the birth rate in rich countries.

If new mechanisms develop whereby the children repay their parents' investment in them, either privately or through some government mechanism, there will arise an increased incentive to have more children. Any such mechanism is complex, however, and we do not know which would be best. To work that out is a task for the future. And in the meantime in the United States, we would do well to stop the gap with the talented foreigners who wish to come here as immigrants, with great gain to all.

"Except for very specific purposes in very small areas, no attempt to determine a population carrying capacity has attained credence."

It Is Impossible to Measure the "Carrying Capacity" of the Earth

Harold Brookfield

Harold Brookfield is professor emeritus in the Research School of Pacific Studies at the Australian National University. In Brookfield's opinion, all discussions of overpopulation rest on the notion that the earth has a specific sustainable population "carrying capacity." According to the author, this idea has been empirically faulted so many times that it should have been discarded long ago. Brookfield asserts that no attempt to determine population carrying capacity on a large scale has ever gained credence, and predictions about the population capacity limits of specific countries have repeatedly been proven wrong.

As you read, consider the following questions:

1. Most modern thinking on "carrying capacity" relies on the work of Malthus and Ricardo. What, in the author's opinion, did these two scholars contribute to the definition of "carrying capacity"?
2. According to the author, what crucial factors does "carrying capacity" ignore?
3. How does the T.P. Bayliss-Smith model of "carrying capacity" differ from the P.M. Fearnside model, according to Brookfield?

Harold Brookfield, "The Numbers Crunch," *The UNESCO Courier*, January 1992. Reprinted with permission.

When we speak of "overpopulation" or of "underpopulation" the implication is that there must be some level of population in any region or country, or in the world as a whole, at which neither of these conditions exists and at which population is "optimal". When we say that the condition of either land or people is worse than it would be if there were fewer inhabitants, then there must be some "maximum" population, probably higher than the "optimal", beyond which stress becomes palpable. Underlying all this is the notion that our planet has a certain undefined, sustainable population "carrying capacity".

Most modern thinking relies on the different formulations of the problem by Thomas Malthus (1766-1834) and David Ricardo (1772-1823). Malthus propounded the "law", or hypothesis, that population tends to increase to the level which just permits subsistence for the great majority. Ricardo modified the Malthusian theory by a more thorough development of the empirical law of diminishing returns as applied to successive units of labour input, implying that limits are attained through rising scarcities.

Historically, it is certainly possible to find instances of something like the Malthusian law. In overwhelmingly rural early fourteenth-century Europe, every poor harvest resulted in an increase of deaths. In Ireland, in the 1840s, the ease of subsisting on potatoes led to rapid population growth among a peasantry constantly pressing on the limits of famine, across which they were thrust by crop failure in 1845.

In the mid-1960s, a group of researchers, concerned by demographic upsurge and evidence of stress in either society or resource management, or both, began to seek ways to quantify the critical population densities which mark the onset of stress conditions. All dealt with mainly self-sufficient agrarian societies using pre-industrial technology and with land-rotation farming in which the fallow period was a critical element.

The pioneer work was carried out in Africa where a system first developed in 1949 in Zambia by W. Allan, with the object of determining the need for land reallocation and rehabilitation, was later extended to societies in other tropical parts of the continent. Anthropologists and geographers used and elaborated formulae, similar to those Allan used to calculate critical population density, to quantify the productive capacity of an environment, the number of people it could support at given per capita requirements, and hence the degree of pressure on resources.

Criticism of the "Carrying Capacity" Concept

Substantial criticism of the whole group of concepts embraced under the notions of "carrying capacity", "critical population levels" and "population pressure on resources" was, however, already building up. Increasingly it came to be understood that a static population-resource equation concealed more than it revealed.

Technical problems with early attempts to make carrying capacity an effective, applicable indicator were summarized in 1986 by P.M. Fearnside. They addressed only one class of agriculture and an essentially subsistence economy. Although some authors introduced caveats, they nevertheless calculated on the tacit assumption that patterns of consumption, income and employment, crop and livestock mix and agrotechnology were fixed. Few considered natural resource degradation or took account of year to year variability in the biophysical conditions of production. Most studies were based on limited periods of field research and there were deficiencies in the data used on yields, the fallow period and the qualities of land and its resilience under human use. Unfortunately, some of these deficiencies have been carried forward into more recent work.

Ted Rall is reprinted by permission of Chronicle Features, San Francisco, California.

The UNESCO/MAB Eastern Fiji project of 1974-1976, which the writer headed, was assigned the task of improving carrying capacity estimation. It was felt, not unreasonably, that islands would provide the best laboratory. Within the project, T.P. Bayliss-Smith took an important step away from the old approaches, including his own, by recognizing that the output obtained by people from any resource-area is not a fixed quantity, but is relative to the intensity of input. The Bayliss-Smith model is not specific to any particular cultivation system and is applicable to open as well as closed economics. It abandons the deterministic approach of the 1960s and creates the potential to take account of both natural and economic variability.

The price of progress towards realism was a greater need for data, more complex calculations and a result made up of choices rather than a single figure. The stage was set for a new computer-based methodological step forward. This was taken by P.M. Fearnside, who tackled the problem of carrying capacity in a very different environment from islands—that of clearings made by settlers in lowland rain forest along the trans-Amazon highway in Brazil.

In this rather specific case Fearnside used as his indicator the statistical probability of colonist failure under specific population densities. He determined this probability through a complex computer model which simulated the whole agrosystem of the settlers, employing data collected over more than ten years to examine the causal relationships between over sixty variables rather than an independent condition of the environment. This was a far remove from the work of twenty years before.

Fearnside's method is very demanding of data, research time and computer time, but it approaches realism by turning the question away from the simple numbers that can be supported under a given and static set of conditions. Instead, it focuses on issues such as levels of support obtainable from environmental sources under varying conditions, or density limits on success among poor settlers in a new environment. It shifts away from determinism towards questions of sustainability, but in very specific contexts.

It would not, however, be reasonable to wait on such intensive enquiries in all situations and certainly not in the face of the large population, development and environmental problems that now confront much of the world. There is a need for answers to questions posed by another doubling of the global population and a desire to know the sustainable carrying capacity of environments and regions for use as a development planning tool.

How Many People Can the World Sustain?

A very fair first approximation to a global estimate of carrying capacity was made by E.G. Ravenstein in 1891. He made reasonable estimates of the world's cultivable area, its capabilities and capacities and of yield improvements, to arrive at a global capacity of close to six billion people which he thought might be reached about the year 2070, at the then current rates of growth, without much loss or gain in living standards.

Since Ravenstein made his estimation, the global situation has been transformed, not least by the "green revolution". This and other factors for change were taken into account in what was probably the most ambitious attempt at large-area measurement of carrying capacity ever made. This major task, carried out in the early 1980s by the Food and Agriculture Organization (FAO), in collaboration with the International Institute for Applied Systems Analysis (IIASA), covered the whole developing world apart from east Asia and sought to determine the physical potential population-supporting capacities of all these countries and of soil and climate regions within them. Soil associations derived from the FAO/UNESCO soil map of the world were used together with a climatic inventory created to classify lands by mean length of growing period.

Calculating Potential Crop Yields

Potential yields for a range of crops were calculated on three bases: of "low inputs", assuming only manual labour, no fertilizer and no pesticides; of "intermediate inputs", with draught animals, some chemical inputs and simple soil conservation measures; and of "high inputs", assuming complete mechanization, full use of optimal genetic material and all necessary farm chemicals and soil conservation measures. Consideration was also given to fallow periods and to the effects of both irrigation and land degradation on productivity. Two time periods were used to determine the relation of actual population to carrying capacity—1975, to represent "the present", and 2000, using United Nations "medium" projected populations.

Results from each soil/climate zone, aggregated by country, suggest that by 2000 most developing countries could support their populations from their own resources only if high levels of input were employed, but also that a number of countries would face inevitable shortage of food; to reach these projections, trade within countries was assumed. Evaluation of the method is best based on the accompanying maps of major regions, which show carrying capacity as persons per hectare for each soil/climate zone, at each level of input. The sheets for a "Southeast Asian" region that extends west as far as Pakistan provide a good basis for analysis; this area exhibits great internal contrasts.

In the entire region, the map for low levels of inputs shows virtually only the north coast of Java as capable of supporting as many as five people per hectare. Almost the whole of Java, Bhutan and Bangladesh, most of Nepal, India and lowland Viet Nam, large parts of the Philippines and several upland areas throughout Southeast Asia have calculated capacities less than their 1975 populations. On the basis of high levels of inputs, only a few small, mainly upland areas are in the latter category, though it is a different story with projected 2000 populations.

More remarkably, however, on the high input assumption most of Sumatra, peninsular Malaysia and the Philippines and the whole south of Kalimantan (Borneo) are shown as having higher capacity (ten or more persons per hectare) than all but limited areas of eastern Java and the north coast of that island. Similarly, most of Kampuchea is shown as having greater capacity to support population at high levels of input than any part of Viet Nam. This information flies in the face not only of present population distribution, but also of a great deal of additional information on the quality of soils and water in certain of these regions, particularly eastern Sumatra and southern Kalimantan, where serious problems have been encountered by transmigrant schemes.

Despite the great body of data handled and the vast resources employed, the methodology differs little from that of the early carrying-capacity calculations of the 1960s. On the basis of incomplete environmental data and a uniform set of assumptions about agricultural technology and basic consumption requirements, a deterministic result is produced. Only food supply is taken into account and industrial and trading capacities are virtually ignored. Moreover, the necessary assumption of the high input levels case, that the best agrotechnology can be applied everywhere and by everyone, displays remarkable lack of realism. As a statement about carrying capacity, this one—based on a one-sector, closed-economy model—merely reveals the impossibility of determining or even conceptualizing what it is in a real, interdependent world.

An Empirical Notion That Should Be Discarded

Although there have been several further estimates, nothing like the FAO/IIASA project has ever been attempted again. Discussion of carrying capacity, however, goes on and has taken on a new lease of life in the modern context of sustainability. In the new wave of environmental concern it is often argued that population pressure contributes causally to degradation and depletion. It has also been shown that degradation can arise under both high and low population densities and under both poverty and affluence, while restorative management can also occur in these circumstances.

Part of the damage now being done to more and more of the environment is due not simply to increased numbers, but to the greater mobility of people and their activities and the enhanced means they have of dealing damage through such simple innovations as the chain-saw, as well as the tools of modern industry. Growing numbers are certainly a major element, but are not themselves a sufficient explanation.

Setting aside speculation about future global warming, there are already ways in which the environment of the whole planet is changed by human activity, with growing population pressure as a major element. Even the advances of the green revolution have reached something of a plateau, though worldwide there is still vast scope for improvement in both production and conservation.

To focus only on one element, however, is to ignore questions of access to resources and capital as causes of poverty and also to disregard the scope for adaptation provided by the rapidly growing division of labour, with its potential for a more intelligent use of technology. Environmental variability is increasingly shown to have major effects on human welfare and we must allow for the possibility that it will increase with global change. To rely for decision-making on carrying capacity determined on the basis of present conditions is a recipe for disaster.

Except for very specific purposes in very small areas, no attempt to determine a population carrying capacity has attained credence. Repeated predictions have been made concerning the population capacity limits of country after country for at least half of this century. In almost every significant case these limits have been exceeded, while in most cases the present people are now better off than their less numerous predecessors.

Carrying capacity is an empirical notion and it has been empirically faulted so many times that it should already have been discarded, at least as a planning tool for local application. It is an impediment to rational planning for a more sustainable future. Carrying capacity for the whole world may be another matter and on this the last word still seems to be with Ravenstein and the system he employed in 1891. His limits need expansion in the light of what has transpired since, but his very simple methods, using quantities that can readily be changed and updated according to circumstances, are all that so transparently simplistic and conditional a notion deserves. The real problem is much larger; population pressure is as much result as cause, and population numbers, though important, are only one part of the whole.

"Uncertainty about the exact dimensions of future carrying capacity should not constitute an excuse to postpone action."

It Is Imperative to Estimate the Earth's "Carrying Capacity"

Gretchen C. Daily and Paul R. Ehrlich

Gretchen C. Daily is a Winslow/Heinz Foundation Postdoctoral Fellow in the Energy and Resources Group, University of California at Berkeley. Paul R. Ehrlich is the Bing Professor of Population Studies at Stanford University. His 1969 book *The Population Bomb* initiated the modern debate on population growth and its effects. In the following viewpoint, Daily and Ehrlich argue that we should attempt to measure the planet's carrying capacity and adjust our economic and social behavior in accordance with that capacity. The authors conclude that we have probably already exceeded the earth's carrying capacity and must, as a species, attempt to rectify the situation.

As you read, consider the following questions:

1. What do Daily and Ehrlich see as the relationship between "I" (the impact of any population on the environment), "P" (the population's size), "A" (its affluence or per capita consumption), and "T" (the environmental damage)?
2. According to the authors, what evidence is there to support the claim that the earth's carrying capacity has already been exceeded?

From Gretchen C. Daily and Paul R. Ehrlich, "Population, Sustainability, and Earth's Carrying Capacity," *BioScience*, vol. 42, no. 10, November 1992, pp. 761-70. Copyright ©1992 American Institute of Biological Sciences. Reprinted with permission.

The twentieth century has been marked by a profound historical development: an unwitting evolution of the power to seriously impair human life-support systems. Nuclear weapons represent one source of this power. Yet, even the complexities of global arms control are dwarfed by those inherent in restraining runaway growth of the scale of the human enterprise, the second source of possible disaster. Diminishing the nuclear threat involves relatively few parties, well-established international protocols, alternate strategies that carry easily assessed costs and benefits, short- and long-term incentives that are largely congruent, and widespread recognition of the severity of the threat. In contrast, just the opposite applies to curbing the increasingly devastating impact of the human population. In particular, the most personal life decisions of every inhabitant of the planet are involved and these are controlled by socioeconomic systems in which the incentives for sacrificing the future for the present are often overwhelming. . . .

Uncertainty about the exact dimensions of future carrying capacity should not constitute an excuse to postpone action. Consider the costs being incurred today of doing so little to halt the population explosion, whose basic dimensions were understood decades ago.

The Current Population Situation

The human population is now so large and growing so rapidly that even popular magazines are referring to the possibility of a "demographic winter." The current population of 5.5 billion, growing at an annual rate of 1.7%, will add approximately 93 million people this year [1992], equivalent to more than the population of Mexico.

Growth rates vary greatly from region to region. The combined population of less-developed nations (excluding China) is growing at approximately 2.4% annually and will double in 30 years if no changes in fertility or mortality rates occur. The average annual rate of increase in more-developed nations is 0.5%, with an associated doubling time of 137 years. Many of those countries have slowed their population growth to a near halt or have stopped growing altogether.

The regional contrast in age structures is even more striking. The mean fraction of the population under 15 years of age in more-developed countries is 21%. In less-developed countries (excluding China) it is 39%; in Kenya it is fully 50%. Age structures so heavily skewed toward young people generate tremendous demographic momentum. For example, suppose the total fertility rate (average completed family size) of India plummets over the next 33 years from 3.9 to 2.2 children (replacement fertility). Under that optimistic scenario (assuming no rise in death rates), India's population, today some 870 million, would continue to grow until near the end of the next century, topping out at approximately 2 billion people.

The slow progress in reducing fertility in recent years is reflected in the repeated upward revisions of United Nations projections. The current estimate for the 2025 population is 8.5 billion, with growth eventually leveling off at approximately 11.6 billion around 2150. These projections are based on optimistic assumptions of continued declines in population growth rates.

Despite the tremendous uncertainty inherent in any population projections, it is clear that in the next century Earth will be faced with having to support at least twice its current human population. Whether the life-support systems of the planet can sustain the impact of so many people is not at all certain.

Environmental Impact

One measure of the impact of the global population is the fraction of the terrestrial net primary productivity (the basic energy supply of all terrestrial animals) directly consumed, coopted, or eliminated by human activity. This figure has reached approximately 40%. Projected increases in population alone could double this level of exploitation, causing the demise of many ecosystems on whose services human beings depend.

The impact (I) of any population can be expressed as a product of three characteristics: the population's size (P), its affluence or per-capita consumption (A), and the environmental damage (T) inflicted by the technologies used to supply each unit of consumption.

$$I = PAT$$

These factors are not independent. For example, T varies as a nonlinear function of P, A, and rates of change in both of these. This dependence is evident in the influence of population density and economic activity on the choice of local and regional energy-supply technologies and on land management practices. Per-capita impact is generally higher in very poor as well as in affluent societies.

Demographic statistics give a misleading impression of the population problem because of the vast regional differences in impact. Although less-developed nations contain almost four-fifths of the world's population and are growing very rapidly, high per-capita rates of consumption and the large-scale use of environmentally damaging technologies greatly magnify the impact of industrialized countries.

Because of the difficulty in estimating the A and T factors in isolation, per-capita energy use is sometimes employed as an imperfect surrogate for their product. Using that crude measure, and dividing the rich and poor nations at a per-capita gross national product of $4000 (1990 dollars), each inhabitant of the former does roughly 7.5 times more damage to Earth's life-support systems than does an inhabitant of the latter. At the extremes, the impact of a typical person in a desperately poor country is roughly a thirtieth that of an average citizen of the United States. The US population has a larger impact than that of any other nation in the world.

The population projections and estimates of total and relative impact bring into sharp focus a question that should be the concern of every biologist, if not every human being: how many people can the planet support in the long run?

The Concept of Carrying Capacity

Ecologists define carrying capacity as the maximal population size of a given species that an area can support without reducing its ability to support the same species in the future. Specifically, it is "a measure of the amount of renewable resources in the environment in units of the number of organisms these resources can support" and is specified as K in the biological literature.

Carrying capacity is a function of characteristics of both the area and the organism. A larger or richer area will, *ceteris paribus* [other things being equal], have a higher carrying capacity. Similarly, a given area will be able to support a larger population of a species with relatively low energetic requirements (e.g., lizards) than one at the same trophic level with high energetic requirements (e.g., birds of the same individual body mass as the lizards). The carrying capacity of an area with constant size and richness would be expected to change only as fast as organisms evolve different resource requirements. Though the concept is clear, carrying capacity is usually difficult to estimate.

For human beings, the matter is complicated by two factors: substantial individual differences in types and quantities of resources consumed and rapid cultural (including technological) evolution of the types and quantities of resources supplying each unit of consumption. Thus, carrying capacity varies markedly with culture and level of economic development.

We therefore distinguish between biophysical carrying capacity, the maximal population size that could be sustained biophysically under given technological capabilities, and social carrying capacities, the maxima that could be sustained under various social systems (and, especially, the associated patterns of resource consumption). At any level of technological development, social carrying capacities are necessarily less than biophysical carrying capacity, because the latter implies a human factory-farm lifestyle that would be not only universally undesirable but also unattainable because of inefficiencies inherent in social resource distribution systems. Human ingenuity has enabled dramatic increases in both biophysical and social carrying capacities for *H. sapiens*, and potential exists for further increases.

Carrying Capacity Today

Given current technologies, levels of consumption, and socioeconomic organization, has ingenuity made today's population sustainable? The answer to this question is clearly no, by a simple standard. The current population of 5.5 billion is being maintained only through the exhaustion and dispersion of a one-time inheritance of natural capital, including topsoil, groundwater, and biodiversity. The rapid depletion of these essential resources, coupled with a worldwide degradation of land and atmospheric quality, indicate that the human enterprise has not only exceeded its current social carrying capacity, but it is actually reducing future potential biophysical carrying capacities by depleting essential natural capital stocks.

The usual consequence for an animal population that exceeds its local biophysical carrying capacity is a population decline, brought about by a combination of increased mortality, reduced fecundity, and emigration where possible. A classic example is that of 29 reindeer introduced to St. Matthew Island, which propagated to 6000, destroyed their resource base, and declined to fewer than 50 individuals. Can human beings lower their per-capita impact at a rate sufficiently high to counterbalance their explosive increases in population?

Carrying Capacity for Saints

Two general assertions could support a claim that today's overshoot of social carrying capacity is temporary. The first is that people will alter their lifestyles (lower consumption, *A* in the $I = PAT$ equation) and thereby reduce their impact. Although we strongly encourage such changes in lifestyle, we believe the development of policies to bring the population to (or below) social carrying capacity requires defining human beings as the animals now in existence. Planning a world for highly cooperative, antimaterialistic, ecologically sensitive vegetarians would be of little value in correcting today's situation. Indeed, a statement by demographer Nathan Keyfitz puts into perspective the view that behavioral changes will keep *H. sapiens* below social carrying capacity:

> If we have one point of empirically backed knowledge, it is
> that *bad policies are widespread and persistent*. Social science
> has to take account of them [our emphasis].

In short, it seems prudent to evaluate the problem of sustainability for selfish, myopic people who are poorly organized politically, socially, and economically.

The second assertion is that technological advances will sufficiently lower per-capita impacts through reductions in T that no major changes in lifestyle will be necessary. This assertion represents a level of optimism held primarily by nonscientists. (A 1992 joint statement by the US National Academy of Sciences and the British Royal Society expresses a distinct lack of such optimism.) Technical progress will undoubtedly lead to efficiency improvements, resource substitutions, and other innovations that are currently unimaginable. Different estimates of future rates of technical progress are the crux of much of the disagreement between ecologists and economists regarding the state of the world. Nonetheless, the costs of planning development under incorrect assumptions are much higher with overestimates of such rates than with underestimates.

Cultural Carrying Capacity

One . . . fundamental [concept about population] rests on the idea of carrying capacity—the limit to the number of animals a given territory can safely support for an indefinite period . . . without damage to the environment. Unless the limitedness of carrying capacity is admitted, there is little point in counting the number of living bodies. When we come to the human species, the concept of carrying capacity must be enlarged to that of the cultural carrying capacity. Human beings are not content to live at the lowest possible level of resource exploitation. . . . We prefer to use resources with some extravagance. . . . The greater the extravagance—the higher the material standard of living—the lower must be the cultural carrying capacity of the environment.

Garrett Hardin, *The Washington Post*, July 25, 1991.

A few simple calculations show why we believe it imprudent to count on technological innovation to reduce the scale of future human activities to remain within carrying capacity. Employing energy use as an imperfect surrogate for per-capita impact, in 1990 1.2 billion rich people were using an average of 7.5 kilowatts (kW) per person, for a total energy use of 9.0 terawatts (TW; 10^{12} watts). In contrast, 4.1 billion poor people were using 1 kW per person, and 4.1 TW in aggregate. The total environmental impact was thus 13.1 TW.

Suppose that human population growth were eventually halted at 12 billion people and that development succeeded in raising global per-capita energy use to 7.5 kW (approximately 4 kW below current US use). Then, total impact would be 90 TW. Because there is mounting evidence that 13.1 TW usage is too large for Earth to sustain, one needs little imagination to picture the environmental results of energy expenditures some sevenfold greater. Neither physicists nor ecologists are sanguine about improving technological performance sevenfold in the time available.

There is, indeed, little justification for counting on technological miracles to accommodate the billions more people soon to crowd the planet when the vast majority of the current population subsists under conditions that no one reading this would voluntarily accept. Past expectations of the rate of development and penetration of improved technologies have not been fulfilled. In the 1960s, for example, it was widely claimed that technological advances, such as nuclear agroindustrial complexes, would provide 5.5 billion people with food, health care, education, and opportunity. Although the Green Revolution did increase food production more rapidly than some pessimists predicted, the gains were not generally made on a sustainable basis and are thus unlikely to continue. At present, approximately a billion people do not obtain enough dietary energy to carry out normal work activities.

Furthermore, as many nonscientists fail to grasp, technological achievements cannot make biophysical carrying capacity infinite. Consider food production, for example. Soil can be made more productive by adding nutrients and irrigation; yields could possibly be increased further if it were economically feasible to grow crops hydroponically and sunlight were supplemented by artificial light. However, biophysical limits would be reached by the maximal possible photosynthetic efficiency. Even if a method were found to manufacture carbohydrates that was more efficient than photosynthesis, that efficiency, too, would have a maximum. The bottom line is that the laws of thermodynamics inevitably limit biophysical carrying capacity if shortages of inputs or ecological collapse do not intervene first. . . .

The Need for Interdisciplinary Evaluations

Because further degradation of the global environment is inevitable, interdisciplinary evaluations of the relative costs of alternative evils and their communication to the public is necessary. Some provision of insurance should be taken in proportion to the level of uncertainty and the severity of possible deleterious effects of given activities. In the meantime, no further net loss of essential elements of natural capital should be incurred.

Several potentially effective social (especially market) mechanisms have been suggested to make short-term incentives consistent with long-term sustainability. These mechanisms include fees for use of common-property resources, taxes on the depletion of natural capital, and flexible environmental assurance bonding systems for regulating activity that may be environmentally damaging, but whose effects are uncertain. Implementation and further development of such methods of avoiding social traps is essential.

Frequently lacking, however, is a vision of a desired world that would establish a basic social carrying capacity for human beings. In the short run, efforts must be made to minimize the damage to Earth's systems, while providing the requisites of a decent life to the entire global population. In the long run, however, public discussions should be encouraged to guide policy on sustainable resource management. Sound science is central to the estimation of carrying capacities and the development and evaluation of technologies, but it can give minimal guidance at best regarding the issues surrounding the question of the kinds of lives people would choose to live.

The current decade [1990s] is crucial, marking a window of environmental and political opportunity that may soon close. Environmentally, each moment of inaction further entrains irreversible trends, such as the global extinction of biodiversity and alteration of the gaseous composition of the atmosphere. Though it is certainly possible that intensifying human impact on the planet will precipitate a sudden disaster, it seems more likely that humanity will just gradually erode Earth's life-support capabilities over the next few decades. The more important window may thus be a political one for laying the institutional foundations for desired change. Right now, in the wake of United Nations Conference on Environment and Development, citizens and national governments may be at a peak in receptivity to acknowledging environmental problems and tackling their solutions. Let us seize the day.

> *"Uncontrolled population growth . . . must not be fought from inside . . . any nation or group of nations; it must be attacked from the outside—by international agencies."*

International Agencies Should Work to Curb Population Growth

Jacques-Yves Cousteau

Jacques-Yves Cousteau is a renowned oceanographer and environmental educator who has written books and made films about the sea and the life within it. He continues to explore the oceans with his research ship *Calypso*. Cousteau argues that our species has been successful—indeed, too successful—in learning how to circumvent laws of nature. We've learned how to lower mortality rates dramatically, but have not been as successful in lowering the fertility of our species. Cousteau calls for the diversion of money spent on armaments and illegal drugs to international agencies and non-governmental organizations that can attack the twin problems of population control and poverty.

As you read, consider the following questions:

1. According to Cousteau, what lesson did we fail to learn from Easter Island?
2. What laws of nature did our species learn how to defy, in the author's view?
3. What fundamental changes does Cousteau call for in order to stop rapid population growth?

Jacques-Yves Cousteau, "The Greatest Adventure of All Time," *Populi*, November 1992. Reprinted with permission.

The world population problem is studied in detail by several competent organizations. All the figures concerning all nations are available, and the forecasts for the next 40 years are reliable. Any new factor, however important, may modify the long-range guesses but will have little influence on the estimates for the next three or four decades.

Malthus's Prediction Has Come True

What is happening now is a consequence of the exponential nature of population growth while available resources obey a linear progression and are ultimately limited, as the British economist Thomas Robert Malthus prophesied almost 200 years ago. The warnings were repeated by the Club of Rome after World War II, and substantiated by Norman Borlaug, father of the Green Revolution; in his acceptance speech of the Nobel Prize in Stockholm, addressed to the leaders of the world, he insisted that they had only 30 years to harness the demographic threat.

Twenty years have passed since, Borlaug told me, and not only have the leaders taken no action whatsoever, they have even avoided discussing the subject. Since then, the situation has worsened. Deforestation becomes necessary to create farmland; cities burgeon past 20 million, non-renewable resources are depleted, biodiversity shrinks to alarming levels, energy is in unreasonable demand—and above all, poverty spreads, illiteracy generalizes in poor countries, education is unaffordable and for two-thirds of humankind, the quality of life decreases at a disquieting pace.

At the present rate, it will take only 41 years [from 1992] for the world's population to double. But the breakdown of the doubling time for population is striking: 338 years for Europe, 23 years for Africa! Whatever efforts will be made, nothing will prove as efficient in such short times as 20 or 30 years.

How has it been possible that such an unrelenting threat had never motivated any reaction, any serious decision, any consternation among the leaders, the intellectuals, the diplomats, the philosophers? Why have such clear warnings as the collapse of Easter Island's population been ignored?

First occupied by Polynesians in the seventh century, and discovered in 1772 by Roggeveen, Easter Island lived a success story for about 1,000 years, but culminated in genocide brought about by the exhaustion of resources due to an explosive population growth. What a lesson to humankind, outlining what will happen to "Island Earth" if we do not strictly control our demography!

It is only recently that the work of the United Nations Fund for Populations Activities (UNFPA) has been given the attention it deserves; and in its 1991 State of World Population report, it has sadly stated that population growth is even faster than forecast in its 1984 report. And it is regrettable that the recent United Nations Conference on Environment and Development in Rio de Janeiro has not taken seriously enough the influence of demography on the sustainability of humankind's future.

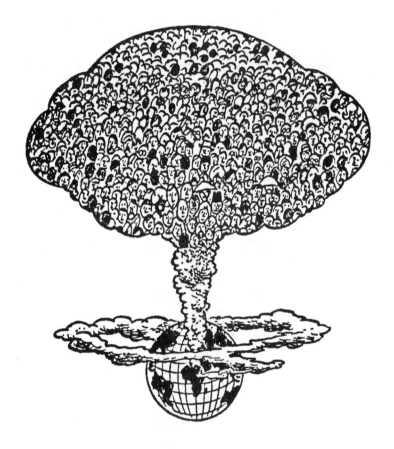

ATOMIC POPULATION EXPLOSION.

Behrendt/Netherlands. Reprinted by permission of Cartoonists & Writers Syndicate.

However, a remarkable joint statement by the Royal Society of London and the United States National Academy of Sciences was recently published, declaring that "if population growth and patterns of human activity on the planet remain unchanged, science and technology may not be able to prevent either irreversible degradation of the environment or continued poverty for much of the world." These two eminent institutions "wish to stimulate debate among scientists, decision-makers, and the public." In addition, they propose to organize a scientific conference to explore these issues in detail.

Such statements and resolutions are to substantiate the 1994 Cairo International Conference on Population and Development. They will permit the international institutions to seriously cope—at last—with what Borlaug calls the "population monster."

Is the public ready to participate actively, aggressively in the debate proposed by the British and American academies? Are not the people at large victims of fatalism, in the wake of apathy shown by their leaders? I believe they must be told a magnificent story—their own story—the greatest adventure of all times.

A Species That Defies the Laws of Nature

We can all be proud to belong to a species that has dared defy the fundamental laws of nature. This idea was originally expressed to me by Prof. Jean Hamburger, president of the French *Academie des Sciences* a few months before he died. In nature, individuals are constantly sacrificed to the survival of the species. Submitted to the harsh law of the jungle, Man—whose design, lacking shell, fangs or claws, made him a victim—resented his own precariousness. As soon as he settled into communities and felt safe from all natural dangers, he divorced from nature and decreed his own rules. We want to respect individuals, Hamburger wrote; we haughtily refuse the sickness, premature death, and natural selection that warranted the quasi-miraculous demographic equilibrium among the innumerable living species. We seek justice, while the story of life was built on the disparity of chances of each. This breach of contract with natural, proven standards is extremely recent, maybe only 100 centuries old, and probably was at the origin of morals.

Almost all our social evils, famines, shocking differences between rich and poor communities, desertification, decrease in biodiversity, increase in the number of hereditary taints, and even the warming up of our planet, originate in the population explosion. And that population explosion is due to the fact that our new set of anti-natural values—generosity, solidarity, pride in our first medical victories over traditional evils—had been enthusiastically applied long before we developed their logical counterpart, birth control.

Our lack of synchronism between part and counterpart shows that we have been very slow to understand that our revolutionary new course, replacing harsh natural rules with our own ideals of equality, fraternity and justice, implied new duties and perils. From victims of nature, we had to become relentless protectors of nature. By refusing for ourselves the law of the jungle, we committed ourselves to making sure that the natural vegetal and animal kingdoms around us would still benefit from that very law of the jungle they cannot survive without.

We have not yet fully realized that our recent divorce from nature is irreversible. Our ancestors have long ago burned the bridges and there is no possible return to nature. This implies for modern man the overwhelming burden to invent from scratch a behaviour at the same time acceptable biologically, and satisfying to his moral ambitions.

Solutions Must Be Found to Curb Population Growth

If we want our precarious endeavour to succeed, we must convince all human beings to participate in our adventure, and we must urgently find solutions to curb the population explosion that has a direct influence on the impoverishment of the less-favoured communities. Otherwise, generalized resentment will beget hatred, and the ugliest genocide imaginable, involving billions of people, will become unavoidable.

We must have the courage to face the situation: either the leaders of the world, having participated in the Rio Conference, understand that what is at stake is literally to save the human species, and accept the need to take drastic, unconventional, unpopular decisions, or the impending disaster dreaded by the British and American scientific academies will precipitate.

Our rejection of the law of the jungle came from our mind, not from our genes. Somehow, in the complex structure of our DNA is engraved our instinct to submit to the harsh laws and principles that have made the success and the diversity of life. The moral laws and principles that we have invented, preferred, and adopted will take a long time to conquer our genetic heritage. A subtle trail of our original wildcat nature has been saved, has grown, and finally blossomed in the free market principle, the cornerstone of all our modern economy.

The free market economy is by far the most efficient system. The collapse of the Communist world is mainly due to the fact that the liberal economy of the West was much more efficient than the planned economy of the East.

However, a closer look leads to unanswered problems: Efficiency? What for? To boost the wealth of the rich quarter and sacrifice the poorer three-quarters of humankind? Efficiency to favour the currency speculators? Efficiency to increase unemployment, to create millions of poor and homeless in the richest countries? To waste resources here that are lacking elsewhere? Efficiency to provide youngsters with only one moral idea: get rich?

94

As long as the free market economy is not far more severely controlled and submitted to our new set of moral values, it will be as cruel, as unjust, and will kill as much as the law of the jungle we have rejected. The international trade in weapons hypocritically enters this free market's set of arguments to flout all moral principles. The armaments market is the trade of death. Nothing else. And it has suddenly increased in the aftermath of the Gulf War.

The two largest industries of the world, the military and the drug markets, are both parasitic, in the sense that they contribute very little or not at all to the well-being of the world. Their turnovers total almost US$1.8 trillion a year. About three times what is necessary to solve the two most pressing problems: population and poverty. The real challenge, even more than reducing or suppressing these ill-omened activities, would be to channel the savings to the vital sectors, in spite of concerted efforts by special interest groups to camouflage their misappropriation,

Uncontrolled population growth and poverty must not be fought from inside, from Europe, from North America or any nation or group of nations; it must be attacked from the outside— by international agencies helped in the formidable job by competent and totally independent non-governmental organizations.

A world policy inspired by eco-biology and eco-sociology is the only one capable of steering our perilous course towards a golden age, and protecting cultural and biological diversity while proudly hoisting the colours of humankind.

"If you listen to most Western economists, then, the dire threats of overpopulation are wildly exaggerated and a laissez faire approach will suffice."

International Population Control Measures Are Harmful

David S. Toolan

David S. Toolan, associate editor of the Jesuit weekly magazine *America*, writes that the dire predictions made a generation ago about a "population bomb" have largely been offset by advances in technology and discovery of new resources. Thus the arguments for a pressing need to find a quick, cheap solution to population growth lose their validity, he maintains—especially when the proposed solution is government-imposed population control. Many government and international programs to curb population growth have harmed women's health, he charges, while failing to support health, education, and social welfare measures that would naturally cut birth rates.

As you read, consider the following questions:

1. Why, according to Toolan, have the dire predictions of Malthus and the Neo-Malthusians been incorrect?
2. How, in the author's opinion, has the United Nations abused third world women, in an effort to control population growth?
3. What results does Toolan foresee from increased literacy and improved economic status for women?

David S. Toolan, "Second Thoughts on the Population Bomb," *America*, March 16, 1993. Reprinted with permission.

In 1803, when the Rev. Thomas Robert Malthus first asserted that "the power of population is indefinitely greater than the power of the earth to produce subsistence for man," a Frenchman, the Marquis de Condorcet, objected that necessity is the mother of invention: Technology—"new instruments, machines and looms"—would prove Malthus wrong, as indeed, so far, it has. The debate continues today in only slightly different form. Environmentalists and their biologist allies take the dismal Malthusian line, threatening us with ecological meltdown and extinction if we do not control the exponential growth of numbers, whereas practitioners of economics optimistically tend to favor Condorcet's faith in the power of science to save us from that fate. Curiously enough, these economists, usually so disdainful of government in other areas, trust it to be competent in matters of population overload—as if city governments in Los Angeles and Nairobi were reliable overseers.

Dire Predictions

The argument goes something like this: Remember Paul Ehrlich's scary *Population Bomb* of 1968, and soon after, the Massachusetts Institute of Technology experts who projected in *The Limits of Growth* that the world would run out of oil in 1992, arable land in 2000, and civilization would collapse in 2070? Yes, in the 25 years since Mr. Erhlich wrote, world population has risen by half, from 3.4 billion people to 5.3 billion—and that may be bad enough, already a strain on local resources here and there (say in sub-Saharan Africa). But the point is that thanks to things like the "green revolution" and new oil discoveries in Alaska and the North Sea, few of 1968's doomsday predictions have materialized. Indeed, in the interim, worldwide per capita food production rose by more than 10 percent, the chronically malnourished fell by 16 percent, and the fertility rates of the poor nations dropped by 30 percent, from an average per woman of 6.0 children to 4.2. Moreover, if this drop in fertility rates continues (as it may not), by the year 2005 it should hit a rate of 2.1, which is the standard rate of replacing a population. Now that may still give us a global population of 10 billion by the year 2025, but it is worth noting that some experts estimate that if the third world used modern methods of agriculture, it would be capable of sustaining a population of 30 billion!

If you listen to most Western economists, then, the dire threats of overpopulation are wildly exaggerated and a laissez faire approach will suffice. Population is a "neutral" factor, they commonly say. Just look at Japan, with one of the highest population densities around (860 per square mile, worse than impoverished Rwanda's!). The problem is not population, they contend, but government policy. The economists (who rarely figure the "social costs" of energy use in their equations) have a limited point. Both sides in this argument might well agree that high fertility is not the primary or only cause of endemic poverty, nor will lower propagation rates automatically lead to prosperity. Clearly, however, for most poor nations, there is a two-way reinforcing relationship between economic development and responsible fertility behavior, each promoting the other.

Reprinted by permission of Matt Wuerker.

To honor that connection would mean that the environmentalists' litany of land, air and water degradation have a more momentous point, and hence there is no time to lose in refunding the U.N.'s Fund for Populations Activities (U.N.F.P.A.) and the International Planned Parenthood Federation that the Reagan Administration abandoned in 1984-85. It is at this juncture, however, that the temptation arises to rush in with a quick technical fix "on the cheap." And this is where the Vatican enters the debate, along with certain women's advocacy groups, both with caveats.

The problem is that even if you agree that birth control ought to be a top priority, the record of U.N.F.P.A.-sponsored action, even apart from the notorious case of China's coercive sterilization and abortion program, provides a record of treating women's health as a dispensable luxury. In many countries such as Brazil and Bangladesh, contraceptive pills and devices were virtually thrown at women without instruction or proper medical care, with the result that the program either backfired, producing greater fertility, or resulted in a high incidence of stroke and infection. The common horror is that U.N. birth control programs are usually part of an International Monetary Fund austerity regime that curbs the local government's spending on education, health and social welfare—the very things that, as is well known, help cut birth rates. For this very reason, some feminist groups like Bella Abzug's New York-based Women's Environmental and Development Organization oppose government-imposed population control and advocate instead a "voluntary reproductive health approach with women at its center."

Environmentalists and the population establishment acknowledge the abuses, but accuse Ms. Abzug and her cohorts of throwing sand in the works. On the eve of the Earth Summit in Rio de Janeiro, Jessica Matthews of Washington, D.C.'s World Resources Institute chided feminists for "playing into the hands of people who are the enemy . . . people who would like to kill population control programs altogether, like . . . [Senator] Jesse Helms and the Vatican." Guilt by association! Heresy!

A Smokescreen to Mask Overconsumption

To be sure, the Vatican's stance in this matter is anything but popular among most feminists, who would sooner be caught dead than be aligned with the Holy See. With many in the third world, however, the Vatican fares better. For its resolute criticism of "scandalous patterns of consumption" in the first world, together with its defense of "the inalienable right of all peoples to development" and the necessity of "an equitable sharing of technology," put it squarely on the side of those third world governments that see the population issue as a smokescreen by which the first world distracts attention from its own overconsumption and casts blame for ecological degradation upon the backs of the poor. At least through the 1970's, therefore, many nonaligned nations resentfully embraced the slogan that "development is the best contraceptive" and demanded a "new international economic order" consisting of transfers of aid and favorable terms of trade. In the last decade, however, third world governments, heeding a rising grassroots demand, have shown an increasing interest in population control. The stage is thus set for Bill Clinton to implement his campaign promise to "restore funding for the United Nations' population stabilization efforts." Supporting abortion need not be a part of such funding.

The Vatican policy on artificial contraception involves a subtle (perhaps too subtle) distinction: It does not intend to kill birth control programs, just to limit severely the options. "The position of the Holy See regarding procreation," said Archbishop Renato R. Martino, the head of the Vatican's delegation to the Rio Earth Summit, "is frequently misinterpreted. The Catholic Church does not propose procreation at any cost. It keeps insisting . . . that the aim of public policy is to enhance the welfare of families; that it is the right of spouses to decide on the size of the family and spacing of births, without pressure from governments or organizations. . . . What the Church opposes is the imposition of demographic policies and the promotion of methods for limiting births which are contrary to the objective moral order and to the liberty, dignity and conscience of the human being."

No doubt this statement implies that the Holy See supports female literacy and the improved economic status for women that feminists espouse, and which usually bring down the birth rate. What neither the Vatican nor many misogynist, macho third world cultures can countenance is that an educated and economically resourceful woman will inevitably learn all the reproductive choices available to her. The world of no choice at all, or of that single choice of natural family planning that the Vatican has in mind, will have vanished forever. Women will have become, many of them for the first time, moral subjects—with all the risks that that entails.

Periodical Bibliography

The following articles have been selected to supplement the diverse views presented in this chapter.

Jesse H. Ausubel

"2020 Vision (Global Population Growth and Technological Remedies to Over-population)," *The Sciences*, November/December 1993. Available from Two E. 63rd St., New York, NY 10021.

Roger L. Conner

"Demographic Doomsayers: Five Myths About Population," *Current*, February 1990. Available from Heldref Publications, 1319 18th St. NW, Washington, DC 20036-1802.

E.W. Foell

"'Z,'" *World Monitor*, May 1992.

Lindsey Grant

"In Search of Optimum Population," *USA Today*, September 1992.

Marguerite Halloway

"Population Pressure," *Scientific American*, September 1992.

Carl Haub

"New UN Projections Show Uncertainty of Future World," *Population Today*, February 1992. Available from 1875 Connecticut Ave. NW, Suite 520, Washington, DC 20009.

Mark Hertsgaard

"Still Ticking . . . the Vatican's Dark Marriage to Islam Has Kept Birth Control off the International Agenda," *Mother Jones*, March 1993.

Charles C. Mann

"How Many Is Too Many?" *The Atlantic Monthly*, February 1993.

Joseph A. McFalls

"Population: A Lively Introduction," *Population Bulletin*, October 1991.

Nafis Sadik

"World Population Continues to Rise," *The Futurist*, March/April 1991.

John C. Schwarz

"Population, the Church, and the Pope," *America*, March 6, 1993.

Julian Simon, interviewed by James Cook

"The More the Merrier," *Forbes*, April 1990.

James Swaney

"Julian Simon Versus Ehrlichs: An Institutionalist Perspective," *Journal of Economic Issues*, June 1991.

Is Overpopulation Responsible for Hunger, Poverty, and Environmental Problems?

Population

Chapter Preface

As much as scholars disagree on whether the world's population is growing too fast, they disagree even more on whether population growth is the root cause of many serious problems. For example, population growth has been causally linked to an environmental crisis by some researchers, while others maintain that the whole "crisis" is a manufactured one.

Population growth has also been causally linked to hunger and poverty. Two hundred years ago Thomas Malthus, in his *Essay on the Principle of Population*, painted excess population as the primary culprit responsible for poverty and hunger. Many contemporary scholars also view population growth as a major factor—perhaps the most important one—in these problems. They maintain that trying to find solutions to world hunger and poverty without addressing population growth is like treating cancer with a Band-Aid—it is futile. Other scholars strongly disagree. Like Karl Marx, they argue that population growth is a convenient scapegoat and that the real explanation for poverty and hunger is inefficient and outdated political and economic systems.

Whether population growth should be blamed for hunger, poverty, and environmental problems is debated in the following chapter.

"Environmentalism is the nice crisis. It's the one that a civilization arrives at when there is no war, when the totalitarian threat is shriveling, when the economy is doing pretty well."

There Is No Environmental Crisis

Ben J. Wattenberg

There is no environmental crisis, Ben J. Wattenberg maintains in the following viewpoint. Humans need to have a crisis at hand, he says; and when there is no available *real* crisis, like war, one must be invented. The "environmental crisis" is just such an artificial construction, Wattenberg maintains, created by academics, politicians, religious leaders, and the press. Wattenberg, a prolific columnist, is the author of *The Birth Dearth*.

As you read, consider the following questions:

1. What does the author think the "environmental crisis" reveals about modern society?
2. What examples does Wattenberg give to support his view that the environmental crisis is a "trendy" concern?
3. What evidence does the author offer to show that the environmental crisis is actually less severe than it was in the past?

Ben J. Wattenberg, "Thanks, Environmentalists," a syndicated column from November 1, 1989. Reprinted by permission of NEA, Inc.

Do not doubt, not for a moment, that environmentalism is the hottest game in town, sweeping all before it, in hallowed groves of academe, in holy places of religious thought, in legislative bazaars, on entertainment soundstages, and in the sacred temple of the free press.

It's a great crisis all right, and what it all shows is just how very healthy modern society is.

At a conference, Charles Alexander said, "As the science editor at *Time*, I would freely admit that on this issue we have crossed the boundary from news reporting to advocacy." (Surprise.)

A full-page advertisement by the Jewish Theological Seminary (J.T.S.) at the time of the Jewish New Year headlined "WHAT ARE WE DOING?" quoted Psalm 104 counterpoised against the horror of modern despoliation. Some examples: "You make the grass grow for the cattle and herbage for man's labor, that he may get food out of the earth" (toxic pesticides). "There is the sea, vast and wide, with its creatures beyond number, living things small and great" (oil spills).

So, the J.T.S. has divined that the divine will is anti–modern-agronomy, and anti–marine-transportation-of-petroleum-products. (Does that mean God is for rotted crops and expensive energy?)

A leading Washington private school canceled the release of helium balloons during its Halloween program. The balloons might ultimately come down in the Potomac and harm marine life. (You should see what happens to marine life when it is broiled, squirted with lemon, and eaten.)

Television is never far behind a trendy trend. In 1990 we will be able to tune out environmental specials, environmental kiddie shows, and trillionaress Barbra Streisand co-hosting a two-hour Earth Day program entitled "A Practical Guide to How You Can Save the Planet." (Probably by putting the second Rolls on blocks.)

The president [George Bush] and Congress are seeking new standards for pesticides in a rhetorical atmosphere that one public health worker calls "anti-science."

All this proves not pollution, but health.

People Crave Crisis

Modern people crave crisis; it is a tropism not unlike a green plant bending toward the sun. Sometimes the crisis is potent and immediate—like war. When such crises are not available, catastrophes of lesser magnitude come to the surface. Such is the case with the environment.

The environmental crisis, remember, is a crisis engendered by people living better. If you're going to have a crisis, that's the place to start.

Next, in terms of what has been measured by the Environmental Protection Agency, the environment is healthier than it used to be by far. Pollution has diminished in fairly direct proportion to the amount of money spent to diminish it. That's not something that can be said for every crisis.

Another "Environmental Crisis"?

[Criticizing environmentalists who are fighting against a water-diversion project that they say would imperil the endangered squawfish, but which she says would benefit her tribe, the Mountain Ute Indians of Colorado]: The environmentalists tell us: "Wait, this isn't the right project. There is something better for your people." But they have yet to tell us what that better thing is. For 100 years, we did not have running water on this reservation. Where were the environmentalists then? They weren't hollering about the terrible conditions for our children. But now, suddenly, the squawfish is so important. More important than the Indian people, apparently.

Judy Knight Frank, *The New York Times*, December 28, 1991.

Moreover, near as can be figured, environmental pollution has not been very harmful. Elizabeth Whalen, of the American Council of Science and Health, says that of the 1 million annual preventable deaths in America, most are due to smoking and alcohol. Those due to pesticides or chemicals in the food supply, she says, account (by the best scientific estimate) for zero. And, she says, air pollution as a general cause of illness or death "provides an extremely minor or hypothetical contribution."

And finally, despite all that, there isn't much of a down side to paying some attention to the panic-mongers. It's probably even good for us if we don't go overboard. (It's certainly good for whales and elephants.)

A few hundred billion dollars for environmental spending won't hurt us much. We're rich. At worst, it will make things somewhat nicer for the aesthetically minded, and somewhat tighter for the poor.

Environmentalism is the nice crisis. It's the one that a civilization arrives at when there is no war, when the totalitarian threat is shriveling, when the economy is doing pretty well.

Environmentalism is the residual crisis. So, thanks environmentalists. Thanks for a crisis that is never-ending, never provable or disprovable, perennially partially conquerable, and psychologically necessary when there is no other game in town.

"The destruction of our environment and resources cannot be stemmed unless the growth of the world's population is stemmed."

The Environmental Crisis Is Real

Henry W. Kendall

Henry W. Kendall, who shared the 1990 Nobel Prize in physics, is the J. A. Stratton Professor of Physics at the Massachusetts Institute of Technology and chair of the Union of Concerned Scientists. According to Kendall, the planet is experiencing serous environmental problems: ozone depletion, depletion of groundwater, soil degradement, and the destruction of the rain forests. These environmental problems are tied very closely to the ever-increasing size of the world's population, he contends, and any effort to solve these problems is doomed unless the population problem is solved first.

As you read, consider the following questions:

1. What specific resources does Kendall list as being critically stressed?
2. How are these stresses directly related to population growth, in the author's analysis?
3. Does Kendall believe the world's environment can withstand present patterns of development? Why or why not?

Henry W. Kendall, "Environment, Resources, Population: The Three Great Problems," *Populi*, June 1992. Reprinted with permission.

Human activities now threaten biological and geophysical systems that all life depends on for food, energy, and a tolerable environment. These activities, if carried on unchecked, will put at serious risk the future that we wish for ourselves and for future generations. They may well leave the world unable to sustain life in the manner that we know.

World Population Growth Must Be Stemmed

The destruction of our environment and resources cannot be stemmed unless the growth of the world's population is stemmed. This growth is putting demands on resources and pressures on the environment that will overwhelm any efforts to achieve a sustainable future. Population growth rates, while declining, are still too large to allow adequate protection for our environment. The United Nations has concluded that the world population could reach 14 billion, a near tripling of today's [1992] numbers. Yet today one person in five lives in absolute poverty and does not get enough to eat, while one in ten suffers serious malnutrition. The obstacle posed by population growth is well appreciated by knowledgeable people although it is not yet fully understood by the world at large.

Critical Stresses

The environment and essential resources are being critically stressed:

- Stratospheric ozone depletion is leading to ultra-violet levels against which much of the natural world has little protection; air pollution near ground level, including acid precipitation, is causing widespread injury to humans, forests and crops.
- We are exploiting and contaminating depletable ground water supplies heedlessly; heavy pressure on the world's surface waters has become a serous concern.
- Agricultural and animal husbandry practices are leading to soil impoverishment, loss of soil productivity, and extensive abandonment; per capita food production in many nations is now decreasing.
- Tropical rain forests, as well as tropical and temperate dry forests, are being destroyed rapidly with the concurrent loss of large numbers of plant and animal species. This irreversible loss—which may approach one-third of all species now living by the year 2100—is an especially serious concern. Forms of life that contribute to the astonishing beauty of Earth are disappearing, and with them the potential for medicinal and other products they might provide, along with much of the genetic diversity that gives robustness to the world's biological systems.

- Pressure on marine fisheries from over-exploitation is increasingly severe. Oceanic regions near the coasts, which produce most of the world's food fish, are being injured by pollution from soil erosion, as well as industrial, municipal, agricultural, and livestock waste.

Tampering with the Web of Life

Much of the damage is permanent or irreversible on a scale of centuries. Other processes appear to pose important threats in the years ahead: Carbon dioxide and other gasses released by human activity into the atmosphere have the potential to alter climate on a global scale. While the predictions of coming warming are still uncertain, the possible risks are very great. Our massive tampering with the world's interdependent web of life could trigger widespread adverse effects, including unpredictable collapses of biosystems that we depend on.

Uncertainty over these possibilities is no excuse for complacency or delay in moving to abate them.

Present patterns of economic development, in both industrialized and developing countries, with the environmental and resource damage they now bring, cannot be sustained because limits on the capacities of vital global systems will soon be reached.

When this occurs, there is great risk that some will be damaged beyond repair and trigger catastrophe that would sweep all into its fold. No more than one or a few decades remain before the chance to control the prospect we now confront will be lost and the prospects for humanity immeasurably diminished.

"Of the 80 million people added to the world's population each year, far too many are destined to be among the poorest and hungriest people on Earth."

Overpopulation Is a Primary Cause of Poverty

Sally Struthers

Sally Struthers, known nationally for her work in television, is Children's Ambassador for Save the Children, an organization devoted to reducing poverty among the world's disadvantaged children. Struthers asserts that rapid population growth has resulted in poverty for much of the world. That many of the poorest countries have seen a rapid rise in population, far beyond their ability to feed their citizens, is a problem made worse, she attests, by a decline in food production in those areas. One answer to meeting this crisis—although a controversial and difficult one, she admits—is to slow population growth.

As you read, consider the following questions:

1. Why does Struthers say the UN estimates of world population are "a tragic figure"?
2. If the world produces enough food to feed all its inhabitants, as Struthers asserts, why are hunger and malnutrition still widespread?
3. What factors does the author list as contributing to a decline in food production?

Sally Struthers, "Saving the Poor," the First Word column in the November 1990 issue of *OMNI*. Reprinted by permission of *OMNI*, ©1990 OMNI Publications International, Ltd.

In Charles Dickens's *A Christmas Carol*, Scrooge is approached in his dank and chilly office by a London charity seeking to help the poor at Christmastime. Scrooge inquires whether the prisons and workhouses of London are still in operation as accommodations for the destitute. His visitor responds that many of the poor would rather die than go to such places. Scrooge's reply echoes in my memory: "If they would rather die," he snarls, "they had better do it and decrease the surplus population."

Not even Dickens, so sensitive to the plight of London's poor, could have pictured how much Scrooge's macabre solution to poverty and overpopulation would become reality. The population of the earth continues to grow while the poor continue to die in unprecedented numbers.

The United Nations Fund for Population Activities estimates [1990] that the number of people on Earth has passed 5 billion. It is a tragic figure: 150 babies are born every minute, 150 new mouths to feed in a world that already cannot feed a fifth of its people adequately. By New Year's Eve, 1999, the number of people inhabiting the earth will reach 6 billion. By 2010 there will be 7 billion of us occupying ourselves with the business of living and dying, loving and hating, being rich and being poor, and trying to solve problems linked to global crowd control. Our great-grandchildren will be contemplating statistics in 2025 of a global population nearing 8 billion. A century from now the world's population will have reached 10 billion. Where, if ever, will it end?

Of the 80 million people added to the world's population each year, far too many are destined to be among the poorest and hungriest people on Earth. From them will come the more than 14 million Third World children under the age of five who die each year because they are too poor to be healthy. These are the kids who will die from diseases spawned by malnutrition—diseases we in the developed nations have long since eliminated as threats to our well-fed youngsters.

Unfortunately, I've seen what malnutrition does to the children of the Third World. In Guatemala, Thailand, Kenya, and Uganda I've looked into the tired eyes of malnourished youngsters who have forever lost the chance to grow straight and strong. But I've also hugged and been hugged by boys and girls who have been rescued from starvation and disease by relief efforts. These are children who will not die because of poverty and neglect. These are the children who have been given the chance to become educated, healthy, confident citizens of their developing nations.

Nearly 20 years ago I made a commitment to do what I could to fight poverty and hunger. I was driven by the misery such a plight inflicts upon children. That commitment seems even more important to me today as world population continues to escalate. Slowing the growth rate is a logical, desirable goal, but the process is agonizingly slow. There *is* much we can do now.

The problem is not a lack of food. The world produces enough food to feed its 5 billion inhabitants, but we need to grow it where it can do the most good. How frustrating to realize that there are hundreds of millions of tons of grains in storage—right now—around the world. We've got to allow more people access to world food supplies.

The irony, the sadness, is that in the countries where the most rapid increases in population are taking place and the poorest people live, food production continues to decline. Years of drought have contributed to the decline, but so, too, has ignorance.

Population, Poverty, and the Environment

The failure of the world community to stem the rising tide of world poverty has many roots. Rapid population growth is one. . . .

The once separate issues of environment and development are now inextricably linked. Environmental degradation is driving a growing number of people into poverty. And poverty itself has become an agent of ecological degradation, as desperate people consume the resource bases on which they depend.

Lester R. Brown, Christopher Flavin, and Sandra Postel, *Saving the Planet: How to Shape an Environmentally Sustainable Global Economy*, 1991.

When I've traveled to make television programs and spot announcements, I've seen farmers still using ancient tools to scratch the dry earth to plant seeds. And too often there are only the most primitive ways of utilizing what little water is available.

What is actually happening, especially in Africa, is that the population is outgrowing the ability of farmers to grow food. In Kenya, where population growth is highest, there will be six times as many people in the year 2025 as there are today. But will there be six times as much food?

Slowing population growth is certainly one answer to the problems of hunger, poverty, and ignorance in the world. How to lower the birthrate is a question fraught with controversy, a question that must be answered separately by nations, peoples, religions, and, ultimately, individual families. But in the meantime the pressures created by the expanding global population have to be relieved as much as possible. Ensuring education, healthy bodies, and sufficient nutritious food for impoverished children is a crucial step in that direction.

"Poverty is not caused by too many people, but by misguided economic and political systems and by a shortage of capital."

Poverty Is Not Caused by Overpopulation

Cal Thomas

Conservative syndicated columnist Cal Thomas asserts in the following viewpoint that the worldwide "population crisis" is a myth. Poverty is not caused by overpopulation, he charges, but by a lack of capital and of economic development—the results of economic and political systems, not of too many people. Thomas contends that U.S. proposals to push a program of population control on Third World countries—especially when such efforts include an emphasis on abortion—are clearly a selfish and distorted response to the problems of poverty. Thomas is the author of several books, including *The Things That Really Matter*.

As you read, consider the following questions:

1. What change took place in U.S. international population policy in 1993, as reported by Thomas?
2. What connection does the author describe between overpopulation and poverty?
3. Whose responses to the changes in U.S. international policy does Thomas describe? How have those changes been received, according to Thomas?

Cal Thomas, "Poverty Is Not Caused by Overpopulation," *Conservative Chronicle*, June 2, 1993, ©1993, Los Angeles Times Syndicate. Reprinted with permission.

One of the first official acts of the Clinton Administration in 1993 was to reverse the Mexico City Policy, prohibiting U.S. funding of international organizations that offer abortions as part of their "family planning" programs. Now the Administration has announced its intention to promote "birth control," including abortion, as a means of "stabilizing" world population growth.

Timothy Wirth, the State Department's counselor, told the U.N. committee planning a major conference on population in Cairo in 1994 that the Administration will resume support for the U.N. Population Fund. Wirth also said that abortion is a necessary component of any global population effort.

Population controllers have succeeded in persuading many people that there are too many humans on the planet, especially in poor countries, and that the answer to poverty is a reduction in the birth rate. In fact, poverty is not caused by too many people, but by misguided economic and political systems and by a shortage of capital.

During the Cold War, the United States was frequently criticized for its intervention in the affairs of some poor countries. Critics said the United States exhibited a spirit of colonialism and paternalism that offended many Third World nations. For the United States to resume "population control" efforts after a hiatus of 12 years would revive those charges on a different and more serious level.

A Population Control "Invasion"

There are signs that the Administration's efforts are already being perceived as an "invasion" of these nations. In March 1993, 61 Catholic bishops, from all parts of Latin America, endorsed an earlier letter of protest to President Clinton written by Cardinal Lopez Rodriguez, president of the Latin American Bishops' Council. Rodriguez pleaded with Clinton to reconsider his revocation of the Mexico City Policy.

The bishops' letter included this: "While we admire the defense of human rights on the part of the government of the United States, we do not understand the denial of the most fundamental of these, the right to life. At the same time we do not concur with the policy which attempts to resolve the dire situation of poverty that afflicts Latin America by imposing a culture of death."

The bishops, influential in mostly Catholic Latin America, are detecting signs that outside efforts to control births are unwelcome. In Guatemala in early 1993, the legislature passed a population-policy law that President Jorge Serrano rejected because of protests, especially from the indigenous Mayan organizations that make up 65 percent of the population.

In the Dominican Republic in March 1993, pro-family and

church groups persuaded the government to put a hold on $10 million of U.S. Agency for International Development money for population control in that country.

The Myth of Overpopulation

Commenting on efforts to use abortion and other means of population control to combat poverty, Pope John Paul II has written that they emanate from a "distorted view of the demographic problem and (come from) a climate of absolute lack of respect for the freedom of decision of the parties involved, frequently subjecting (the people) to intolerable pressures . . . in order to force them to submit to a new form of oppression."

The notion of a worldwide "population crisis" is a myth. People are not a burden. They are a natural resource. If the poor are such a problem, why not just kill them all now and be done with it? Poor people aren't the problem. Economic and political systems that do not let them escape from poverty are.

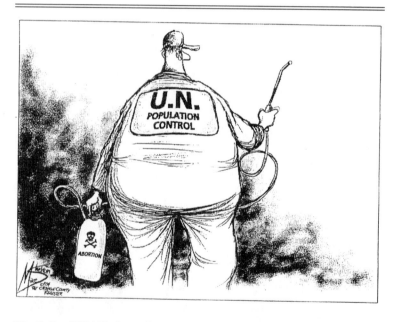

Mike Shelton, ©1994 *The Orange County Register*. Reprinted with permission.

The No. 1 contributor to poverty is a lack of economic development and, in some countries, external debt. That was the point made eloquently by Marcia Ccocllo (cq) of Lima, Peru, in a Feb. 4, 1989, letter to the *New York Times:* "We don't need birth control. We need to end poverty. I witness daily that the intrauterine devices and pills that the United States floods our country with only create more frustrations for women and many times serious harm to their health, which worsens their financial condition even more. At times, I view with sadness that many women bring their children with an injury or a burn to health centers that don't even have gauze or antiseptics, but shelves filled with birth-control pills. . . . Our country needs technical and economic assistance to make progress."

A Selfish Agenda Undermines Foreign Relations

By pursuing a "population control" agenda, the United States risks undermining already delicate relations with Latin America and other countries. They see our promotion of abortion while refusing aid for economic development as an effort to preserve our own affluent lifestyle that ignores the legitimate aspirations of people whose poverty will not be cured by not having babies.

*"There is enough food to feed 40 billion to 50
billion people annually—nearly 10 times the
present world population."*

There Is No
Shortage of Food

David Osterfeld

The vast majority of nations, including India and China, have suc-
cessfully increased agricultural output to keep up with population
growth over the past few decades, reports David Osterfeld.
Worldwide food consumption is up, he maintains; in fact, enough
food is produced now to feed four or five times the world's current population. Only Africa has endemic problems with food production, he declares, and these problems result from tribal and
regional conflicts and inefficient socialist economies—not population growth. Osterfeld was a professor of political science at St.
Joseph's College in Rensselaer, Indiana, and a Bradley Resident
Scholar at the Heritage Foundation, a conservative think tank.

As you read, consider the following questions:

1. Why did the agricultural output of India and China begin to
   increase dramatically in the late 1970s and early 1980s,
   according to Osterfeld?
2. What evidence does the author offer to support his point that
   Africa's food shortages are not the result of overpopulation?
   What specific reasons does he offer for Africa's shortages?
3. What does the author mean by a "birth dearth"? Does he
   indicate that the number of people on the planet is
   decreasing?

David Osterfeld, "Crowding Out the Species," *The Washington Times*, March 29, 1992.
Reprinted by permission of the author's estate.

Ringing with the moral authority of a papal encyclical, the U.S. National Academy of Sciences and the Royal Society of London have announced that if current predictions of population growth prove accurate, "science and technology may not be able to prevent either irreversible degradation of the environment or continued poverty for much of the world."

That just goes to prove that scientists may be good at science, but lousy at public policy.

The Polls vs. the Facts

The message is not new. The Chicken Little gang has been heralding the need for zero population growth for decades. Unfortunately they have been quite successful: Polls show that most Americans believe that the world is overpopulated, that population growth must be halted, that there are too many people relative to food, resources and living space.

Now, let's forget the polls, and dwell on the facts. Data from the U.N. Food and Agriculture Organization and the U.S. Department of Agriculture show that per capita food production and consumption have been increasing by about 1 percent a year since the 1940s. Between 1965 and 1985, per capita food consumption increased in 80 percent of the nations of the world—even as the world population was steadily increasing.

China and India, the world's two most populated countries, are doing a much better job of feeding their people than they were even a decade ago, in the early 1980s. Since the abolition of the Chinese collectives in the late 1970s farm output has been increasing by about 12 percent per year. Similarly, agricultural output in India shot up dramatically following the lifting of price controls and other agricultural restrictions in the early 1980s.

Africa's Problem Is Not Overpopulation

Of the countries showing either no improvement or a drop in food consumption, the majority were in Africa. But most of the agricultural problems on the continent are not a result of overpopulation: Africa, one of the world's least densely populated continents, was a food exporter during the first half of the 20th century.

Instead, Africa's food shortages are traceable to other factors. One is war: Since the end of the colonial era, dozens of countries have been embroiled in tribal or regional conflict. Another is inefficient socialist economies. Until recently, the private sale of farm products was prohibited or severely restricted in Tanzania, Nigeria, Zaire, and elsewhere; in Ghana and other states, governments routinely have seized more than half of farmers' income through taxation and regulation.

A growing number of countries actually have food surpluses.

That's why worldwide food prices have fallen by more than 25 percent since 1950. According to many agricultural experts, there is enough food to feed 40 billion to 50 billion people annually—nearly 10 times the present world population. Food supplies, in short, are increasing.

Reprinted by permission of Chuck Asay and Creators Syndicate.

What about natural resources? Like food, resources are becoming more, not less, plentiful—thanks largely to technological advances. Aluminum, for example, can be substituted for tin and zinc, rubber and plastic for lead, and plastic and glass for wood. The result has been a long-term decline in average prices for natural resources, particularly over the last decade. Even the price of gasoline, when adjusted for inflation, is lower now than in 1972, the year before the Arab oil embargo.

The Birth Dearth

The population explosion has, in fact, turned into a birth dearth, as fertility rates have dropped to 1.8 children per family in the developed world and are declining even more rapidly in the Third World. At the same time, supplies of food, resources and even living space have been increasing. Dare we say it? Yes, the world actually is becoming relatively less populated.

The deafening demands to encourage—or to force—couples to have fewer children is the triumph of ideology over fact. It is an unwarranted interference with the most intimate and personal decision human beings can make. If such a choice is left to scientists or government bureaucrats, then a Brave New World has arrived—a dark world ruled by a disdain for life itself.

"Satisfying the food needs of 90 million more people each year is possible only by reducing consumption among those already here."

Food Yields Are Shrinking as Population Grows

Lester R. Brown

According to Lester R. Brown, the world's population continues to expand while per capita food production has begun to decline. Although dramatic increases in grain harvest, seafood catch, and beef production since mid-century have led to a "golden age" of consumption, no more such increases are on the horizon, he warns. In fact, Brown reports, natural systems are faltering under the stress of these high yields, while the increases in agricultural output have reached the limit of foreseeable growth. He concludes that it is necessary to reduce both consumption and population growth. Brown is president of Worldwatch Institute, an environmental research group in Washington, D.C., that annually publishes *The State of the World, Vital Signs,* and *The Environment Alert.*

As you read, consider the following questions:

1. How does the growth in world grain production from 1950 to 1984 compare with the production from 1984 to the present, according to Brown? What similar comparisons does he make for seafood and meat production?
2. What limits to food production does the author discuss?
3. What consequences does Brown foresee if current trends in population growth and food production continue?

When the history of the last half of this century is written, population growth is likely to get far more attention than it does now. Those of us born before mid-century have witnessed unprecedented worldwide rises in incomes, steady gains in food consumption and a dramatic extension of life expectancy. But this golden age may be coming to an end for reasons that we do not well understand. And that is what will fascinate historians.

Slowdowns in Food Production

After mid-century, the world's farmers more than doubled the grain harvest, something no previous generation had done. Raising the harvest from 631 million tons in 1950 to 1,650 million tons in 1984, they increased grain production by 40 percent per person, reducing hunger and malnutrition around the world. Since 1984, however, grain production has fallen behind population growth, falling roughly 1 percent a year.

An even more abrupt slowdown is restricting supplies of seafood, the world's principal source of animal protein. Between 1950 and 1989, the world catch climbed from 22 million tons to 100 million tons. As a result, we have enjoyed a doubling of seafood consumption per person.

Since 1989, however, the catch has declined—to an estimated 97 million tons in 1992, or a decline of 8 percent per person. For some time, marine biologists at the United Nations Food and Agriculture Organization have warned that the oceans could not sustain a catch of more than 100 million tons a year.

With grasslands, the other natural system on which we depend heavily for animal protein, demands are also straining the limits on every continent. From 1950 to 1990, world production of beef, most of it from grasslands, went from 19 million to 53 million tons. But since 1990, production has dropped more than 2 percent. Mutton, the other grass-based meat, has followed a similar trend.

Marine biologists and rangeland agronomists had warned that these natural systems were being pushed ever closer to their limits. The slowing growth in grain output was somewhat less predictable, but growth in the area planted in grain came to a halt in 1981.

The Limits of the "Green Revolution"?

Two other trends are partly responsible. First, the growth of irrigated areas, after more than doubling between 1950 and 1978, fell behind population growth. Since 1978, the irrigated area per person has shrunk by 7 percent. Second, the growth of fertilizer use, the engine that drove the growth in food output, is slowing. Fertilizer use increased ninefold from 1950 to 1984, but since then has increased little. In agriculturally advanced countries, applying more fertilizer now does little to raise output.

As growth in fertilizer use has slowed, so has growth in the world grain harvest. More disturbing, there is no new technology in prospect that will enable farmers to restore the 3 percent annual growth in grain production that prevailed from 1950 to 1984.

This is a matter of deepening concern. In 1992, the National Academy of Sciences and the Royal Society of London issued a report that warned: "If current predictions of population growth prove accurate and patterns of human activity on the planet remain unchanged, science and technology may not be able to prevent either irreversible degradation of the environment or continued poverty for much of the world."

Reprinted by special permission of North America Syndicate.

The world has quietly entered a new era, one in which satisfying the food needs of 90 million more people each year is possible only by reducing consumption among those already here.

The only sensible option may now be an all-out effort to slow population growth. The first step is to fill the family-planning gap by expanding services. But unless the world can go beyond that and attack the conditions that foster rapid population growth—namely, discrimination against women and widespread poverty—reversing the decline may not be possible.

"The populations of the arid and semi-arid countries of Kenya, Ethiopia, and Iran may well double within 25 years, but the amount of available water will remain the same."

Population Growth Is Causing Water Shortages

Mary Mederios Kent

Although water is a "renewable" resource, Mary Mederios Kent cautions that even recycling has its limits. Current population growth and water use patterns threaten not only regional water quality and supplies, but local and global environmental systems, she maintains. Kent warns that while many developing countries are already water-poor, they have some of the highest rates of population growth; this not only creates direct competition for already scarce water but also spurs development that aggravates the problem. Kent is a research demographer at the Population Reference Bureau (PRB), a demographic research organization in Washington, D.C. The data in this viewpoint were drawn from "Population and Water Resources: A Delicate Balance," by Malin Falkenmark and Carl Widstrand, *Population Bulletin*, November 1992, published by PRB.

As you read, consider the following questions:

1. What limits on the "renewability" of water does Kent cite?
2. According to the author, what countries are experiencing the most severe water problems? What causes does she cite?
3. How can water shortages result in land degradation, as described by Kent?

Mary Mederios Kent, "New Report Studies Population, Water Supply," *Population Today*, December 1992. Reprinted by permission of the publishers, the Population Reference Bureau.

The world's population lives at the mercy of the water cycle. Human innovation can make the best possible use of the water that passes through a country's territory, but technology cannot influence the rate at which water is naturally renewed from the global water circulation system. Further, human activities, such as clearing forests, waste disposal, and withdrawal of freshwater, introduce disturbances in the water cycle that resonate throughout local and global environmental systems.

Population Growth Exacerbates Water Problems

These disturbances are accelerated by the world's continuing population growth and consumption patterns. Nearly one-third of the world's inhabitants live in countries with severe water problems. Some of the world's poorest countries lie within regions of North Africa and the Middle East where water is scarce. These regions also have some of the highest rates of population growth in the world. The populations of the arid and semi-arid countries of Kenya, Ethiopia, and Iran may well double within 25 years, but the amount of available water will remain the same. Although birth rates are falling in some countries in these regions, the young age structure of the population—created by decades of high fertility—provides a tremendous momentum for future growth as large young cohorts reach their prime reproductive years.

The Hydrological Margin

One way to quantify the changing relationship between population size and water stress is by comparing a country's population size to its number of flow units of water. (One flow unit equals 1 million cubic meters of water per year.) Most of the water used by people—about 70 percent worldwide—goes to produce food and other necessities through agriculture. The production of goods through industry accounts for about 23 percent of use. People require about 8 percent of the water supply for direct household use.

If the population per flow unit remains low—below 100—water supply is generally not a problem. As population numbers increase, some water management is required to assure quality and equal distribution. The countries of central and southern Europe—at about 300 persons per flow unit—are at this level of water resource competition. As population per flow unit increases to over 600, signs of stress begin to appear. At over 1,000 persons per flow unit, a country experiences chronic water shortage. Under current technology, extreme scarcity occurs if the ratio exceeds 2,000 persons per flow unit.

Many North African and Middle Eastern countries already face water scarcity. In Jordan and Israel, over 3,000 people compete for every flow unit of renewable water. In Africa and

126

Myths About Water

Myth: Water is an endlessly renewable resource.
Fact: Water is renewed within the global cycle, but the renewal rate of water is fixed and extremely slow. The amount of water entering an area each season depends on geography and climate. There are no untapped reserves of water, but there may be unused flows that could be developed. Deep underground aquifers (such as Libya's Nubian Aquifer) refill so slowly after water is pumped out that they must be classified as nonrenewable resources.

Myth: Water is a static resource.
Fact: Water is a dynamic, not static, resource. The renewal rate, not the global volume of water at a given time, determines how much water is available for use. The volume of a lake does not determine the amount of water that can be withdrawn, but rather the flow of rivers and springs that feed the lake.

Myth: Water and the availability of water is a purely technical issue.
Fact: Many of our economic and resource problems have been solved by technology, but water is not solely a technological issue. If technology produces rain over one country, a neighboring country is deprived of its rainfall. If Ethiopia builds a dam near the source of the Nile, that would diminish the supply of water for Egypt, thousands of miles downstream.

Myth: Availability of water is mainly an economic question governed by market forces.
Fact: About 90 percent of the world's water supplies are not amenable to metering and thus elude current market economies.

Mary Mederios Kent, *Population Today*, December 1992.

southern Asia, rapid population growth will push many countries into higher stress ratios and eventually to chronic water shortages if they don't make substantial water-management improvements. Kenya had 905 people per flow unit in the 1970s, but this ratio should exceed 2,000 by the year 2025, when its population is expected to quintuple from the 1970 level. Over 1 billion people in Africa and southern Asia will live under conditions of water scarcity by 2025. All countries of western Asia, except Turkey, will be affected.

Threats to Water Quality

In water-scarce countries, population size along with water management will become a major determinant of the quality of life. Yet, even in water-rich countries, pressures from modern farming technology, urbanization and industry may undercut water quality, creating health and environmental hazards. For example, the overuse of nitrogen-rich fertilizers has caused algae blooms which rob the water of oxygen in the Baltic and North Seas, raising public concern about water quality and its effect on the fishing industry in Scandinavia. Acid rain is another human-induced chemical disturbance, caused by the buildup of chemicals in the air from the burning of fuels for energy production, industry, and auto exhaust. This process has disrupted forest growth in the Adirondack Mountains in the United States and in Czechoslovakia.

Where rivers and prevailing winds flow across national boundaries, the pollution problems of one country may originate in another. The water supply for the Netherlands, for example, is vulnerable to the huge amounts of pollutants carried into the region by the Rhine River from the upstream countries of Switzerland, France, and Germany. Many of the pollutants that cause Canada's acid rain originate in the United States.

In developing countries, rapid urbanization and industrialization can increase the stress on water resource quality. The average population pressure on water resources in most Latin American countries appears moderate, for example. But a majority of Latin Americans live in cities, which often are subject to serious water pollution from industrial and household wastes. Natural increase plus a constant stream of migrants from the countryside is causing rapid growth in these urban areas, often encompassing informal squatter settlements that lack sanitary water systems. Explosive growth in cities such as Alexandria and Cairo in Egypt or Lagos and Ibadan in Nigeria exacerbates the problems of providing sanitary water for domestic use and needed industrial expansion, as well as the disposal of human and industrial wastes.

In water-poor countries, the pressure of rising populations can set off a cycle that reinforces the effects of other sources of water scarcity. Population growth can aggravate deforestation and overgrazing, resulting in changes in microclimate such as rainfall fluctuation, drought conditions, and the loss of topsoils that retain water. Such conditions can lead to land degradation and recurrent droughts that decrease food production.

What can countries do to protect their water supply? Slowing population growth is an important step for fast-growing countries. For example, in Nigeria and Uganda, where family size averages six children per woman, the governments have set the goal of reducing family size to four. But demographic change occurs slowly because of the momentum for growth built into the current age structure. In the short term, the impending shortages can be ameliorated by adopting management techniques to increase the amount of available water, use water more efficiently, and reduce human-induced disruption of global water systems.

"Using water more efficiently, in effect, creates a new source of supply."

Conservation Measures Can Alleviate Water Shortages

Sandra Postel

Water conservation is not only more ecologically sound than developing new supplies of water, contends Sandra Postel, it is also a better economic investment. Agricultural, industrial, business, and residential users of water have all been encouraged to use this increasingly scarce resource wastefully, she charges. While there have been scattered instances of successful conservation efforts around the world, Postel argues for a comprehensive strategy to ensure that water use policies protect the ecology and the integrity of worldwide water systems. A former vice president of the environmental research organization Worldwatch Institute in Washington, D.C., Postel is the author of *Last Oasis: Facing Water Scarcity*, from which this viewpoint is adapted.

As you read, consider the following questions:

1. What methods does Postel mention for conserving water used in agriculture? How much water does she say can be saved?
2. How does the author suggest water can be conserved by industry and in residential and commercial buildings?
3. What policies and laws does the author say need to be changed to encourage water conservation?

Conservation, once viewed as only an emergency response to drought, has been transformed in recent years into a sophisticated package of measures that offers one of the most cost-effective and environmentally sound ways of balancing water budgets. Using water more efficiently, in effect, creates a new source of supply. Each liter conserved can help meet new water demands without damming another stretch of river or depleting more groundwater. And aside from being more ecologically sound, most investments in water efficiency, recycling, reuse, and conservation now yield more usable water per dollar than do investments in conventional water supply projects.

Tremendous Saving of Water Possible in Agriculture

Because agriculture claims two-thirds of all the water removed from rivers, lakes, streams, and aquifers, making irrigation more efficient is a key to achieving more sustainable water use. The savings possible in agriculture constitute a large and mostly unexploited new source of supply. Reducing irrigation needs by one-tenth, for instance, would free up enough water to roughly double domestic water use worldwide.

A wide variety of measures exists to boost agriculture's water productivity. For example, in Texas, which faces long-term depletion of the Ogallala aquifer, many farmers have adapted old-fashioned furrow systems to a new surge technique that reduces percolation losses at the head of the field and distributes water more uniformly. Savings in the Texas Plains have averaged 25%, and the initial investment of about $30 per hectare (1 hectare = 2.47 acres) is typically recouped within the first year. Israel has pioneered the use of drip irrigation, a thrifty technique that delivers water through a network of porous or perforated piping directly to the crops' roots, often achieving efficiencies of about 95%.

Worldwide, since the mid-1970s the use of drip and other microirrigation techniques has grown 28-fold. Nearly 1.6 million hectares are now watered by these methods. Israel has about half of its total irrigated land under drip. This has helped farmers reduce their water use on each irrigated hectare by one-third, and they have even increased crop yields at the same time.

In addition to spreading these technologies, raising the efficiency of the extensive surface canal systems that dominate the world's irrigated lands is very important. Because many irrigation works are poorly maintained and operated, some lands get too much water and others get none. In India, for instance, improvements in the infrastructure and operation of its large canal systems could expand the irrigated area by nearly a fifth without the building of any new dams.

Collectively, industries account for nearly a quarter of the world's water use. Most industrial water is used for cooling, processing, and other activities that may heat or pollute water but do not consume it. This allows a factory to recycle its supplies, thereby getting more output from each cubic meter delivered or allocated to it.

Japan, the United States, and former West Germany are among the countries that have achieved striking gains in industrial water productivity. After a period of rapid industrialization following World War II, total water use by Japanese industries peaked in 1973 and then dropped 24% by 1989. Meanwhile, industrial output was climbing steadily. As a result, in 1989 Japan got $77 worth of output from each cubic meter of water supplied to industries, compared with $21 (in constant dollars) in 1965. In just over two decades, the nation more than tripled its industrial water productivity.

Water Resources Management Requires Teamwork

The most critical need to solve problems of water resources management is leadership, including leadership in the integration of problem-solving teams involving different disciplines and points of view. . . . Research will be needed at the problem-solving level to discover how natural and man-made systems interact. The contributions of each discipline on the problem-solving team, engineering, economic, legal, ecological, financial, political, are needed to find the best solutions. Research can help to reduce conflicts to those that require policy debate and political action by providing information, unraveling complexity and pointing out how to reach integrated decisions.

Neil S. Grigg, in Katherine Hon, ed., *Water Management in the '90s*, 1993.

Homes, apartments, small businesses, and other municipal enterprises account for less than one-tenth of the world's total water use. But their demands are concentrated in relatively small geographic areas and in many cases are escalating rapidly. Cities as diverse as Singapore, Boston, Mexico City, Jerusalem, and Los Angeles have shown conservation to be a money-saving way of meeting their residents' water needs. In the greater Boston area, for instance, the installation of water-efficient fixtures in homes, industrial water audits, systemwide leak detection and repair, and public education reduced total annual water demand by 16%, bringing it back to the level of the late 1960s and postponing the need to develop new water sources.

Altogether, with the tools and technologies readily available, farmers could cut their water needs by 10-50%, industries by

40-90%, and cities by a third with no sacrifice of economic output or quality of life. Yet we are stuck at the brink of this transformation because of policies and laws that encourage wastefulness and misuse rather than efficiency and conservation.

New Policies and Laws Are Needed

Reducing water subsidies, especially in irrigation, is a top priority. Many farmers pay less than a fifth of water's true cost, and thus have no incentive to use it wisely. Real-cost pricing is also critical in municipal water systems to encourage industries and homeowners to conserve. In addition, encouraging open markets for water trading would help reallocate scarce supplies and promote efficiency. In the United States, 127 water transactions were reported in 12 western states during 1991; most of the water was sold by farms and bought by cities.

Where groundwater extractions exceed recharge [natural renewal], pumping regulations or depletion taxes are needed to achieve water balance. And public action is also needed to ensure that ecological systems get the water they need to remain healthy. Montana, for instance, has a law that allows the state and federal governments to reserve water for "instream" uses. As a result, about 70% of the average annual flow in the upper basin of the Yellowstone River and half to two-thirds of the lower basin flow have been reserved to protect aquatic life, water quality, and other ecological services.

Here and there, pricing, marketing, and regulatory actions are being used effectively to promote conservation and sustainable water use. But nowhere have all the elements been brought together into a strategy ensuring that human use of water remains within ecological bounds and that the overall integrity of water systems is protected. The challenge now is to put as much human ingenuity into learning to live in balance with water as we have put into controlling and manipulating it.

Periodical Bibliography

The following articles have been selected to supplement the diverse views presented in this chapter.

Lester R. Brown and Werner Fornos
"The Environmental Crisis: A Humanist Call for Action," *The Humanist*, November/December 1991.

Anna Maria Gillis
"Forecasting the Future," *BioScience*, January 1991.

Cynthia P. Green
"The Environment and Population Growth: Decade for Action," *Population Reports*, May 1992. Available from Office of Health, Research, and Statistics, Box 3378, Honolulu, HI 96801.

Daniel E. Keshland Jr.
"Clean Thoughts on Clean Air," *Science*, September 1993.

Maurice King and Charles Elliot
"Legitimate Double-Think," *The Lancet*, March 13, 1993. Available from Williams & Wilkins, 428 E. Preston St., Baltimore, MD 21202.

Richard D. Lamm
"The Future of the Environment," *The Annals of the American Academy of Political and Social Science*, July 1992.

Ronald D. Lee
"The Environmental Challenge," *The Unesco Courier*, January 1992. Available from Unipub, 4611-F Assembly Dr., Lanham, MD 20706-4391.

Bobbi S. Low and Joel T. Heinen
"Population, Resources, and Environment: Implications of Human Behavioral Ecology for Conservation," *Population and Environment*, September 1993.

Wanga Mumba
"Viewpoint: Women, Population, and the Environment," *Environmental Action*, Summer 1992. Available from 6930 Carroll Ave., Suite 600, Takoma Park, MD 20912.

David Norse
"A New Strategy for Feeding a Crowded Planet," *Environment*, June 1992.

Nafis Sadik
"Poverty, Population, Pollution," *The Unesco Courier*, January 1992.

Mira Shiva and Vandana Shiva
"Population and Environment: An Indian Perspective," *Women and Environments*, Winter/Spring 1993. Available from Centre for Urban and Community Studies, 455 Spadina Ave., Toronto, Ont. M5S 2G8.

What Are the Effects of Immigration into the United States?

Population

Chapter Preface

As recent political maneuvering in such "entry" states as Florida, California, and Texas demonstrates, immigration is a volatile topic—especially during times of economic hardship or instability. The United States may be a nation of immigrants, but Americans have a checkered history in their welcome and respect for newcomers to the country.

Debates on immigration—legal or illegal—often focus on the effects of immigrants on the rest of the nation, their cost to the nation, and whether and how immigration should be controlled—all issues that are debated in the following viewpoints. Occasionally arguments are made from the point of view of the immigrant (arguments, for example, on how bad or dangerous conditions must be in an immigrant's native country before he or she should automatically be admitted to the United States). Most of the arguments, though, assume that migration to the United States is a desirable thing, an ultimate good for the immigrant; why else would he or she wish to migrate?

Ruben G. Rumbaut, in an anthology edited by Barry Edmonston and published by the National Academy of Sciences, suggests that that "ultimate good" may well be attenuated, that immigration to the United States may even threaten the health of some immigrants. "The good life," it seems, includes unhealthy lifestyle options: Rumbaut reports on rising cholesterol levels among Vietnamese in Connecticut, increasingly unhealthy diets among Mexican farmworkers in California, and progressive development of bad habits—smoking, drug and alcohol use—of Latino immigrants in Los Angeles.

So, while the nation—including the authors of the following viewpoints—debates whether and how to allow immigrants to enter the country, some who have already arrived are holding up a mirror to their new compatriots, outlining by contrast to their old lives the results of the "American way of life."

"Diversity is the opposite of unity, and unity is a prime requirement for national survival."

Excessive Immigration Undermines National Unity

Garrett Hardin

Misguided attempts to avoid the appearance of racism have led to an uncritical celebration of diversity, maintains Garrett Hardin in the following viewpoint. Those who applaud diversity often promote increased immigration from non-European cultures to the United States, he says, which leads to cultural clashes. Diversity should be supported among nations, he declares, but it should be approached cautiously within each nation. Hardin, a professor emeritus of ecology at the University of California, Santa Barbara, is the author of several books, including *Population, Evolution, and Birth Control* and *Living Within Limits: Ecology, Economics, and Population Taboos.*

As you read, consider the following questions:

1. What examples does Hardin cite of ways non-European immigrants could produce conflict in the United States?
2. What kind of social and cultural diversity would the author like to see promoted? In his view, how do the effects of this kind of diversity compare with the effects of increased immigration?

Garrett Hardin, "How Diversity Should Be Nurtured," *The Social Contract*, Spring 1991. Reprinted with permission.

The word "diversity" has become, as Shelby Steele says, one of the "golden words" of our time—words like motherhood and apple pie that we are supposed to accept unthinkingly as sound coinage. But doubt-free acceptance is always dangerous.

Biologists are partly responsible for the prestige of "diversity." Seeking the highest yields, American corn-growers at one time greatly reduced the genetic diversity in their hybrid cornstocks. "Monocultures"—pure stands of grains—became the rule. Unfortunately, monocultures are a standing invitation to the evolution of new plant diseases. In 1970 a mutant fungus suddenly appeared and almost wiped out the U.S. corn crop. (A few more days of warm, humid weather and it would have.) Then agricultural scientists backpedaled fast and introduced more genetic diversity into the stocks (even though it meant somewhat less productivity in the short term). "Diversity" became a golden word in agriculture.

Now some critics are saying we need more diversity in human populations—specifically, in the American population. But even the most casual inspection of our people reveals an amount of variety that greatly exceeds that in cultivated crops. Uniformity is not our problem. Why, then, this cry for more diversity?

Affirmative Action Is Racist

It's safe to say that most of the proponents of diversity are emotionally opposed to racism. But are their actions anti-racist *in their effect*? The non-racist way to assign jobs to people is to distribute them according to individual merit. Unfortunately, of course, the problem of ascertaining merit is a difficult one; it is easily warped by prejudice. Seeking to thwart prejudice, fair-minded people evade the problem by distributing positions on the basis of the relative frequencies of identifiable groups.

For a while the mandated numbers were called "quotas." Then sensitive people dropped "quotas" and used the golden phrase "affirmative action." As the second term became recognized as the equivalent of the first, a third golden term was adopted: "diversity." But whatever term is used (and no doubt there will be others), the operational meaning is clear: society is asked to assign positions on the basis of group membership rather than individual merit. Whatever words one may attach to such a policy, operationally it amounts to racism.

What irony—that emotional anti-racism should end in operational racism! (In the same way anti-sexists, by calling for job assignments by the numbers, promote sexism in practice.) An old saying warned us of such tragedies: "We become what we hate."

It would be a mistake, however, to pursue this line of argument further; it could easily degenerate into a war of golden words. Instead, let's see what the actual consequences would be

137

of promoting diversity in our already very diverse population by greatly increasing the amount of immigration.

Promoters of more diversity maintain that the more immigrants the better, and the greater the variety the richer America will become. Many of these promoters are "Europhobic"—fearful of, or revolted by, European civilization and values. They say we should stop taking in North Europeans, urging us instead to solicit the Filipinos, the Taiwanese and the Salvadorans. "And why not more Sikhs, more Turks, more Somalis, more Chileans, more Maoris, more Ibos, and more Malaysians?"

A Brazil of North America

By 2050, according to the Census Bureau, whites may be near a minority in an America of 81 million Hispanics, 62 million blacks and 41 million Asians. By the middle of the next century, the United States will have become a veritable Brazil of North America. . . .

Supporters of open immigration contend that Hispanic, Asian and Arab immigrants often bring with them the same strong family ties, respect for authority, and work ethic Americans have always cherished and celebrated.

Undeniably true. But it is equally true that many Third World immigrants are living off public services, and many are going into crime. . . .

Looking back down the 20th century, we see that all the great multinational empires have fallen apart. Now, the multinational states—Canada, Czechoslovakia, India, Russia, Yugoslavia, South Africa, Ethiopia—are breaking apart. Are we immune to all this?

Pat Buchanan, *Conservative Chronicle*, June 16, 1993.

Diversity triumphant! How exciting! Anyone who opposes such proposals risks being called a racist. But possible genetic differences are not the issue. Even if there are no significant genetic differences, there are formidable cultural differences. When we admit a Sikh or a Muslim, for instance, we are admitting more than a human body. We are admitting a person imbued with cultural values that are significantly different from our own.

All across central Africa there are people who believe in the justice of "female circumcision," that is, the mutilation of the genitalia of young women. The object is to make intercourse painful to women so that wives won't be tempted to be unfaithful to their husbands. Were we to admit large numbers of cen-

138

tral Africans would they not insist on continuing the practice here? Some of them might even justify it on religious grounds. Are we really so tolerant of other religions and other cultures that we would permit the transplantation of female mutilation into our own country? I doubt it. Moreover I don't think we should be that tolerant. I submit that many increases in diversity should be rejected at the outset.

The Salman Rushdie Affair

But that dreadful scenario has not been enacted here yet. Let's look at a story that developed recently in England—the Rushdie affair. The novel *The Satanic Verses*, written by Salman Rushdie, an expatriate Indian, has much disturbed the Muslim world with its alleged blasphemy of the Koran. Muslims are not willing to allow extra latitude to the expression of obnoxious sentiments by fictional characters. In 1988 the Ayatollah Khomeini, the ruler of Iran, condemned Rushdie's book, and soon a non-governmental Iranian organization offered $3 million to any true believer who assassinated Rushdie *anywhere in the world*. The threat was taken seriously because there were thousands of Iranians and other Muslims living in Europe and the Americas. The author went into hiding in England and the British government assigned agents to protect him. The expense of protection must have been considerable. Worse, the Muslim threat must have had a chilling effect on the creativity of other authors and artists.

Muslim and non-Muslim logics met in a fascinating clash. Muslim governments are theocracies: religion and state are Siamese twins. What religious leaders decree in Islam, secular leaders execute. In such a world there is no freedom of religion or speech because an anti-religious act is an act of treason. It was, therefore, not surprising when a Muslim association in England called upon the local judiciary to invoke the existing English laws against blasphemy to punish Rushdie.

An English court pointed out that English laws against blasphemy refer only to blasphemy against the official English religion, Protestant Christianity. There is no world state, or global religion, so there can be no such thing as "global blasphemy." If a Muslim state wants to kill Muslim blasphemers within its own borders, that is its own business. But Muslims must not expect to be allowed to reach across borders and kill Muslim blasphemers within our sovereignties. Such action is tantamount to an act of war.

Refusing to Tolerate Intolerance

Nations differ greatly in their attitudes toward tolerance. Here we encounter a paradox. *A tolerant government can survive only if it is intolerant of intolerance.* It cannot stand idly by while intolerant visitors agitate against tolerance. Tolerant people must live with this apparent inconsistency, otherwise tolerance will be destroyed.

Among the many nations much diversity should be permitted, for several reasons. For one thing, since we cannot be sure that we have all the right answers to social problems, it is desirable that the human species carry out different experiments in different countries. Each country can then observe the results of experiments elsewhere.

Conceivably, the Muslim ideals of the theocratic state and criminal blasphemy might produce more happiness in the long run than our Western ideas of free speech and the separation of church and state. Allowing for this possibility we permit Muslim states to govern themselves (while we watch), and we expect them to allow us to govern ourselves (while they watch).

This is not an isolationist position. We have not forgotten that much harm was done by the complete isolation of Japan during the Tokugawa period. From 1624 to 1867 Japan "went it alone" and fell further and further behind the rest of the world in technology. When Japan finally reopened her doors it took her almost a century to catch up. We don't want to repeat that error.

Sharing Ideas, Not People

What every progressive nation wants from others is ideas and information. But ideas don't have to be wrapped in human form to get them from one place to another. Radio waves, printed documents, film and electronic records do the job very well indeed. There is no need to risk the civil disorder that can so easily follow from mixing substantial bodies of human beings in the same location, when these beings bring with them passionately held beliefs and practices that are irreconcilable with those of the receiving nation. Perhaps really small numbers of immigrants of almost any belief are safely admissible, but the rate of admission should be slow enough to allow assimilation of immigrants and ideas to take place peacefully.

Any proposal to limit diversity in the population is sure to be criticized as provincial, parochial or chauvinistic. In a sense, it may be. But notice that diversity-limitation passes this test of a good policy: "Sauce for the goose is sauce for the gander."

Should, for instance, a theocratic Muslim country admit large numbers of American immigrants who believe passionately in free speech and the separation of church and state? Should a central African country that practices "female circumcision" admit large numbers of immigrant American feminists? Should a polygamous country admit large numbers of outspoken Christians who condemn polygamy? Should a country that practices animal sacrifice admit large numbers of immigrants who belong to the Society for the Prevention of Cruelty to Animals?

The answers to these questions should be beyond dispute. Diversity is the opposite of unity, and unity is a prime requirement for national survival in the short run. In the long run, beliefs must be susceptible to change, but massive immigration is a dangerous way to bring about change in ideas and practices.

To nurture both unity and progress a double policy should be embraced: *Great diversity worldwide; limited diversity within each nation.*

"Immigration does not substantially alter American institutions and culture. Rather, the immigrants absorb American ways and are absorbed into them."

Immigration Does Not Decrease National Unity

Julian L. Simon

Thomas Jefferson, like many Americans over the centuries, worried that immigrants to the United States would not blend in with American society. This worry is unfounded, says Julian L. Simon, professor of business administration at the University of Maryland and a leading author on immigration issues. Simon argues that immigrants always have been, and always will be, absorbed into American culture: They learn to speak English, they become involved in the two-party system, they learn and follow American customs, and they celebrate national holidays. In fact, he maintains, the best way to spread American values throughout the world is to welcome immigrants so that they can share their assimilated culture with those who remain in their native countries.

As you read, consider the following questions:

1. What, according to the author, is the basis for Americans' worries about the addition of immigrants to the American population?
2. According to the author, the state of Hawaii is more "American" than the state of Louisiana. What examples are given by Simon to support this claim? Why does he find this ironic?
3. What, according to Simon, are the positive effects of immigration?

Thomas Jefferson worried that immigrants would not "harmonize" with natives "in matters which they must of necessity transact together." He believed that the immigrants "bring with them the principles of the governments they leave . . . or if they throw them off, it will be in exchange for an unbounded licentiousness. . . . These principles, with their language, they will transmit to their children."

The nightmare vision is of "us" being overwhelmed by "them," and it has taken on new life in the last few years. Pat Buchanan has written that aliens alter "the ethnic character of California and the United States." He quotes with approval the magazine *Chronicles:* "High rates of non-European immigration . . . will swamp us all."

When Margaret Thatcher closed the door to the people of Hong Kong—British subjects—who wanted to leave before the Communist takeover in 1997, she used the same wording as Buchanan: the British fear "being swamped by people of a different culture."

People across the political spectrum think that immigrants change our country. The "liberal" Arthur Schlesinger writes: "In the twenty-first century, if present trends hold, non-whites in the U.S. will begin to outnumber whites. This will bring inevitable changes in the national ethos."

Anti-immigration advocates such as the Federation for American Immigration Reform (FAIR) lean heavily on the idea that the country should restrict immigration in order to maintain our customs and institutions. Immigrants, they say, will not "make an irrevocable commitment to the language and political system of America." And the American Immigration Control Foundation distributes scary pamphlets warning about "whites becoming a minority group in America."

People Like Us

Such nativism is psychologically understandable. It is like wanting our own children to resemble us. But the supposed facts used to justify it are quite disproven by the history of immigration—into the United States, at least. Immigration does not substantially alter American institutions and culture. Rather, the immigrants absorb American ways and are absorbed into them.

For starters, ask yourself: Which state is more quintessentially "American" now—Hawaii, with its majority of non-European stock of fairly recent immigration, or Louisiana, with little recent immigration?

Let's consider our distinctive central institutions one by one. We'll see that our ways are little different from what they would be if no immigrant had arrived in the past half a century, though of course immigrants have contributed many American-type innovations.

Law. U.S. law clearly is an organic growth from its Anglo-Saxon beginnings. The only state whose law is noticeably different is Louisiana, a result of its origins two centuries ago.

Language. Every child born here now (though not in the nineteenth century) speaks English as a first language, no matter what his parents speak. The only exception is Puerto Rico. Its original Spanish continues to dominate despite immigration of English-speakers from the mainland. Words like chutzpah and Mafia creep into the national language, but they are at most a light spice on our native tongue.

THE UNITED IMMIGRANTS OF AMERICA

Reprinted by permission of Kirk Anderson.

Customs. We all shake hands, and we don't embrace much, just the way Americans have always done. Yes, we high-five on the basketball court in imitation of Magic Johnson. But no black or white yuppie high-fives at a business lunch, except perhaps with a basketball buddy. And we continue to play American football no matter how many people come from soccer-playing lands or are better fitted by physique for European football than for American football or basketball.

Politics. We still have the same old two-party political system, even after Ross Perot. We have not descended into an anarchic

144

national system imported by foreigners, despite the hysteria that contributed to the convictions of Sacco and Vanzetti [anarchists executed for murder in 1927] and the expulsion of Emma Goldman [a Russian-born political activist deported to Russia in 1919]. Nor have immigrants imposed an "alien" mode of government onto any of our states.

Holidays. Lots of our forebears came here without a Christian tradition from Moslem and Jewish religions, and from African and Asian ways. But are the department stores of any city in doubt about whether Christmas is our national holiday? Yes, there is some variation in religious holidays celebrated in various states—Good Friday, for example. But the relative insignificance of this variation in our national life emphasizes how little effect immigration has.

The only religiously based holiday that affects public life markedly is Mardi Gras in Louisiana. This illustrates the power of origins to set the pattern, and highlights the imperviousness of institutions to change by minority immigration.

Of course the WASP [white Anglo-Saxon Protestant] settlers swamped the religious traditions of the Native Americans. But that was because the immigrants quickly became the majority, and because their material culture was superior to that of the earlier residents.

Same Theme, New Variations

The previous two paragraphs contain the seeds of a general theory explaining why immigrants have had so little noticeable effect upon American life patterns. The pattern of civic life remains what it was before a wave of immigration, unless the immigrants are greater in numbers or riches than the prior residents. The chance that any immigration into the United States will meet these conditions is nil.

Notice how I, the grandson of immigrants, naturally write "us" and "our," and how you—whether a descendant from the Mayflower folks, or almost fresh off the boat yourself—feel it natural to use these same pronouns while you discuss with me this or other issues. What greater proof could there be that, rather than altering our national life, immigrants intensify it and make us more like ourselves?

Immigration does increase *diversity* in a variety of ways—foods eaten, ethnic festivals celebrated, types of schools operated privately, foreign-language newspapers published. But this is variation *around* the main line, rather than an alteration in the central tendencies of national life. Nativists confuse the one with the other, in error or purposely for its scare power. . . .

If you don't enjoy seeing foreign-looking faces on the street or subway, neither economics nor demography proves you "wrong" or illogical. But . . . the facts cited above disprove the argument that keeping out non-Caucasian immigrants preserves those ways of public life that Americans consider "American."

Many of us care more about making the United States a "shining city on the hill" than about the origins of the people who help attain that goal. For those who care about the strengthening of American values of liberty, constitutionalism, and democracy so that they will spread throughout the world, the most effective step is to bring persons from the rest of the world here, so that their light can go back to where they came from, and make those places more like "us."

"For 1993 alone, the net costs [of immigrants into the United States] were $44.18 billion in excess of taxes paid."

Immigrants Cost More Than They Pay in Taxes

Donald Huddle

Donald Huddle, a professor emeritus of economics at Rice University in Houston, Texas, has emerged as one of the key researchers who argue that the financial costs of immigration into the United States outweigh the economic benefits realized by our society. The primary reason for this, according to Huddle, is that the costs of assisting or incarcerating immigrants exceed the taxes paid by these newcomers. Huddle also argues that native citizens of the United States are being occupationally displaced by immigrants and that this represents an additional cost to U.S. society.

As you read, consider the following questions:

1. What three categories of immigrants does Huddle utilize in his study?
2. How does the author estimate the costs attributable to immigrants into the United States?
3. How does the author estimate taxes paid by immigrants into the United States?

From Donald Huddle's June 27, 1994, updated Executive Summary of *The Net National Costs of Immigration in 1993*, a study of the Carrying Capacity Network, Washington, D.C. Reprinted with permission.

Rising public concern over the fiscal costs of immigration at both national and local levels has intensified a search for political and administrative answers. Major states of immigration settlement are pressing Washington in the courts and in Congress for reimbursement of the costs to them of public assistance to rising numbers of legal and illegal immigrants and refugees arriving under federal policy or because of federal inaction. Pressed to find new savings, Congress has tightened eligibility conditions for some immigrant public assistance programs and is considering other steps.

In a study conducted in 1993 of the public sector costs of immigrants entering the country since 1970, I found that the 19.3 million immigrants caused direct and indirect public assistance and service costs in 1992 of $42.5 billion in excess of the $20.2 billion they paid in taxes. My updated study found that for 1993 alone, the net costs were $44.18 billion in excess of taxes paid. . . .

Key Findings: Overall 1993

This study estimates public assistance and displacement costs and revenues at all levels of government that are attributable to the following groups, each with differing income profiles and entitlements to public assistance: legal immigrants, including refugees and other humanitarian entrants; legalized or "amnesty" immigrants; and illegal immigrants. The study builds its estimates on the following specific assistance and taxation programs:

- *Assistance and Services to Immigrants:* Twenty-five major federal, state and local government assistance programs, including a package of county and city assistance and services, that are open entirely or in part to both legal and illegal immigrants.
- *Assistance to Displaced U.S. Workers:* Five major federal and state assistance programs available to U.S. residents displaced from jobs by immigrants.
- *Revenues from Immigrants:* Estimated federal, state and local income, sales, excise, Social Security, and property tax contributions of the three sub-populations under study.

The report estimates net costs associated with different sub-populations of immigrants, currently for 1993 (Table 1).

Assessing Immigrant Poverty and Use of Public Assistance

Costs for the legal, illegal and amnesty immigrant subpopulations were estimated in a two-step process. *Step one* involved

1. calculation of an annual nationwide cost per beneficiary—citizen and immigrant—for each program, using 1993 government data, or the most recent available, adjusted for inflation;
2. determination of the probability of immigrant recipiency in

each program. Thus, the combination of the per-recipient cost data in step one with the probable number of immigrant recipients in each assistance program yielded the immigrant cost estimates.

Step two, to calculate the probability of immigrant public assistance use, was based on

1. determination of the overall national recipiency rate stated as a percentage of the particular sub-population at risk, such as over 65, school-age children, persons in the labor force, and so on;
2. estimation of the extent to which the recipiency rate of immigrants varies from the general use rate, based on factors such as income, poverty status and propensity to use public assistance.

Thus, the combination of the per-recipient cost data in step one with the probable number of immigrant recipients in each assis-

Table 1: Overall Immigrant Sub-Population Size and Current Costs

Legal Immigrants Settling Since 1970, Including Refugees and Other Humanitarian Entrants

Estimated population size in 1993	12.76 million
Net cost for 1993	$16.19 billion

Illegal Immigrants

Estimated population size in 1993	5.1 million
Net cost for 1993	$19.34 billion

Amnesty Immigrants

Estimated population size in 1993	2.81 million
Net cost for 1993	$8.64 billion

Total Tax Revenues from Immigrants

Contributions for 1993	$76.90 billion

U.S. Workers Displaced from Jobs by Immigrants

Displaced workers in 1993	2.35 million
Cost for 1993	$11.92 billion

Overall Assistance and Displacement Costs After Taxes

Net costs for 1993	$44.18 billion

Note: Net costs refer to the fact that costs have been subtracted from revenues collected.

tance program yielded the cost estimates for immigrants.

Data on poverty and public assistance use were taken from a variety of sources:

- samples of the 1990 U.S. Census microdata and Census publications on conditions of the foreign born in 1990;
- studies of immigration researchers such as George Borjas, Leif Jensen, and Frank Bean.

Data from the 1990 Census place the poverty rate of the foreign-born population 42.8 percent higher than the native-born, and the average value of public assistance recipiency and income received from public assistance 44.2 percent higher than those of the *native-born.*

Heavy flows of refugees and illegal immigrants since the early 1970s and preference for relatives of prior immigrants rather than skilled persons account for the *rising incidence of poverty in the post-1970 stock of immigrants.* According to Borjas, the poverty rate of cohorts [groups sharing statistical or demographic characteristics] measured since 1975, using 1980 census figures, is 151.0 percent greater than that of the native-born. The 1990 Census showed equally high differential poverty rates, with the poverty rate of immigrants entering after 1985 being 149 percent higher than for the native-born.

Estimating Tax Revenues from Immigrants

Immigrants pay 52.4 percent of their taxes to the federal government, 17.7 percent to the states, and 29.8 percent to local governments. The federal income tax is the largest single source of revenue from immigrants, commanding 25.1 percent of revenues. Social Security contributions are the second-largest single source of revenue from immigrants, representing 22.8 percent of all immigrant tax payments. Legal immigrants pay a far greater share of their taxes as income taxes than do illegal aliens. Illegal immigrants make their major revenue contributions through sales and property taxes.

Tax payments of the various immigrant sub-populations in this study were estimated by using individual and household income and tax data from the Census and Internal Revenue Service, *Statistics of Income,* adjusted to 1993. Federal income tax payments were calculated by grouping immigrant households according to income categories. The effective tax rate for each category times the number of tax-paying immigrant households in it yielded the tax contribution. To estimate federal excise tax payments, the author determined the average amount of excise tax paid for each $1000 of income. This rate was applied to the average adjusted gross income of immigrants in each income category.

State and local tax payments were calculated by determining an adjusted national average of state, county and city taxes paid per $1000 of income. These rates were then applied to the per capita income of each immigrant sub-population. The resulting individual average tax contributions were generalized to all households in the study population.

Social Security Revenues

The study of 1992 costs did not include social security contributions (FICA) of immigrants as revenues, considering them an investment or "premium" for a future benefit. Outlays for Old Age, Survivors and Disability and Health Care (OASDI) were, accordingly, not apportioned to the immigrant study population. The 1993 study does include as revenue an estimated $17.55 billion in FICA contributions from working immigrants in the study population, along with $18.92 billion in outlays chargeable to the study population.

Reprinted by permission of Chuck Asay and Creators Syndicate.

A key assumption is that the employee bears 75 percent of the total FICA payroll contribution of 15.3 percent. The study immigrant population's share of the total pay-in 1993—$17.55 billion—was 6.86 percent of total worker contributions to the fund in 1993, 14.7 percent less than their representation in the population as a whole.

The immigrants' share of $305.2 billion in overall OASDI outlays in 1993 was based on their proportional share of the U.S. labor force. This amount was then adjusted downward by the ratio of the immigrant sub-population's per capita income to the overall per capita income to reflect the present lower rate of immigrant use of Social Security. Under this formula, the share of Social Security pay-out attributable to study immigrants in 1993 was $18.92 billion, $1.37 billion more than that population's contribution.

Assistance Programs of Heaviest Use

Immigrant use of public assistance and services varies with their eligibility, the availability of the service, and need. Free public primary and secondary education is guaranteed to all immigrants regardless of legal or illegal status by a 1982 Supreme Court decision. Public education, including bilingual, adult and compensatory education, higher education and student aid, in 1993 was 25.4 percent of all outlays for immigrants. County and city services, including indigent medical care, mental health, and family and child welfare services, accounted for 26.9 percent of immigrant costs. OASDI outlays were 17.3 percent. These three programs, together with Medicaid (8.3 percent) and unemployment compensation (2.6 percent) accounted for over 80 percent of total public outlays for immigrants.

Illegal and Amnesty Immigrants

Illegal immigrants or their 550,000 U.S.-born school-age children are eligible for some costly major federal and state benefits, such as AFDC (Aid to Families with Dependent Children) and public housing, but are denied others such as unemployment compensation and supplemental security income and, in some states, benefits such as general assistance.

Average individual cost of public assistance to illegal immigrants in 1993 was $4890, while per-capita tax payments were only $1951. This deficit is due to [illegal immigrants'] dramatically higher poverty rates, lower tax compliance, and relatively high propensity to use public assistance programs and services not barred to them.

Amnesty immigrants are former illegal immigrants and have similar low skills and weak earning power. But unlike illegals, as of May 1992 they were no longer barred from public assistance. About one third of this number, seasonal agricultural workers (SAWS), were never barred from federal benefits. Cost estimates for this population, like estimates for legal immigrants, encompass twenty-five federal, state and local programs, including a package of city and county services. Methods for determining recipiency rates are the same. . . .

The estimated costs of services to the three immigrant sub-populations [legal immigrants, illegal immigrants, and amnesty immigrants] in every case significantly exceeded revenues received from them, a trend projected to continue as the stock of immigrants grows into the next century.

Costs of Public Assistance to U.S.
Workers Displaced by Immigrants

Entry of sizable numbers of immigrants into the labor market displaces some resident workers, particularly the least skilled, by substitution of immigrants for resident workers in jobs or by closing off resident workers' access to prospective job vacancies. The unemployed or discouraged workers then require public assistance. The labor displacement rate is defined [here] as the number of citizen workers who are not able to work as a result of the presence of 100 immigrant job holders in the labor market.

The displacement rate varies with wage and unemployment levels, job conditions and amenities, and the skills and opportunities involved. *Under economic conditions prevailing in 1993, the displacement rate is estimated to have been at least 25 percent for low-skill U.S. citizen workers.* Displacement also occurs among certain classes of skilled workers and professionals, though no generally acceptable methods have been devised for determining the rate.

The study currently does not calculate the large revenue losses due to immigration-induced depression of wage rates in unskilled trades where competition for jobs is fierce, according to researchers such as Borjas and Joseph Altonji and David Card. Wage depression in high-immigration states pushes many unskilled citizen minorities into poverty, thus triggering the use of additional public assistance resources.

To compute displacement, the study determines from INS [Immigration and Naturalization Service] data the percentage of less-skilled immigrants in the three sub-populations. In 1993 the percentage of less skilled in that year's flow of non-farmworker migrants was 62.2 percent. Of the estimated 7.23 million post-1969 legal immigrants in the labor force in 1993, 4.55 million have low skills. Applying a displacement coefficient of 25 percent to the number of low-skill foreign workers produces estimated unemployment among U.S. workers occasioned by legal immigrants in 1993 at 1.14 million.

Public assistance and service costs for 1.14 million displaced U.S. workers are estimated by using the same two-step method applied to legal immigrants. *Displacement in 1993 by less-skilled legal immigrants produced one-year public assistance costs of $5.77 billion in five assistance programs* [Medicaid, Aid to Families with Dependent Children, Unemployment Compensation, Food Stamps, and General Assistance].

Because illegal and formerly illegal immigrants have markedly lower skills than legal immigrants and higher labor force participation, their displacing effect on less-skilled citizen workers is more severe. The number of less skilled among 5.84 million illegal and amnestied immigrant labor force members is about 4.86 million, or 83 percent. Applying the same displacement rate of 25 percent, 1.22 million low-skill U.S.citizen workers are jobless because of illegal immigration. The costs of public assistance to U.S. workers and dependents displaced by illegal and amnestied immigrants totals $11.92 billion.

"Contrary to the public's perception, . . . immigrants generate significantly more in taxes paid than they cost in services received."

Immigrants Do Not Cost More Than They Pay in Taxes

Michael Fix and Jeffrey S. Passel

Michael Fix and Jeffrey S. Passel are researchers associated with the Urban Institute, a nonprofit, nonpartisan policy research organization located in Washington, D.C. Fix and Passel find fault with the numerous studies that conclude that the net cost of immigration into the United States exceeds the amount paid in taxes by immigrants. First, they contend, these studies overestimate the costs in social services to immigrants. Second, they assert, these studies seriously underestimate the amount of taxes paid by immigrants.

As you read, consider the following questions:

1. According to Fix and Passel, how do studies of immigration costs overestimate the cost of social services to immigrants?
2. According to the authors, how do studies of immigration costs underestimate the amount that immigrants pay in taxes?
3. What are the authors' main criticisms of Donald Huddle's study?

From Michael Fix and Jeffrey S. Passel, "Immigrants and Public Sector Impacts," in *Immigration and Immigrants: Setting the Record Straight*. Washington: Urban Institute, May 1994. Reprinted with permission.

The public costs of immigrants—in particular their costs to the welfare system—are drawing increasingly critical attention as lawmakers seek to reduce the federal deficit and control public sector spending. Tension between the federal government and states and localities is also mounting under the fiscal pressures of tight state budgets and stagnant local economies in some high-immigration areas, particularly California. State and local governments in several areas have argued that the federal government's right to control legal and illegal immigrant flows and to mandate state payments for cash welfare and Medicaid should carry with it the responsibility to provide sufficient financial support to cover immigrant costs.

Adding further to the heat of this debate is a set of recent studies attributing enormous public costs to immigrants. These studies are widely cited in calls to restrict immigrants' access to public benefits, impose stricter immigration controls, and increase the federal revenues going to states. Because these studies have themselves become part of the debate, it is important to understand and correct their errors so that the policy debate can proceed on a firm factual basis. This viewpoint also focuses on the current debate regarding welfare and immigrants. Specifically, we investigate the degree to which immigrants actually receive welfare payments and examine potential impacts of some proposed welfare reforms.

Public Misperceptions

Contrary to the public's perception, when all levels of government are considered together, immigrants generate significantly more in taxes paid than they cost in services received. This surplus is unevenly distributed among different levels of government, however, with immigrants (and natives) generating a net surplus to the federal government, but a net cost to some states and most localities. This misperception regarding immigrants' net fiscal impact has been reinforced by several highly publicized recent studies that overlook three basic facts about immigration. First, integration of immigrants is dynamic; their incomes and tax contributions both increase the longer they live in the United States. Second, incomes vary considerably for different types of immigrants with legally admitted immigrants, as a group, generally having significantly higher incomes than illegal immigrants or refugees. Finally, the studies do not take into account the indirect benefits of job creation from immigrant businesses or consumer demand.

One of the myths often cited to support the contention that immigrants cost more than they contribute is that they are heavy users of welfare. The facts are very different. When refugees are excluded, it becomes clear that immigrants of working age are considerably less likely than natives of working age to receive welfare. Refugees are explicitly entitled to such benefits on arrival and are, not surprisingly, much more likely than natives to be welfare recipients. Again, the failure to differentiate immigrants according to their legal status contributes greatly to misperceptions of reality and to proposals of potentially ineffective policies.

Immigrant Welfare Costs and Other Public Sector Impacts

There is no doubt that estimating the economic costs and benefits of immigrants is extremely difficult. The data required to develop direct estimates for local areas, states, or the nation are generally unavailable. Consequently, researchers must fill in the gaps with assumptions. There is nothing inherently biased about this exercise. But most current studies use assumptions that maximize the apparent costs of immigrants. Alternative assumptions—often more plausible—produce very different results.

Immigrants Are Drawn by Jobs, Not Benefits

Do immigrants overuse welfare and other social programs and underpay taxes? . . .

Most research has found that immigrants are overwhelmingly drawn by the hope of better jobs, not by U.S. benefits programs. When job prospects dim, many (especially Mexicans) return home.

For refugees without that option, such as the Vietnamese, program usage is more common, at least during the resettlement period. Undocumented aliens are legally barred from most such programs, and seem to largely avoid contact with government agencies out of fear of detection.

Many legal immigrants also think twice about seeking government benefits, since a record of welfare usage can increase their risk of deportation and decrease their ability to sponsor the entry of other relatives. Moreover, since immigrants tend to arrive at young ages, they have less need for many services than do natives, especially the growing number of elderly citizens.

Gregory DeFreitas, *Dollars & Sense*, January/February 1994.

The body of literature available through 1991 paints a fairly consistent picture of the costs of immigrants across differing levels of government. Most *national* studies suggest that immigrants are not an overall fiscal burden on the native population. At the *state* level the picture is mixed, resulting in part from the differing responsibilities assumed by different state governments. At the *local* level, analyses completed in the 1970s and 1980s have invariably found immigrants to be a net fiscal burden. They found the same for native populations.

Recent analyses by government agencies interested in "recovering" the public sector costs of immigrants and nonprofit groups committed to reducing levels of immigration uniformly find that immigrants impose fiscal burdens on governments and on native-born taxpayers. Although some studies are better than others, all overstate the negative impacts of immigrants for one or more of the following reasons:

- Tax collections from immigrants are *understated*.
- Service costs for immigrants are *overstated*.
- Benefits of immigrant-owned businesses as well as the economic benefits generated by consumer spending from immigrants are *ignored*.
- Job displacement impacts and costs are overstated.
- Parallel computations for natives, which would show that natives are also net tax users, are *not done*.
- The size of the immigrant population—particularly the undocumented immigrant population—is *overstated*.

The following discussion illustrates how much these types of errors can affect the estimates of immigrant public sector costs.

Los Angeles County—Fiscal Impacts

Recent legal immigrants, immigrants granted legal status under the Immigration Reform and Control Act of 1986, and illegal immigrants and their U.S.-born children contributed $139 million in taxes to Los Angeles County, according to a study conducted by the Los Angeles County Internal Services Division (ISD). At the same time, the study estimated that the county spent $947 million on services for the same population, leaving a deficit to the county of $808 million. The study also noted that only 3.2 percent of the taxes paid by this population went to the County, with the federal and state governments getting virtually all the rest.

Most of the ISD study was done with care, and it uses the best demographic assumptions. Even so, it overstates costs and understates revenues to a substantial degree. The study

- Understates revenues from immigrants by as much as 30 percent, because it underestimates the income of recent legal immigrants;
- Omits the contribution of long-term legal immigrants, who represent 15 percent of the county's population and pay 18 percent of the taxes;
- Overstates the costs for recent legal immigrants by 60 percent, about $140 million;
- Fails to clarify that the county-level "deficit" generated by the

native population is larger than that generated by immigrants;
• Fails to clarify that the county received a *greater* share of all taxes paid by these immigrants than it did of taxes paid by natives.

San Diego County—Fiscal Impacts

Two studies of San Diego County by Rea and Parker rely on methods and assumptions that also overstate costs and underestimate revenues. For example, the studies assume that there are over 200,000 undocumented aliens in San Diego County—far more than can be supported by data. This figure would imply, by the authors' own reasoning, that there are over 4 million undocumented immigrants in California and 8 million to 12 million in the United States. The latter figure is between 5 and 9 million more than estimated by the Immigration and Naturalization Service (INS). In addition, the revenue estimates for San Diego County omit several taxes (notably property taxes), underestimate other revenues, and base most estimates of service use levels—and costs—on small, nonrepresentative samples.

United States—Fiscal Impacts

According to the most controversial study of those discussed here, the benefits and costs of immigration to the United States in 1992 added up to a total net cost to all levels of government of $42.5 billion. This study, by Donald Huddle, was sponsored by the Carrying Capacity Network, a nonprofit group that advocates major reductions in immigration to the United States. "The Costs of Immigration" uses estimation procedures that include a variety of errors. When these errors are corrected, the post-1970 immigrants in Huddle's study actually show a surplus of revenues over social service costs of at least $25 billion. How did Huddle develop his estimates and why are they so wrong?

Revenue Estimation Errors. Three major errors affect Huddle's revenue estimates. First, he generalizes from the wrong immigrant population. Huddle relies on the ISD study's income estimates for legal immigrants in Los Angeles County. The ISD estimates are for Los Angeles' legal immigrants who entered during the 1980s, but Huddle uses them to represent all legal immigrants who entered the United States during the period 1970-1992. The incomes of these groups, in fact, differ substantially. The assumptions underlying the ISD figures used by Huddle yield an average income estimate for legal immigrants entering L.A. County between 1980 and 1990 of about $9,700 a year. Census data for 1990 yield income estimates of legal immigrants entering the U.S. between 1970 and 1990 averaging more than $14,000 a year, or almost 45 percent more than the ISD estimates. Second, underestimating incomes leads inevitably to an understatement of the rates at which immigrants are taxed. Third, in addition to undercounting taxes paid, the study omits several significant revenue sources that are included in the ISD study—notably Social Security contributions, unemployment insurance, and gasoline taxes. These taxes all have large impacts on people who are in the low- and middle-income brackets—including most immigrants.

This combination of errors leads Huddle to estimate that post-1970 immigrants (legal, illegal, and amnesty) paid $20.2 billion in taxes, or more than *$50 billion* below the $70.3 billion estimated with better data, assumptions, and methods. The shortfall consists of:

- $21.3 billion from understating the incomes of legal immigrants and misspecifying tax rates;
- $28.8 billion from omitting other taxes paid by immigrants (FICA, unemployment insurance, vehicle registration and fees, and state and federal gasoline taxes).

Even this corrected estimate accounts for only a little over 80 percent of all taxes collected by all levels of government, because it omits corporate income taxes, local income taxes, commercial property taxes, utility taxes, and a number of other sources of government revenues.

Since Huddle estimates a "net cost" for immigrants in 1992 of $42.5 billion, his underestimation of revenue by $50 billion more than offsets his entire net cost estimate. Within the context of his own methods, in other words, immigrants show a net surplus.

Cost Estimation Errors. Huddle overstates the service costs of immigrants by almost $10 billion. The major sources of cost overstatement include:

- Application of ISD's inflated per capita service costs for recent legal immigrants to all immigrants, thereby overstating service costs by 60 percent—$2.6 billion;
- Use of overstated participation rates and unit service costs for certain programs that include AFDC [Aid to Families with Dependent Children], Food Stamps, and Head Start—$2.4 billion;
- Overstating immigrant enrollment in public schools—$3.4 billion;
- A 50 percent overstatement of the size of the illegal population in estimating program participation and costs—$3 billion.

Huddle's assessment of immigrant costs fails to take into account the impacts of programs on natives or society at large. The single largest component of immigrant-related public sector costs is the cost of providing public primary and secondary education, which is approximately $11 billion annually for immigrants. The actual recipients of these expenditures are, for the most part, native-born teachers, school administrators, maintenance staffs, and others employed in school administration, maintenance, and construction. In addition, the benefits realized by society from the additional education given to the immigrant children are not recognized in the analysis.

Indirect Impacts of Immigration. In addition, contrary to the strong research consensus that immigrants have little overall impact on U.S. job opportunities, Huddle includes displacement costs of $12 billion for social services to natives who have permanently lost their jobs to immigrants. This result is based on Huddle's own, small-scale, limited studies in Houston and his misinterpretation of another study. Huddle fails to include any estimate of the sizeable positive impacts of immigration already described.

*"Illegal migration can be significantly reduced
with a few effective measures."*

Illegal Immigration into the United States Can Be Curtailed

Michael T. Lempres

According to Michael T. Lempres, the notion that the use of land mines and tanks along the border is the only way to stop illegal immigration into the United States is simply wrong. Lempres, a Washington, D.C., attorney who served as an official in both the Reagan and Bush administrations, asserts that a coordinated effort—including such steps as requiring citizenship papers for all citizens and revoking the constitutional right to citizenship for anyone born in the United States—could significantly reduce illegal entry. However, he warns, a piecemeal approach to controlling illegal immigration by using only some of the suggested steps would fail.

As you read, consider the following questions:

1. Why and how, according to Lempres, can interdiction at the border be successful?
2. According to the author, how must the deportation process and the treatment of criminal aliens be changed in order to reduce illegal entry into the United States?
3. What does the author have to say about the limits placed on both legal and illegal migration into the United States.

Michael T. Lempres, "Getting Serious About Illegal Immigration," *National Review*, February 21, 1994. Copyright ©1994 by National Review, Inc., 150 E. 35th St., New York, NY 10016. Reprinted by permission.

Seven years after the Federal Government thought it solved the problem, sustained high levels of illegal immigration have again become a hot political issue. One need only look around the world to see that public opposition to extraordinary levels of uncontrolled migration can lead to destructive policies and the rise of irresponsible leaders. In the United States today, politicians of both parties recognize the potency of a promise to reduce illegal immigration. Unfortunately, there remains a chasm between a politician's flamboyant promises and an effective public-policy response.

That chasm reinforces the belief that it is impossible to reduce illegal migration significantly without using land mines and tanks at the border. President Clinton apparently shares this belief, as he said, on a recent visit to California, that the United States lacks the resources to control its borders. The President is wrong.

While there is no painless magic answer, illegal migration can be significantly reduced with a few effective measures. Some of those measures require money; some require political will; many can be accomplished by the President without new legislation. Adopted as part of a comprehensive approach, these measures will be effective. Adopted selectively, they will fail.

As a first step, however, current law and regulations must be clarified. Employers are caught between competing legal mandates when hiring non-citizens; aliens with only a tenuous claim to presence in the United States remain here for years under the color of law; and some government officials do not know whether they are obliged to report information to or withhold it from the Immigration and Naturalization Service (INS). Congress and the regulators must simplify legal requirements so that the average person, citizen or alien, can know what the rules are.

Interdiction at the Border

The first component of any effective program has to be interdiction at the border. Policies that rely exclusively on interdiction, however, are doomed to failure.

Interdiction can be effective because of the nature of the flow of illegal migration. Over 95 per cent of illegal border crossers come through Mexico, where the terrain funnels traffic into several crossing points. By far the busiest crossing point in the nearly 6,000 miles of land border is the 13 miles near San Diego, California. Over 40 per cent of the Border Patrol's total interdictions occur in that 13-mile strip of land. Moreover, the Border Patrol estimates that over 90 per cent of its total apprehensions occur in just 100 miles of border segments.

The concentration of illegal traffic means that interdiction efforts can be focused for greater effectiveness. Physical structures such as lights, fences, and anti-automobile barriers can be placed along the high-traffic crossing points. Without new legislation, the Administration can build these structures and add Border Patrol officers at the hot spots.

The Border Patrol recently targeted the border near El Paso for a focused interdiction effort. Operation Blockade, as it was called, reduced illegal migration dramatically. Local polls indicate an astonishing 98 per cent approval of the operation.

Effective interdiction will deter illegal crossers who seek to stay in the United States for a short period, most likely to work for a few days or weeks. Interdiction will not, however, effectively deter those who intend to remain for a longer period of time. This distinction between "sojourners" and "settlers" should become part of the policy response to illegal migration.

Interior Enforcement

The principal goal here is to deny illegal migrants the jobs and public benefits that cause them to enter the United States in the first place. The Immigration Reform and Control Act of 1986 (IRCA) moved in the right direction by making it against the law to hire illegal aliens. Virtually every developed country in the world requires proof of work authorization based on citizenship status. Unfortunately, IRCA's susceptibility to fraudulent documents has dramatically undercut the law's effectiveness.

Fraudulent documents are available in Mexico and in most major cities in the United States, often for as little as $20. The INS requires employers to accept any of 29 different documents as proof of work authorization, and rules intended to curb discrimination prohibit employers from looking beyond the face of any document that is not transparently fraudulent.

It seems clear that the best way to prevent illegal aliens from working in this country is to provide some fraud-resistant method of providing work authorization. The best system currently available appears to be a fraud-resistant document. Everyone entitled to work in the United States, citizen and alien alike, would have to present the document in order to take up a new job. The technology for a counterfeit-resistant card (no document is counterfeit *proof*) has been available for years, and the cost is not prohibitive.

Deportation Process Reform

Aliens have no absolute right to remain in the United States. They have a privilege. Their privilege must be balanced against the right of the American people to integrity in their immigration laws. And yet the current system of deportation is such that, as a practical matter, almost no aliens are deported unless they are in government custody.

The deportation process should be streamlined, and the rules should be clarified to avoid manipulation. There should be only one level of administrative appeal and limited judicial appeal. The standard of review should be limited to asking whether the original adjudicator abused his discretion in finding deportation appropriate. Aliens who wish to pursue other issues should apply for reentry, from outside this country.

Deport Criminal Aliens

All aliens who abuse the privilege of presence in this country by committing felonies should be deported. Today, that is neither the law nor the practice: 25 per cent of the federal prison population and over 10 per cent of the state prison populations are aliens. Sentencing for criminal convictions should include an order of deportation to be carried out when the sentence has been served. Plea bargains should include stipulated orders of deportation. Appeals should focus only on the underlying felony conviction, and there should be no discretion to fail to deport an alien felon.

Inter-Government Cooperation

Lack of cooperation among federal, state, and local governments on immigration goes far beyond the usual dismal level of cooperation. Some agencies make an affirmative decision to oppose immigration-law enforcement. This is notoriously true of the so-called "sanctuary cities," but also true of federal agencies such as the Internal Revenue Service, the Department of Housing and Urban Development, and the Social Security Administration.

Agencies typically argue that illegal aliens will be deterred from dealing with any agency that cooperates with INS and that this will drive illegal aliens underground. What this argument misses is that discouraging illegal migration may *require* driving illegal aliens underground.

All law-enforcement authorities should have access to appropriate citizenship databases. INS has placed agents in arraignment and trial courts in a pilot program, which has been very effective in identifying aliens accused or convicted of crimes. At an absolute minimum, cooperation would permit the United States to say to illegal aliens: Obey our laws or face certain deportation.

Real Caps on Immigration

Most Americans believe that there should be a limit to the number of migrants, however labeled, that this country accepts each year. The distinction between legal and illegal migration is important, but less so than the impact of the total number.

And yet the limit that U.S. law currently puts on immigration applies to only a minority of those who migrate. A separate limit applies to those who migrate as refugees and those who enter the country without intending to remain permanently. No limit applies to the over 100,000 aliens who will seek asylum this year or the backlog of over 300,000 unadjudicated asylum claims. The limit ignores the estimated three million aliens who cross the border illegally each year.

Amend the Constitution

The federal government has failed miserably at controlling the border. Crossing America's southern border is easier than crossing Prospect Street in La Jolla, California. Millions have done it, and millions more will if we don't take action. . . .

But controlling the border isn't enough. . . . We must fundamentally rethink the very foundation of our immigration laws. The Constitution has been interpreted as granting citizenship to every child born in the United States, even the children of illegal aliens. Some illegals come to our country simply to have a child born on U.S. soil who can then gain American citizenship. That, of course, renders the child eligible for a host of public benefits. Just since 1988, the number of children of illegal aliens on our state's welfare rolls has grown more than four-fold.

It's time to amend the Constitution so that citizenship belongs only to the children of legal residents of the United States.

Pete Wilson, *The San Diego Union-Tribune*, January 9, 1994.

The lack of a comprehensive, freely debated cap on migration undercuts the laws passed by Congress, such as the Immigration Act of 1990, signed by President Bush. That Act imposed a "flexible" cap on the category of legal immigrants to be set at 700,000 per year (the cap was exceeded in its first year), and it sought to change the ratio of skill-based to family-based immigration. Congress failed to recognize that the debate it held over a marginal increase of fewer than 200,000 immigrants had no effect on the majority of aliens who enter the United States every year.

Congress ought to set a comprehensive limit for *all* immigration in a single year. In that way, funding decisions and other trade-offs could be made in a more fully informed manner. The limit should also include reference to illegal migration by requiring the President to certify that illegal migration is being reduced and is currently at an acceptable level. The President could also specify countries that are not cooperating with the United States to reduce illegal migration. In the absence of a presidential certification, the comprehensive cap on immigration to the United

States could be reduced by a set figure, for example 15 per cent. The country-specific limits that exist under current law could also be reduced for countries that do not cooperate.

Birthright Citizenship

Another of the forces that draw aliens to the United States is the grant of citizenship to all people born in this country. Approximately two of every three babies born in California's Los Angeles County hospitals are born to illegal aliens.

Most of the rest of the world determines citizenship based on the citizenship of one or both parents. However, it would most likely take an amendment to the Constitution to achieve that here, so this is not a solution that can be achieved in the short term.

Defense Department Assets

The military cannot be relied upon as a permanent solution to the problem of illegal migration. We are not facing a short-term emergency; the forces leading to high levels of illegal migration are embedded in our laws. We can more effectively change the system of incentives we provide that encourage illegal migration.

In order to be effective, National Guard troops would have to operate inside the United States, detaining and questioning both U.S. citizens and aliens to determine legal status. This would represent a threat to the civil liberties of Americans, and would lead to little benefit unless the current system was amended to put some teeth in the deportation process.

But the military can help civilian law enforcement reduce illegal migration by helping design and build structures for interdiction along the border. Excess military bases could be used for detention or other purposes.

Illegal migration can be reduced without using the Army for law-enforcement purposes or amending the Constitution. It merely requires that we clarify and enforce the law. And once illegal immigration has been reduced, the United States can hold a meaningful discussion on levels of legal immigration.

167

*"Efforts by . . . developed regions to shut the
door on the rising tide of migrants are not only
questionable on ethical grounds but may also
turn out to be impractical."*

Current Migratory Flows
Are Likely to Continue

Alan B. Simmons

Alan B. Simmons, a Canadian sociologist at York University in
Toronto, is a fellow of the Center of Research on Latin America
and a member of the Centre for Refugee Studies. In the following viewpoint, Simmons contends that efforts to tighten the borders of developed countries and to hasten the development of
third world nations will do little to stem the south-to-north tides
of migrants. The flows of migrants will not be stopped, he maintains, at least in part because of the mutuality of interests of the
sending and receiving countries. Instead of trying to prevent migration, Simmons proposes, new procedures to facilitate the
movements of large numbers of people should be adopted.

As you read, consider the following questions:

1. Why, according to Simmons, are efforts to promote
   development and economic growth in less-developed countries
   bound to fail to quickly reduce south-to-north migration?
2. What are the key trends of the "globalization of trade," as
   specified by the author?
3. How does the current international division of labor put
   the less developed countries at a disadvantage, according
   to Simmons?

Alan B. Simmons, "Sixty Million on the Move," *The UNESCO Courier,* January 1992.
Reprinted with permission.

The modern scientific community takes pride in providing answers to world problems, yet, paradoxically, it often makes a greater contribution by the perspicacity with which it continues to ask questions. The premature proposal of simple solutions to difficult problems often does no more than reveal ignorance.

The complex emerging patterns of international migration are a case in point. Efforts by Europe, North America and other developed regions to shut the door on the rising tide of migrants from the Third World are not only questionable on ethical grounds but may also turn out to be impractical as well. Many migrants will find ways round all but the most costly, vigorous and harsh control systems. This is because the very logic of social and economic change tends to create new avenues and opportunities for migrants. Just how this works is only now beginning to be understood.

Equally misguided is the argument that coordinated international development efforts and economic growth in the countries of out-migration will soon lead to a reduction in South-to-North migration. There is a considerable body of historical evidence to contradict this argument. After a long period of economic growth in the South, pressures promoting current migration trends are indeed likely to ease or stop, but in the short to medium term—over twenty to thirty years or even longer—development efforts will probably tend to increase South-North migration. This is because the mechanization and increased efficiency required to boost productivity will mean that large numbers of workers will lose their jobs. As unemployment rises, so too will the numbers of people seeking refuge elsewhere. The process may run over several decades, since even in the best possible circumstances development is gradual.

Sixty Million People on the Move

It is estimated that some 60 million people in the world are currently "on the move". This figure includes people displaced by war, civil strife, political repression, environmental catastrophe, the threat of starvation, economic hardship or the desire to better their circumstances. Some 16 million of these people are political refugees within the definition of the United Nations Charter, that is, they are individuals seeking asylum from a well-founded fear of persecution.

Potential migrants are heavily concentrated in the poor regions of the South—in the previously colonized nations of Africa, Asia, the Caribbean and Latin America, and in the southern regions of the [former] Soviet Union. They not only move to neighbouring countries within their own regions, but, more and more, they are seeking to move to industrially advanced regions such as Europe, North America and Australia.

The Northern nations (and some migrant-receiving nations in the South) are reacting with alarm. In the North, this alarm has been fed by graphic images in the press of Haitian, Albanian and Sri Lankan "boat people" arriving in Florida, Italy and Canada. Some leaders are calling for the expulsion of unwelcome migrants, while others are calling for increased efforts to solve the economic problems in the sending regions so that migrant flows will be stopped at source. In some countries pressure is mounting to stop virtually all immigration.

The concerns underlying these attitudes are complex, ranging from fear that migrants will steal jobs or be a burden on social services, to xenophobia and even racism.

The "Globalization" of Trade

There is a tendency to blame current South-to-North migration on development failures in the South and, indeed, the 1980s, the "Decade of Development", were marked by economic stagnation and declining levels of real per capita income in Africa, the Caribbean and Latin America. The decade will also be viewed historically as a period of dramatic shift towards "globalization" of markets and a related global co-ordination of national economic policies.

Key trends, which are still under way, include: globalization of production (final assembly based on parts manufactured in various parts of the world); globalization of consumer markets (goods assembled in one nation are sold in many others); the spread of "structural adjustment" programmes (to favour export-oriented development); the rise of international trading blocs (Europe, the North American Free Trade Agreement, the Southern Cone trading bloc in Latin America, etc.). Clearly globalization is not an accident. It is the result of deliberate policies promoted by the developed nations, by major international institutions and by many less developed countries that have taken their lead from one of the major players.

One of the principal effects of globalization has been to differentiate more sharply between the "winners" and the "losers" in economic development. Globalization and the policies supporting it have, for example, worked to benefit the fast-growing economies of the Pacific Rim (The Republic of Korea, Hong Kong, Taiwan, Singapore, Malaysia and Thailand) because they combined political stability, progressive policies on education, low wages and other elements to attract investors and promote exports. Mexico may gain in the near future from globalization due to the size of its labour force, industrial infrastructure and access to the United States.

Other regions have clearly been losers in the new global trade and development game. Africa, for example, has such poorly developed economic infrastructures and such underdeveloped labour force skills that even its very low wages and geographic proximity to Europe did not attract many new investors in the 1980s. Development aid has been insufficient to fill this gap. Foreign direct investment in Africa actually declined over the 1980s, as it did in most countries of Latin America.

International Linkages Encourage Migration

Current immigration policy in developed countries is increasingly at odds with other major policy frameworks in the international system and with the growth of global economic integration. . . .

The policy framework for immigration treats the flow of labor as the result of individual actions, particularly the decision to migrate in search of better opportunities. Such a policy puts responsibility for immigration on the shoulders of immigrants. Policy commentary which speaks of an immigrant "influx" or "invasion" treats the receiving county as a passive agent. The causes of immigration appear to be outside the control or domain of receiving countries; immigration policy becomes a decision to be more or less benevolent in admitting immigrants. Absent from this understanding is the notion that the international activities of the governments or firms of receiving countries may have contributed to the formation of economic linkages with emigration countries, linkages that may function as bridges not only for capital but also for migration flows. That older view emphasizes individual "push" factors and neglects systemic linkages.

Saskia Sassen, *Crossroads*, November 1993.

Third World countries that have experienced economic growth in recent decades have also generally experienced long periods of high unemployment and significant out-migration, although there are some exceptions. Puerto Rico since the 1950s, Mexico in the 1960s and 1970s, and Korea in the 1970s and 1980s all experienced rather spectacular economic growth, while at the same time losing large numbers of workers and their families through international migration. High rates of natural population growth and the impact of mechanization in agriculture and industry created far more workers in these countries than could be absorbed in the local economy. In the late 1970s, on the other hand, Malaysia's economic growth was so fast that it actually suffered from labour shortages. This, however, was an exceptional case and cannot be taken as a general model.

Over the 1980s, a much larger number of countries lost ground economically, and rising unemployment and falling real incomes in these nations generated political crises and rising pressure for emigration. We have no crystal ball to indicate which countries will be tomorrow's winners and losers in the global development game. What does seem clear is that development in the new era of globalization will be inherently uneven and will inevitably continue to generate large pressures for international migration. The places of origin of the migrants will shift as global circumstances change. . . .

An International Division of Labour

Globalization of production has reinforced an international division of labour in which scientific, technological, design, finance, management and control jobs are concentrated in the North, while labour-intensive and manual manufacturing jobs are concentrated in the South. Economic growth in the North leads to an expanding demand for low-cost service and support activities in the developed countries themselves. These are jobs which workers in the developed countries do not want, or will not take at the prevailing wage level—in building, cleaning, gardening, garbage collection, etc. This situation lends itself to the sub-contracting of services to smaller companies which in turn may hire foreign-born workers, including illegal immigrants.

The demand for drugs and other illicit international commodities arises mainly in the North. This has led to a globalization of underground commerce, creating further employment opportunities in both the exporting and importing countries. Illicit commercial opportunities in the importing countries favour migrants since they are well placed to work across languages and to link vendors in their home countries with buyers in their new countries of residence.

A further effect of the globalization of trade and international commerce has been to bring about a dramatic fall in travel and communications costs. Information flows across international boundaries have increased enormously and have given rise to an unprecedented level of information in the South about informal job niches and economic opportunities in the North. This, together with the globalization of consumer products and advertising, has generated a rising demand for income and purchasing power, all of which fuels motivation of potential migrants in poor countries.

An additional level of complexity arises in some major migrant-receiving regions in the North, where the presence of large ethnic communities changes the politics of immigration. Families and ethnic groups originating in Third World countries press the State to open the door to ethnic kin. These pressures are most evident in the multiethnic receiving countries—the United States, Canada and Australia.

The conclusion that current trends in South-North migration are part of a global system of changing social and economic relationships, favoured and promoted by the North, will not please those who see the current migration crisis as a process that can be stopped by stiff migration controls or by short-term development programmes.

A Changing Social and Economic World

Solutions to the current crisis must include a longer-term perspective. It must be recognized that, although international development efforts will probably reduce migration in the longer term, these same efforts will almost certainly increase pressures for South-to-North migration in the short to intermediate term.

The overall international system, and the way in which the economies of the Northern countries function within it, imply at least moderate levels of international migration. Levels that are too low will be opposed internally as well as externally and will work against economic development and co-operation in the international system.

It is difficult to imagine how economic growth can take place in the South without extensive and rising trade, technical exchange and co-operation with the North. Similarly, it is difficult to imagine how the North can achieve greater security without fair and just co-operation with the South. This mutuality of interest in the new global context will require legitimate procedures to permit the short- and long-term movement of rather substantial numbers of people from South to North as new international institutions and arrangements are forged and strains arising from uneven international development are compassionately dealt with. To image otherwise is to go back to a state of greater isolation of nations, conflict between States and international chaos.

Periodical Bibliography

The following articles have been selected to supplement the diverse views presented in this chapter.

Virginia Abernathy — "Population Politics," *Population and Environment*, September 1992.

Kate Dallen — "How America Will Change over the Next Thirty Years," *Fortune*, June 17, 1991.

C. Lloyd Francis — "The Costs of Maintaining a Free Society," *The American Journal of Economics and Sociology*, October 1991. Available from 41 E. 72nd St., New York, NY 10021.

Robert Graham and Paul Beattie — "The Main Brain Drain," *The Journal of Social, Political, and Economic Studies*, Spring 1991. Available from 1133 13th St. NW, Suite Comm. #2, Washington, DC 20005.

Garrett Hardin — "Zero Net Immigration as a Goal," *Population and Environment*, November 1992. Available from Human Sciences Press, 72 Fifth Ave., New York, NY 10011.

Andrea Honebrink — "Migrants Create a New World Order with Their Feet," *Utne Reader*, May 1993.

Donald Huddle — "Dirty Work: Are Immigrants Only Taking Jobs That the Native Underclass Does Not Want?" *Population and Environment*, July 1993.

Gene Koretz — "The Upside of America's Population Upsurge," *Business Week*, August 9, 1993.

Richard D. Lamm — "Saint Martin of Tours and the New World of Public Policy," *The Humanist*, September/October 1993.

William Montalbono — "A Global Pursuit of Happiness," *Los Angeles Times*, October 1, 1991.

Ruben Rumbaut — "Origins and Destinies: Immigration to the United States Since World War II," *Sociological Forum*, December 1994. Available from Plenum Press, 233 Spring St., New York, NY 10013.

Julian Simon — "The Case for Greatly Increased Immigration," *The Public Interest*, Winter 1991.

Lydio Tomasi — "Population Growth, Immigration, and the National Interest," *Migration World*, March 1992. Available from 209 Flagg Pl., Staten Island, NY 10304-1188.

What Population Policies Should Be Pursued?

Population

Chapter Preface

Population policy refers to the guiding principles or courses of action adopted toward demographic objectives. Those objectives may include trends in fertility, mortality, migration, and total population size. Individual nations as well as the international community can have population policies, which tend to be ever-changing, not static.

The Programme of Action adopted by the 1994 United Nations Conference on Population and Development held in Cairo, Egypt (excerpted in this chapter), is illustrative of how the international community can formulate policy. By comparing this with prior population policy statements of the international community (the 1974 Population Conference in Bucharest, Romania, and the Population Conference in Mexico City in 1984), one can see how international population policy changes over time.

National population policy, especially in a country as large and diverse as the United States, can originate from local political initiatives. California's Proposition 187 is a good example. This initiative, which bans medical, social, and educational assistance to illegal immigrants in California, passed overwhelmingly when it was placed on the ballot in November 1994. Immediately challenged legally, it is likely to be tested eventually in the U.S. Supreme Court.

"Prop 187" was a response to the deep-seated frustrations of many Californians over the perceived lack of federal control of the U.S./Mexican border. With the state in an economic recession, tensions mounted over the supposed impact of hundreds of thousands of illegal immigrants in California and the federal mandate that the state supply them with certain benefits. Many political pundits believe that because of the high degree of popular support for the proposition, it will have a major impact on the future immigration policy of the United States—demonstrating not only the influence of local and regional concerns but also the effects of changing economic conditions on national population policy.

The authors of the following viewpoints debate some of the many issues that can provoke controversy when attempts are made to formulate population policy.

"It would be perverse if extremist feminist groups managed to deflect a worldwide effort to address the population question head-on."

The Feminist Agenda Detracts from Population Control Efforts

Charles F. Westoff

Charles F. Westoff is professor of demography and sociology at Princeton University and is the author of numerous articles and books on population, including *The Contraceptive Revolution* with Norman B. Ryder, and *From Now to Zero: Fertility, Contraception, and Abortion in America* with Leslie Aldridge Westoff. While Westoff agrees with feminists on the legitimacy of issues such as gender equality, women's rights, and the inadequacies of reproductive health and women's health services, he argues that the feminist agenda minimizes the importance of population control, to the detriment of the planet.

As you read, consider the following questions:

1. How does population momentum guarantee future growth in the world's population, according to the author?
2. How, according to the author, does the feminist agenda detract from population control?
3. According to Westoff, what is needed, in addition to family planning programs, to bring down world fertility levels?

In September of 1994 delegations from governments throughout the world convened in Cairo for the United Nations' third International Conference on Population and Development. The first such conference took place in 1974 in Bucharest; the population of the world at that time had reached four billion.

At the Bucharest meeting, the United States and other Western representatives emphasized the problems of rapid population growth and promoted fertility targets and family planning. A third-world contingent replied that this was an attempt at a cheap fix for the enormous economic inequities between the developed and developing nations, and coined the slogan "Development is the best contraceptive."

Once again, leading scientists are increasingly concerned about the additional billions of people expected in the next generation and thereafter—a prospect they say can no longer be ignored. World population is now 5.6 billion and growing at a rate that, if continued, will double in 43 years. The increase of one billion people expected in the 1990's alone is the greatest of any decade in history, even though the growth rate is continuing to decline from its peak in the 1960's. If fertility remains constant at the 1990 level, the total could reach 21 billion by the year 2050—a sobering number indeed.

The Importance of Population Momentum

Part of the enormous projected growth is due to the sheer demographic momentum created by the large proportion of children in developing countries who will eventually reach reproductive age. Even if, beginning tomorrow, the women of the third world replaced only themselves, their total population would still increase by more than 50 percent before the age distribution flattened out and zero growth settled in. Like the momentum of a huge ocean liner, population growth simply takes time to stop. The important implication of this demographic mechanism is that the world is in for a substantial increase in numbers despite rapid declines in fertility.

President Clinton, within a few days of taking office, reversed the Reagan-Bush policy on population and began steps to restore financing to the International Planned Parenthood Federation and the United Nations Fund for Population Activities. The Reagan-Bush policy, propounded at the 1984 population conference in Mexico City, was based on the laissez-faire ideology that if governments would get out of the way and let the free market operate, population would take care of itself.

But a new divisive issue has surfaced: the feminist agenda. The voices of feminists have been heard before on the subject of population (I first met Betty Friedan at the Bucharest conference 20 years ago); what is different is their increasing power

178

(they have more money now). Their concerns include women's rights; making women the subjects and not the objects of population policies; insisting that women occupy at least half of managerial and policy positions in the population field; the inadequacies of reproductive health and women's health services in general; the provision of legal abortion services; an end to genital mutilation practices; and demands for gender equality and for the empowerment of women in the economic, social and political arenas.

"But, Doctor, I'll be drummed out of my zero population growth chapter!"

These are legitimate concerns, consistent with lowering fertility, but the new rhetoric and political correctness may collide with effective approaches to the population problem. Many feminists ignore or minimize population growth and its presumed consequences, saying efforts to address the issue will inevitably lead to population control programs and fertility rate targets—in other words, to coercion of women by governments. (It's as if the consequences of rapid population growth apply only to men.) Some feminists argue that the emphasis on fertility control is misplaced: the real problems are gender inequality and poverty. Even family planning, long the centerpiece of women's efforts to gain control over reproduction, is not seen as an un-ambiguous benefit; radical feminists are suspicious of many birth control methods.

Feminists Reject Population-Environment Connections

Many feminists also reject population-environment connections. Their influence at the 1992 Rio conference on the environment was summed up by Jessica Tuchman Mathews, a former vice president of the World Resources Institute, who deplored the absence of any strong population component in the final language of that report: "The fate of the population language was sealed, ironically, by representatives of women."

The feminization of reproductive issues has clearly influenced the position of the United States Government. An official statement released on May 11, 1993, emphasized freedom of reproductive choice, including access to abortion, quality of care in women-centered and -managed services, empowerment of women and primary health care. Environmental issues are also addressed, but the high rate of world population growth is only implied, as if it were some kind of underlying, unmentionable disease. The effect of the promotion of abortion rights on international consensus remains to be seen. Thus, even though the current position on population policy is a refreshing step forward from that of Reagan-Bush days, it has lost its focus and is overreacting to organized groups that have a legitimate but also different agenda—an agenda family planning budgets cannot begin to cover.

It is curious that some organized feminist groups, in the name of reproductive rights, seem determined to dilute the population objectives of the United Nations conference. So much potential common ground exists in the goals of the family planning movement and in women's concerns for their reproductive health and rights—as well as for improving their status—that it would be perverse if extremist feminist groups managed to deflect a worldwide effort to address the population question head-on.

Economists vs. Ecologists

Ever since Malthus argued that populations grow geometrically while the food supply grows arithmetically, thus creating periodic imbalances that are corrected by increases in the death rate, the pros and cons of population growth have been hotly debated. It is self-evident that more people means more pressure on land, soils, forests, water and so on; growing populations multiply whatever environmentally destructive behavior is present. Yet even if population stopped growing tomorrow, environmental problems would remain unaltered in the absence of other changes; per capita levels of consumption, prices, technology and Government policy are also key factors. An estimated three-quarters of the world's energy resources is consumed by the one-quarter of the global population that resides in affluent countries. The damage can be reduced by appropriate economic incentives and disincentives and with more sensitive technologies—in short, with sound environmental policies.

But to dismiss the role of population growth in environmental deterioration—an attitude of many social scientists—is obtuse; the opposite view, which regards it as the chief villain, is equally extreme. Part of this continuing debate, typically between economists and ecologists, results from differing professional paradigms. The economist is optimistic that market mechanisms, technological innovation, unlimited human ingenuity and competent political leadership will solve such problems over time; the ecologist is pessimistic about the effects of seemingly relentless growth in numbers on a fragile ecosystem and the very carrying capacity of the globe. There is no little irony in the fact that the reputation Malthus earned for economics as the "dismal science" has shifted to the ecologists, currently the leading proponents of his pessimistic views.

Most future population growth will occur in the world's poorest countries. Many developing countries, including China, have made impressive economic gains despite rapid population growth. But these are largely the same countries that have lowered their fertility, which indicates other related social changes are occurring as well. Despite the complexities and inconclusive evidence connecting the pace of development with demographic changes, it hardly seems likely that additional hundreds of millions of people in China or India will facilitate development, let alone reduce poverty. Had the government of China been more concerned about population growth 30 years ago instead of being locked into the doctrinaire Marxist view that the subject was not a legitimate concern in a socialist economy, their present population policies might be less extreme.

Is it possible to accelerate the decline of fertility that is already occurring in many developing countries? Is family planning enough? Or must we wait for the slower processes of economic and social development to alter the basic conditions of life?

Reducing Fertility in Developing Countries

Significant reductions of fertility can be achieved by satisfying existing demand for family planning. In many East Asian and Latin American countries where fertility has declined sharply, unwanted births no doubt could still be averted, reducing fertility to near replacement. In sub-Saharan Africa, however, the effect of satisfying women's current reproductive preferences would be to reduce fertility from roughly six to five births per woman—a considerable distance from replacement. A similar conclusion would apply to other parts of the world, including Pakistan and much of the Middle East. In China, on the other hand, families are having fewer children than they would like to have.

Satisfying unmet demand for birth control is certainly an important part of any population program. It is politically acceptable; it can serve health needs of mothers and their children; and it is essentially in everyone's interest. Yet it involves more than providing supplies and improving the quality of services. Because there is a great deal of ambivalence in many high-fertility populations about having fewer children, information about methods and their health implications must be readily available. Some women are opposed to contraception on religious grounds; some report that their husbands are opposed; others are fatalistic about the number of children they will have. Motivational efforts are required even for those predisposed to postpone the next birth or to avoid further child bearing. A key role can be played by the media in promoting exposure to modern ideas. One innovative New York City–based organization, Population Communications International, promotes the idea of smaller families through local radio and television soap operas. Evidence from Kenya, Mexico and India suggests that such mass media approaches do work. And if the recent demographic history of parts of Asia and Latin America is any guide, once the idea that fertility can be controlled catches on, it accelerates rapidly.

Greater commitment and effort by concerned governments and international agencies could have a substantial effect in the next few decades, and voluntary programs implemented now could reduce the likelihood of more drastic programs later.

"Women and women's organizations should be involved in the decision-making process . . . where any laws or policies affecting their rights and health are designed and implemented."

The Feminist Agenda Is Necessary for Transforming Population Policies

Participants of Reproductive Health and Justice: International Women's Health Conference

In January 1994, 215 women from 79 countries met in Rio de Janeiro, Brazil, in preparation for the September 1994 United Nations International Conference on Population and Development (ICPD). The New York City–based International Women's Health Coalition and the Rio-based Citizenship, Studies, Information, Action (CEPIA) supported the Rio Conference. One aim of the conference was to "build solidarity and strengthen the women's health movement as an important political actor in the ICPD and beyond." The following viewpoint—"the Rio Statement" hammered out at the conference—demands that the rights and concerns of women be specifically addressed in all laws and policies on population and development.

As you read, consider the following questions:

1. What social development policies did the conference participants agree are needed?
2. How should contraceptive technology resources be redirected, according to the authors?

From the "Rio Statement" of the participants of Reproductive Health and Justice: International Women's Health Conference for Cairo '94. Reprinted by permission of the International Women's Health Coalition, New York.

During the period from January 24 through 28, 1994, 215 women from 79 countries participated in "Reproductive Health and Justice: International Women's Health Conference for Cairo '94" held in Rio de Janeiro. The conference brought together representatives of women's and other non-governmental organizations [NGOs] and networks active in the fields of health, human rights, development, environment, and population. The main objective of the conference was for women to prepare to participate in the International Conference on Population and Development to be held in Cairo in September 1994, and to provide a forum where women could search for and identify commonalities on reproductive health and justice, while recognizing the diversities emanating from different economic, social, political, and cultural backgrounds. The conference also aimed at developing tools and strategies to be used before, during, and after the Cairo conference.

The participants strongly voiced their opposition to population policies intended to control the fertility of women and that do not address their basic right to a secure livelihood, freedom from poverty and oppression; or do not respect their rights to free, informed choice or to adequate health care; [they said] that whether such policies are pro- or anti-natalist, they are often coercive, treat women as objects, not subjects, and that in the context of such policies, low fertility does not result in alleviation of poverty. In fact, a significant number of the participants opposed population policies as being inherently coercive. There was unanimous opposition to designing fertility control measures or population policies specifically targeted at Southern countries, indigenous peoples, or marginalized groups within both Southern and Northern countries, whether by race, class, ethnicity, religion, or other basis.

There was also significant criticism of pressure by donors and efforts to link development aid or structural adjustment programs to the institution and/or implementation of population control policies, and a suggestion that donor countries should not promote in other countries what they do not support for the majority of their own people.

It was agreed that:

1. Inequitable development models and strategies constitute the underlying basis of growing poverty and marginalization of women, environmental degradation, growing numbers of migrants and refugees, and the rise of fundamentalism everywhere. For women, these problems (and their presumed solutions through economic programs for structural adjustment that promote export production at the expense of local needs) have particularly severe consequences:
   - growing work-burdens and responsibilities (whether in

female-headed households or otherwise);

- spiralling prices and worsened access to food, education, health services, and other basic rights;
- greater economic pressures to earn incomes;
- growing victimization through violence, wars, and fundamentalist attempts to control and subordinate women sexually and in a number of other ways.

2. External debt, structural adjustment programs, and international terms of trade sustain Northern domination, increase inequalities between rich and poor in all countries, aggravate civil strife, encourage the corruption of government leaders, and erode the already meager resources for basic services.

3. Environmental degradation was seen to be closely related to inequality in resources and consumption, profit-driven production systems, and the role of the military as a major polluter and user of resources; hence, there is a close rela-

Kevin Kallaugher(KAL)/England. Reprinted by permission of Cartoonists & Writers Syndicate.

185

tionship between the violence and poverty that bedevil people's, particularly women's, lives, and environmental problems. Focussing on women's fertility as a major cause of the current environmental crisis diverts attention from root causes, including exploitative economic systems, unsustainable elite consumption patterns, and militarism. Women in the conference urged governments to diminish military expenditures in favor of social programs. The participants also urged the Northern governments and donors to stop supporting and financing military and undemocratic regimes in the South.

4. There was particular concern about the situation of women migrants who are heads of households, domestic servants, migrant workers, entertainers, and other service workers. It was agreed that while the movement of people should not be constrained by discriminatory and restrictive immigration policies that operate in contexts where migration is often forced by economic hardship, civil strife, war, and political persecution, efforts should be made to address the brutality and violence faced by women and children who are victims of trafficking and sexual exploitation.

5. Alternative development strategies must be identified. In doing so, there is no single blueprint for development strategies but a multiplicity of approaches within a basic framework of food security, adequate employment and incomes, and good-quality basic services, which can be guaranteed through democratic people-centered and participatory processes.

6. The "sustainable and human development models" that are currently being proposed in the official documents of governments and international organizations need to be based on investments and social policies that guarantee the quality of life and well-being of all people.

7. There was general agreement on the need to design social development policies starting from the concerns and priorities of women. These include:
   - the need to redistribute resources in an equitable and just manner without discrimination against women, to remove poverty, and to improve the quality of life of all;
   - the need to design development strategies so that they do not disempower and marginalize people, particularly women;
   - to restore and strengthen basic services (for health, education, housing, etc.) that have been eroded by macroeconomic policies;
   - to provide health services that are of good quality, accessible, comprehensive, and address the reproductive

health needs of women and men of all ages;

- to address reproductive health and rights needs and concerns (including the right to free and informed choice) within the context of social and economic justice;
- to strengthen women's participation and empowerment in political and policy-making processes and institutions with the goal of achieving gender balance in all such processes and institutions;
- to build accountability processes and mechanisms into policies.

8. The discussion of fundamentalism brought strong agreement that, whatever its origins or religious claims, its aim is political. Central to fundamentalist attempts to gain political power is the control of women's lives and in particular of female sexuality, including the right to self-determination and reproductive decisions. There was criticism of the role of major Northern countries in supporting fundamentalist groups for their own political ends. Fundamentalists use religion, culture, and ethnicity in their pursuit of power; such movements represent a new form of war against women and an aggressive attempt to mutilate their human rights.

9. A major site of the fundamentalist war against women is over the meaning of "families." The participants at the conference agreed that a definition of "family" that is limited to a model with a male "head" of household, wife and children does not reflect the life situation of all of the world's people. Instead it was agreed that all those who voluntarily come together and define themselves as a family, accepting a commitment to each other's well-being, should be respected, supported, and affirmed as such.

10. All members of the family have rights, especially to justice and human dignity. Physical, emotional, psychological, or sexual abuse of women, young girls, and children within families constitutes a serious violation of basic human rights under the Universal Declaration of Human Rights. Women's rights within the family include access to resources, participation in decision making, bodily integrity, and security. Women have a right to participate in public life, to social benefits and social insurance, and to have their unpaid work inside and outside the home recognized and shared by all members of the family.

11. Comprehensive and high-quality health services for women, including for reproductive health, are a primary responsibility of governments. They should be available, accessible, and affordable to women in order to reduce maternal mortality, morbidity, child mortality, and unsafe abortion, within a broad women's health approach that addresses

women's needs across the life cycle. Qualitative (as well as quantitative) indicators need to be developed to assess services, and users need to be involved in this.

12. There was clear agreement that quality reproductive health services are a key right for women. However, existing family planning programs cannot simply be redefined as programs of reproductive health. Reproductive health services should include prenatal, childbirth, and postpartum care including nutritional and lactation programs; safe contraception and safe non-compulsory abortion; prevention, early diagnosis, and treatment of sexually transmitted diseases, and breast, cervical, and other women's cancers, as well as the prevention and treatment of HIV/AIDS, and treatment of infertility; all with the informed consent of women. These services should be women-centered and women-controlled, and every effort should be made to prevent the maltreatment and abuse of women users by the medical staff. The UN and other donors and governments should recognize the right to safe and legal abortion as an intrinsic part of women's rights, and governments should change legislation and implement policies to reflect such a recognition.

What Makes Reproductive Rights Meaningful?

In their book *Taking Population Seriously*, Frances Moore Lappé and Rachel Schurman posit that for Third World women, access to and control of reproduction is meaningless if

- security means depending on one's children;
- many births are necessary to guarantee that some children will survive to become adults;
- health care and services remain the privilege of the better-off in urban areas;
- women have few opportunities for self-improvement (education and employment) outside the home and have no choice other than marriage;
- women's power and status are derived from their children, especially sons.

Evelyn Hong, "Behind the Population Debate," *Third World Resurgence*, Winter 1991-92.

13. In the area of contraceptive technology, resources should be redirected from provider-controlled and potentially high-risk methods, like the vaccine, to barrier methods. A significant proportion of the participants also felt strongly that Norplant® or other long-term hormonal contraceptives should be explicitly mentioned as high-risk methods from

which resources should be redirected. Female-controlled methods that provide both contraception and protection from sexually transmitted diseases, including HIV, as well as male methods, should receive the highest priority in contraceptive research and development. Women's organizations are entitled to independently monitor contraceptive trials and ensure women's free, informed consent to enter the trial. Trial results must be available for women's organizations at the different stages of such trials, including the very early stages.

14. Better health services are one element of women's human rights. In addition, sexuality and gender power relationships must be addressed as a central aspect of reproductive rights. Reproductive rights are inalienable human rights that are inseparable from other basic rights, such as the right to food, shelter, health, security, livelihood, education, and political empowerment. Therefore, the design and implementation of policies affecting reproductive rights and health should conform to international human rights standards.

15. Women are entitled to bodily integrity. Within this principle, violence against women; forced early marriage; and harmful practices, especially female genital mutilation, must be recognized as major reproductive rights, health, and development issues. Governments should take measures to combat such practices and should be held accountable for failure to do so.

16. Women have a right to express their sexuality with pleasure and without fear of abuse and risk of diseases or discrimination on the basis of their sexual orientation or disability. Social and economic powerlessness; oppressive cultural, traditional and religious norms and practices; inequitable laws; fundamentalism; and fear of male violence are impediments to women's own sense of entitlement and should be challenged.

17. Women, especially girls, must have equal access to education in general. Such education should not be gender-discriminatory in its objectives, methods, and content. Quality sex education with a gender perspective should be made available to women and men of all ages, in order to create the conditions for equity in social roles and empowerment of women in order to enable them to control their own fertility.

18. For women to be able to empower themselves and fully exercise their rights of citizenship, the underlying inequities in gender relationships must be eliminated. In particular, policies and programs should educate and encourage men

to share family responsibilities, including the responsibility for their reproductive behavior and for the prevention of sexually transmitted diseases.

19. Participants at the conference were concerned that women and women's organizations should be involved in the decision-making process locally, nationally, and internationally where any laws or policies affecting their rights and health are designed and implemented. Governments, the UN, and other international institutions should be held accountable for the design and implementation of social and development policies that guarantee women's reproductive rights and health. Mechanisms for monitoring and regular evaluation should be established, and should provide for participation of women's organizations.

20. Donors and governments should also be held accountable, and their concern for women's health and development should be reflected in their resource allocation and priorities. Donors and governments should revise their funding categories to promote comprehensive women's health programs, rather than narrowly defined programs for family planning. A major requirement is that women-centered programs must have access to a fair share of the financial resources available for reproductive health.

21. The participants recommended a UN commission on women's reproductive rights whose composition should be gender-balanced, and should take account of geographic, ethnic, racial, social class, and other balances. Said commission should be interdisciplinary and should include NGOs, especially women's human rights organizations. Each government should be held responsible for establishing a similar commission at the national level.

"Discussion of population . . . too often leads to the imposition of standards and policies of some nations on other nations."

Global Policies Should Condemn Abortion and Restore the Traditional Family

Mohammed Aslam Cheema and William Keeler

Four days before the United Nations' 1994 International Conference on Population and Development, spokesmen for the Roman Catholic and Muslim faiths urged the conference to discourage abortion and encourage a return to "traditional values." In the following viewpoint, Mohammed Aslam Cheema, president of the American Muslim Council, and William Keeler, archbishop of Baltimore, present the religious views of their denominations on these issues. They urge that the Cairo conference adopt these values in "unambiguous" language for its final text.

As you read, consider the following questions:

1. What was the concern of the authors about how the use of abortion would be treated at the Cairo conference?
2. How do the authors define a family? What place in society do they see for the family?
3. What is the authors' view on sex education for unmarried adolescents?

Excerpted from Mohammed Aslam Cheema and William Keeler, "Interreligious Statement Addresses Cairo Issues," *Origins*, September 15, 1994. Copyright National Catholic News Service.

At the invitation of the American Muslim Council to the National Conference of Catholic Bishops, we, the presidents of these two organizations which have cooperated on several projects in the past, now issue this joint statement on certain aspects of the current public discussion of the upcoming Cairo conference. . . .

In 1991, the participants in the first national dialogue between Catholics and Muslims, which our organizations co-sponsored, attested that this dialogue would seek to join together for the realization of common values. Our organizations co-sponsored a second national dialogue and have cooperated on a number of other projects. . . .

This statement on the Cairo conference, therefore, is that of a partnership with a history and with ongoing consultation. Even now our staff are discussing, in a preliminary way, a proposal to convene our national dialogue on certain aspects of marriage and family life.

The worldwide discussion about the draft program of action for the International Conference on Population and Development, called by the United Nations in Cairo next week [September 5-13, 1994], has motivated us to make this joint statement today. We draw attention to important values which we share with regard to topics on the agenda. Our positions are based on teachings and moral principles rooted in our earliest traditions.

The Sanctity of Human Life

We share a special reverence for life. For Catholics this is often summarized under the expression "the sanctity of human life," which includes respect for the life and dignity of every human being, born and unborn. Muslims fully agree with this; in addition they recite specific passages in the holy Quran against the great evil of the killing of children, which at the time of the prophet often meant female infanticide. Spelled out clearly in the teachings of both traditions is the right of every individual for true development in all dimensions, social, cultural and spiritual, with justice and equality for all, so that every person will have the opportunity to experience the divine gifts of dignity and peace. We agree that care must be taken to distinguish the God-given right to development for every person in the human community and a false individualism that puts self-centered goals before the good of others. Such individualism is antithetical to our understandings of social justice.

We agree that abortion is an evil. The coercion of abortion, whether subtle or overt, is repugnant to us. We join our voices with Pope John Paul II, the scholars of Al Azhar University and leaders throughout the world calling on the Cairo conference to reaffirm the decision of the 1984 Mexico City international conference that all nations should "take appropriate steps to help women avoid abortion, which in no case should be promoted as a method of family planning, and whenever possible provide for the humane treatment and counseling of women who have had recourse to abortion." Our solemn concern is that, in preparation for this meeting on population and development, access to abortion is being discussed as a policy of population control and even as a legitimate aspect of reproductive health care or fertility regulation. We join all those calling upon nations affirming policies of permissive abortion to cease the massive deaths of the unborn and the severe harm to women who undergo abortions.

A Roman Catholic Bishop Speaks on Abortion

Abortion is frequently spoken of as "terminating a pregnancy." Rarely is it described as taking the life of a preborn child—which is what it is. People frequently speak of being "pro-choice" rather than "pro-abortion" or of "supporting a women's right to choose," without acknowledging that this "choice" when made involves ending the life of another human being. . . .

Unless the right to life is acknowledged as inherent, universal and inviolable—that is, due a person simply because he or she is human—no one's right to life is assured and other rights founded on the right to life are also threatened. As Pope John Paul II has said, "The common outcry, which is justly made on behalf of human rights—for example, the right to health, to home, to work, to family, to culture—is false and illusory if the right to life, the most basic and fundamental right and the condition for all other personal rights, is not defended with maximum determination" (*Christifidelis laici*, no. 38).

The Catholic Church has always condemned abortion. It has never wavered from its teaching that abortion is always seriously wrong. It has always understood the commandment, "You shall not kill" (Ex. 20:13) to preclude all direct and intentional taking of innocent human life. The Second Vatican Council upheld and reaffirmed Church teaching on abortion: "Life must be protected with the utmost care from the moment of conception: abortion and infanticide are abominable crimes" (*Gaudium et spes*, no 51).

Robert H. Brom, "Statement on Abortion on the 20th Anniversary of *Roe v. Wade*," January 22, 1993.

For Muslims and Catholics alike, the family is the principal school of virtues, the primary school of religious instruction. We endorse wholeheartedly the rights of the family to organize its own religious life in the home and under the control of the parents. The family is the basic unit not only for society but for a just and holy society.

A family is a sacred relationship among persons. A family proceeds from the marriage between a man and a woman, and this formative bond of families is divinely mandated. We agree that the union of a wife and husband is intended to be an intimate, exclusive, permanent and faithful partnership, even though our traditions may have different practices regarding some of these aspects. Even though we are compassionately aware that there are large numbers of single-parent families, we are distressed at current efforts to redefine family and other developments that devalue marriage.

The Holiness of Human Sexuality

Our views of the family, based upon revelation as we each understand it, also draw attention to our similar teachings on the holiness and integrity of human sexuality. The climate of sexual permissiveness which is prevalent in some parts of the world stands in stark contrast to our teachings on the family and human sexuality. It further underscores with urgency the rights and responsibilities of parents for the moral and sexual education of the future generation. No government or no nongovernmental agency outside the family should provide counsel or services to unmarried adolescents without the knowledge and express consent of their parents.

Our teachings are nuanced differently with regard to methods of family planning, but we agree that one goal of the divinely ordained marriage between a husband and wife is the creation of new life.

Meeting the Needs of the Poor and Women

Development in connection with population growth is indeed the major focus of the Cairo conference. We join all men and women of good will in stating our agreement that true development is based on meeting the needs of every human person and the common good. Muslims and Christians are committed to meeting the needs of the poor; the serious ecological questions and other issues regarding land use, efficient production and distribution of food provide us with the opportunities to affirm our moral principles and to overcome the temptation of selfishness. Every human being has a right to participate fully in economic and social development. Everyone should have the opportunity for an education, and this is equally true for women and for male and female children. These rights and issues should be the primary points for engaging nations rather than means of population control.

The Conference on Population and Development focuses also on the equality of women in dignity and rights. The particular gifts of women as teachers of the faith, bestowers of values, imparters of wisdom, leaders of projects and officeholders have sustained our two traditions from their origins. Development and expansion of the roles of women in society and the educational and health needs of women, which are insufficiently met across the world, should be addressed by nations. Abuse and violence against women, whether individually or collectively, whether motivated by sinfulness or cultural biases, should be condemned and action taken for the eradication of abuse, violence and neglect of women and girls everywhere.

Discussion of population, consumption and resources purely for demographic objectives too often leads to the imposition of standards and policies of some nations on other nations. As members of the two largest religious groups on Earth, embracing the human family extensively on every continent in rich and poor nations alike, we are acutely aware of the need for arriving at universally accepted procedures and policies. Therefore, we plead that the language of the final text on the issues which are of critical concern to us be unambiguous and not open to opposing interpretations.

A Critical Need for the Religious Perspective

It is indeed critical to hear from religious communities because they provide moral and inspirational perspectives on these critical issues. Religion is very much a part of the lives of people in the United States and throughout the world, providing sustenance and knowledge for addressing ultimate questions of meaning and the human condition. With ancient wisdom and extensive resources of knowledge and skills, religious communities are committed to meeting the profound needs of all and to respect for the Earth.

We express together our concern about the crass labeling of the positions of Muslims on population and development issues as "fundamentalists," implying they are extremists, when they indeed are speaking from the heart of their tradition. We also wish to note for the record that the Holy See has had diplomatic relations with countries with Muslim majorities, a practice which can be traced back even to ancient times. Full diplomatic relations with many "Islamic" nations have been on the public record for a long time.

We conclude by noting that there are threats of violence against those who will attend this important International Conference on Population and Development in Cairo. We reiterate these sentences from our 1993 joint statement: "Aggression and terrorism wherever they occur are to be condemned since they constitute an illegitimate use of force and therefore violate the law of God. . . . With equally strong resolve we reject any effort to claim a religious inspiration or sanction for such contemptible acts."

"The aim should be to assist couples and individuals to achieve their reproductive goals and . . . to exercise the right to have children by choice."

Global Policies Should Support a Full Range of Family-Planning Options

UN International Conference on
Population and Development, Cairo

The draft of *The Programme of Action of the United Nations International Conference on Population and Development* was adopted on September 13, 1994, in Cairo, Egypt. The programme presents "basis for action," "objectives," and "actions" sections on population-related issues. The following viewpoint excerpts "actions" sections proposed in the areas of reproductive rights and reproductive health, family planning, HIV prevention, human sexuality and gender relations, adolescents, and abortion. While the conference rejects the use of abortion as a primary method of family planning, it urges that all forms of legal family planning options be made safe and universally available.

As you read, consider the following questions:

1. What position does the conference take on sex education for unmarried adolescents?
2. How does the conference address the use of abortion for unwanted pregnancies?

Excerpted from *The Programme of Action of the United Nations International Conference on Population and Development*, September 13, 1994.

While the International Conference on Population and Development does not create any new international human rights, it affirms the application of universally recognized human rights standards to all aspects of population programmes. It also represents the last opportunity in the twentieth century for the international community to collectively address the critical challenges and interrelationships between population and development. The Programme of Action will require the establishment of common ground, with full respect for the various religious and ethical values and cultural backgrounds. The impact of this Conference will be measured by the strength of the specific commitments made here and the consequent actions to fulfil them, as part of a new global partnership among all the world's countries and peoples, based on a sense of shared but differentiated responsibility for each other and for our planetary home. . . .

Reproductive Rights and Reproductive Health

7.6. All countries should strive to make accessible through the primary health-care system, reproductive health to all individuals of appropriate ages as soon as possible and no later than the year 2015. Reproductive health care in the context of primary health care should, *inter alia*, include: family-planning counselling, information, education, communication and services; education and services for prenatal care, safe delivery, and postnatal care, especially breast-feeding, and infant and women's health care; prevention and appropriate treatment of infertility; abortion as specified in para. 8.25, including prevention of abortion and the management of the consequences of abortion; treatment of reproductive tract infections, sexually transmitted diseases and other reproductive health conditions; and information, education and counselling, as appropriate, on human sexuality, reproductive health and responsible parenthood. Referral for family-planning services and further diagnosis and treatment for complications of pregnancy, delivery and abortion, infertility, reproductive tract infections, breast cancer and cancers of the reproductive system, sexually transmitted diseases and HIV/AIDS should always be available, as required. Active discouragement of harmful practices such as female genital mutilation should also be an integral component of primary health care, including reproductive health-care programmes.

7.7. Reproductive health-care programmes should be designed to serve the needs of women including adolescents and must involve women in the leadership, planning, decision-making, management, implementation, organization and evaluation of services. Governments and other organizations should take positive steps to include women at all levels of the health-care system.

7.8. Innovative programmes must be developed to make infor-

197

mation, counselling and services for reproductive health accessible to adolescents and adult men. Such programmes must both educate and enable men to share more equally in family planning, in domestic and child-rearing responsibilities and to accept the major responsibility for the prevention of sexually transmitted diseases. Programmes must reach men in their workplaces, at home and where they gather for recreation. Boys and adolescents, with the support and guidance of their parents, and in line with the Convention on the Rights of the Child, should also be reached through schools, youth organizations and wherever they congregate. Voluntary and appropriate male methods for contraception, as well as for the prevention of sexually transmitted diseases and AIDS, should be promoted and made accessible with adequate information and counselling. . . .

A Spirit of Compromise in Cairo

After nine days of painstaking debate, the International Conference on Population and Development ended September 13, 1994, with a compromise plan that for the first time stresses the importance of women in efforts to curb the rapid growth of the human family.

The 113-page final "Programme of Action" allows all sides to claim victory: It strengthens the position of the Vatican and its allies on abortion and family; vindicates Muslim countries from charges of extremism by compromising on language relating to homosexuality; and gives women more control over decisions relating to reproduction.

The plan aims to stabilize population at about 7.27 billion in 2015, up from the current level of roughly 5.7 billion, but well below an estimate of 12.5 billion in 2050 if growth rates are not slowed.

Delegates said their aim was to reach a consensus with all nations so that governments could not easily dismiss the document. The text is not legally binding, but is likely to be used as a reference for governments and activists in shaping family-planning policies.

Geneive Abdo, *Christian Science Monitor*, September 15, 1994.

7.10. Without jeopardizing international support for programmes in developing countries, the international community should, upon request, give consideration to the training, technical assistance, short-term contraceptive supply needs and the needs of the countries in transition from centrally managed to market economies, where reproductive health is poor and in some cases deteriorating. Those countries, at the same time, must themselves give higher priority to reproductive health services, including a comprehensive range of contraceptive means, and must address their current reliance on abortion for fertility regulation by meeting the need of women in those countries for better information and more choices on an urgent basis.

7.11. Migrants and displaced persons in many parts of the world have limited access to reproductive health care and may face specific serious threats to their reproductive health and rights. Services must be sensitive particularly to the needs of individual women and adolescents and responsive to their often powerless situation, with particular attention to those who are victims of sexual violence. . . .

Family Planning

7.15. Governments and the international community should use the full means at their disposal to support the principle of voluntary choice in family planning.

7.16. All countries should, over the next several years, assess the extent of national unmet need for good-quality family-planning services and its integration in the reproductive health context, paying particular attention to the most vulnerable and underserved groups in the population. All countries should take steps to meet the family-planning needs of their populations as soon as possible and should, in all cases by the year 2015, seek to provide universal access to a full range of safe and reliable family-planning methods and to related reproductive health services which are not against the law. The aim should be to assist couples and individuals to achieve their reproductive goals and give them the full opportunity to exercise the right to have children by choice.

7.17. Governments at all levels are urged to institute systems of monitoring and evaluation of user-centred services with a view to detecting, preventing and controlling abuses by family-planning managers and providers and to ensure a continuing improvement in the quality of services. To this end, Governments should secure conformity to human rights, and to ethical and professional standards in the delivery of family-planning and related reproductive health services aimed at ensuring responsible, voluntary and informed consent and also regarding service provision. In-vitro fertilization techniques should be provided in accordance with appropriate ethical guidelines and medical standards. . . .

7.19. As part of the effort to meet unmet needs, all countries should seek to identify and remove all the major remaining barriers to the utilization of family-planning services. Some of those barriers are related to the inadequacy, poor quality and cost of existing family-planning services. It should be the goal of public, private and non-governmental family-planning organizations to remove all programme-related barriers to family-planning use by the year 2005 through the redesign or expansion of information and services and other ways to increase the ability of couples and individuals to make free and informed decisions about the number, spacing and timing of births and protect themselves from sexually transmitted diseases.

7.20. Specifically, Governments should make it easier for couples and individuals to take responsibility for their own reproductive health by removing unnecessary legal, medical, clinical and regulatory barriers to information and to access to family-planning services and methods.

7.21. All political and community leaders are urged to play a strong, sustained and highly visible role in promoting and legitimizing the provision and use of family-planning and reproductive health services. Governments at all levels are urged to provide a climate that is favourable to good-quality public and private family-planning and reproductive health information and services through all possible channels. Finally, leaders and legislators at all levels must translate their public support for reproductive health, including family planning, into adequate allocations of budgetary, human and administrative resources to help meet the needs of all those who cannot pay the full cost of services.

7.22. Governments are encouraged to focus most of their efforts towards meeting their population and development objectives through education and voluntary measures rather than schemes involving incentives and disincentives.

7.23. In the coming years, all family-planning programmes must make significant efforts to improve quality of care. Among other measures, programmes should:

(a) Recognize that appropriate methods for couples and individuals vary according to their age, parity, family-size preference and other factors, and ensure that women and men have information and access to the widest possible range of safe and effective family-planning methods in order to enable them to exercise free and informed choice;

(b) Provide accessible, complete and accurate information about various family-planning methods, including their health risks and benefits, possible side effects and their effectiveness in the prevention of the spread of HIV/AIDS and other sexually transmitted diseases;

(c) Make services safer, affordable, more convenient and accessible for clients and ensure, through strengthened logistical systems, a sufficient and continuous supply of essential high-quality contraceptives. Privacy and confidentiality should be ensured;

(d) Expand and upgrade formal and informal training in sexual and reproductive health care and family planning for all health-care providers, health educators and managers, including training in interpersonal communications and counselling;

(e) Ensure appropriate follow-up care, including treatment for side effects of contraceptive use;

(f) Ensure availability of related reproductive health services on site or through a strong referral mechanism;

(g) In addition to quantitative measures of performance, give more emphasis to qualitative ones that take into account the perspectives of current and potential users of services, through means including effective management information systems and survey techniques for the timely evaluation of services;

(h) Family-planning and reproductive health programmes should emphasize breast-feeding education and support services, which can simultaneously contribute to birth spacing, better maternal and child health and higher child survival.

7.24. Governments should take appropriate steps to help women avoid abortion, which in no case should be promoted as a method of family planning, and in all cases provide for the humane treatment and counselling of women who have had recourse to abortion.

7.25. In order to meet the substantial increase in demand for contraceptives over the next decade and beyond, the international community should move, on an immediate basis, to establish an efficient coordination system and global, regional and subregional facilities for the procurement of contraceptives and other commodities essential to reproductive health programmes of developing countries and countries with economies in transition. The international community should also consider measures such as transfers of technology to developing countries enabling them to produce and distribute high-quality contraceptives and other commodities essential to reproductive health services, in order to strengthen the self-reliance of those countries. At the request of the countries concerned, the World Health Organization should continue to provide advice on the quality, safety and efficacy of family-planning methods. . . .

Sexually Transmitted Diseases and HIV Prevention

7.33. Promotion and the reliable supply and distribution of high-quality condoms should become integral components of all reproductive health-care services. All relevant international organizations, especially the World Health Organization, should significantly increase their procurement. Governments and the international community should provide all means to reduce the spread and the rate of transmission of HIV/AIDS infection. . . .

Human Sexuality and Gender Relations

7.37. Support should be given to integral sexual education and services for young people with the support and guidance of their parents, and in line with the Convention on the Rights of the Child, that stress male responsibility for their own sexual health and fertility and that help them exercise those responsibilities. Educational efforts should begin within the family unit, in the community and in the schools at an appropriate age, but must also reach adults, in particular men, through non-formal education and a variety of community-based efforts.

7.38. In the light of the urgent need to prevent unwanted pregnancies, the rapid spread of AIDS and other sexually transmitted diseases, and the prevalence of sexual abuse and violence, Governments should base national policies on a better understanding of the need for responsible human sexuality and the realities of current sexual behaviour. . . .

Adolescents

7.45. Recognizing the rights, duties and responsibilities of parents and other persons legally responsible for adolescents to provide, in a manner consistent with the evolving capacities of the adolescent, appropriate direction and guidance in sexual and reproductive matters, countries must ensure that the programmes and attitudes of health-care providers do not restrict the access of adolescents to appropriate services and the information they need, including on sexually transmitted diseases and sexual abuse. In doing so, and in order to, *inter alia*, address sexual abuse, these services must safeguard the rights of adolescents to privacy, confidentiality, respect and informed consent, respecting cultural values and religious beliefs. In this context, countries should, where appropriate, remove legal, regulatory and social barriers to reproductive health information and care for adolescents.

7.46. Countries, with the support of the international community, should protect and promote the rights of adolescents to reproductive health education, information and care and greatly reduce the number of adolescent pregnancies.

7.47. Governments, in collaboration with non-governmental organizations, are urged to meet the special needs of adolescents and to establish appropriate programmes to respond to those needs. Such programmes should include support mechanisms for the education and counselling of adolescents in the areas of gender relations and equality, violence against adolescents, responsible sexual behaviour, responsible family-planning practice, family life, reproductive health, sexually transmitted diseases, HIV infection and AIDS prevention. Programmes for the prevention and treatment of sexual abuse and incest and other reproductive health services should be provided. Such programmes should provide information to adolescents and make a conscious effort to strengthen positive social and cultural values. Sexually active adolescents will require special family-planning information, counselling and services, and those who become pregnant will require special support from their families and community during pregnancy and early child care. Adolescents must be fully involved in the planning, implementation and evaluation of such information and services with proper regard for parental guidance and responsibilities.

7.48. Programmes should involve and train all who are in a position to provide guidance to adolescents concerning responsible sexual and reproductive behaviour, particularly parents and families, and also communities, religious institutions, schools, the mass media and peer groups. Governments and non-governmental organizations should promote programmes directed to the education of parents, with the objective of improving the interaction of parents and children to enable them to comply better with their educational duties to support the process of maturation of their children, particularly in the areas of sexual behaviour and reproductive health. . . .

Abortion

8.25. In no case should abortion be promoted as a method of family planning. All Governments and relevant intergovernmental and non-governmental organizations are urged to strengthen their commitment to women's health, to deal with the health impact of unsafe abortion [Unsafe abortion is defined as a procedure for terminating an unwanted pregnancy either by persons lacking necessary skills or in an environment lacking the minimal medical standards or both. (WHO/MSM/92.5)] as a major public health concern and to reduce the recourse to abortion through expanded and improved family-planning services. Prevention of unwanted pregnancies must always be given the highest priority and all attempts should be made to eliminate the need for abortion. Women who have unwanted pregnancies should have ready access to reliable information and compassionate counselling. Any measures or changes related to abortion within the health system can only be determined at the national or local level according to the national legislative process. In circumstances in which abortion is not against the law, such abortion should be safe. In all cases, women should have access to quality services for the management of complications arising from abortion. Post-abortion counselling, education and family-planning services should be offered promptly, which will also help to avoid repeat abortions.

"To bring the spiraling population growth under control, China must continue with the family planning programme."

China Still Needs the One-Child Policy

Peng Peiyun, interviewed by Jing Wei

Jing Wei, a staff reporter for the *Beijing Review*, interviewed Peng Peiyun, chair of China's State Family Planning Commission, on the subject of China's burgeoning population. Peng Peiyun maintains that China's one-child-per-family policy has been effective in reducing China's fertility rate, but asserts that because of limited arable land and resources, China must continue to require a limit of one child per couple, at least in urban areas. She contends that any other population policy would be irresponsible, both to China and to the rest of the world.

As you read, consider the following questions:

1. How has China's one-child policy benefited China and the world, according to Peng Peiyun?
2. Why does Peng Peiyun believe that China still needs the one-child policy?
3. What, according to the viewpoint, are the exceptions to the one-child policy? Why are these exceptions made?

"China Still Facing Population Problem," Jing Wei's interview of Peng Peiyun, *Beijing Review*, December 28, 1992-January 3, 1993. Reprinted with permission.

It has now been two decades since China first implemented a family planning programme. What effects has the programme had? Should it be continued? What does the future hold for population growth? Peng Peiyun, chairman of the State Family Planning Commission, was interviewed to find answers to these and related questions now confronting the country.

200 Million Fewer Babies

Peng noted that when New China was founded in 1949 it had a population of 540 million. The figure grew by an average of 13 million annually, hitting 800 million by 1969. Such a sharp rise made the Chinese government realize the seriousness of population growth and prodded it to implement a family planning programme in the early 1970s. Free contraceptives and birth control services were offered, and great efforts were made to publicize the importance of family planning. The programme was also made a part of the national plan for social and economic development, and since 1978 has become an item of basic state policy. New laws and regulations have been enacted and family planning centres have been set up at various levels. People are encouraged to marry and give birth later and to have only one child per couple.

Many successes can be seen. The birth rate has been lowered, and the burden on social and economic development caused by sharp population growth has been mitigated. The 1970 birth rate of 33.43 per thousand had fallen to 19.68 per thousand by 1991, and the average number of births per woman fell from 5.81 to 2.2 during the same period. Based on projections from the 1970 figures, the number of births was reduced by at least 260 million.

China's family planning programme has contributed to the worldwide decrease in birth rate and population growth. The global growth rate of 2 percent in the 1960s has fallen to the present level of 1.7 percent. As a result, the global population bumped the 5 billion mark two years later than it would have without such programmes. The Asian population delayed its arrival at 3 billion by three years.

Experts have estimated the 1990 average birth rate for developing countries to be 31 per thousand, the natural growth rate to be 21 per thousand, and the average number of births per woman to be 4. If China is not included, the figures rise to 35 per thousand, 24 per thousand and 4.6 respectively.

China's programme has also improved the quality of life in the country. Before 1949, the average life expectancy was 35 years. By 1987 it had increased to 69.5 years. The mortality rate has dropped from its pre-liberation level of 20 per thousand per year to 6.67 per thousand. And infant mortality has fallen from an average of 92.55 per thousand during the 1944-49 period to 22.4 per thousand for the years 1985-87, a 76 percent drop.

Still a Heavy Burden

Although great improvements have been made, China is still faced with serious population problems, according to Peng.

- A large base. The population of the mainland had reached 1.15823 billion by the end of 1991, more than double the 1949 figure. Although measures to control increases have been in effect for two decades, the population has still grown at an average annual rate of 16 million, equal to the population of a medium-sized country.
- A large number of women of child-bearing age. The 1990 fourth national census revealed that women in their child-bearing years account for 27.1 percent of China's total population, and the median age for women was 25.25 years. This means China will continue to face a high birth rate in the next decade.
- A large rural population. At present, rural residents make up about 74 percent of the population, and economic and cultural conditions there are not conducive to quick changes. Traditional values expressed in phrases such as "the more children, the happier" and "sons to carry on the family tree" make the implementation of family planning programmes a long and arduous task in farming communities.

China has a huge population, an inadequate amount of arable land and low per-capita natural resources. Its economic and educational levels are lower than those in other countries. A high population growth drains state resources, making development and improvement of people's living standards even more difficult.

China's 22 percent of the world's population has available to it only 7 percent of the world's arable land, a per-capita amount of only 0.086 hectare. This figure is much lower than the world average of 0.3 hectare, and much lower than the United States figure of 0.81 hectare. Exacerbating the problem, China's population has increased by more than 100 million over the last ten years, while land fit for cultivation has decreased at an average rate of 300,000 hectares per annum. The present figure for per-capita arable land is now less than half that of the 1949 amount of 0.18 hectare. If the loss of arable land is not brought under control, there could be serious food supply problems in the future.

Grain production has seen large increases, but it has not kept up with the increase in population. In 1984, per-capita grain output was 394 kg, but this dropped to 362 kg by 1988. Even the figure for the bumper harvest year of 1990 was lower than that of 1984.

Sharp increases in the population also cause problems in employment, education, housing, communications, health care and social welfare. The over 20 million people who reach working age each year have saturated the job market, and surplus labour in rural areas exceeds 100 million. In urban areas, per-capita living space averaged only 6.7 square metres in 1990, and there were only five public buses available to every 10,000 people. In health care, the national average is only 23 hospital beds and 15.6 doctors for every 10,000 people. Rural schools suffer from a lack of funds. Limited living space, transport problems, difficulties in finding employment and inadequate health care have brought home the troubles caused by a huge population.

Reduce Birth Rates to Speed Development

Twenty years ago, just before the 1974 Bucharest conference on population, the head of the Indian delegation distilled the view then held by many leaders from poor and populous countries: "Development is the best contraceptive.". . .

Reality suggests otherwise. The period when East Asia produced the fastest economic growth in the world coincided with a sharp decline in birth rates in the region. From 1965 to 1980, the birth rates in the most successful Asian states dropped by 40% to 50%.

If the Asians had chosen to develop first, then reduce fertility rates, their economic ascent would have been far less dramatic.

Tim Carrington, *Wall Street Journal*, August 8, 1994.

The excessive increase in population has also caused problems in generating funds for economic construction. In the last few years, about one-fourth of newly added revenues were spent on the new additions to the population. Such large increases slow both economic development and the efforts to make improvements in the areas of education, science and technology.

Policies and Prospects

"To bring the spiraling population growth under control, China must continue with the family planning programme while speeding up the development of its economy," said Peng.

During the last two decades, China has worked to perfect its family planning policy. The Chinese Constitution stipulates the goal of family planning is to keep the growth rate at a level suitable to economic and social development plans. Both spouses in a family are responsible for the implementation of the programme.

The family planning policy encourages late marriage, having children at a later age, having only one child and a large age difference between the two children of rural couples allowed additional children because of special situations. It also advises that minority programmes be developed in line with local conditions.

This means the "one child per couple" statement is an oversimplification. The programme is worked out in light of the differing conditions of various urban and rural areas and ethnic groups. It is generally more lenient in rural and minority areas than in urban and Han-inhabited areas. [The Han are the Chinese peoples of China.] For example, in rural areas, which contain 74 percent of the country's population, if the first child of a couple is a girl, they are allowed to have a second child some years later. Farmers and herdsmen of small ethnic groups can have three or four children. And in a few minority areas, the programme is limited to public education about the life and health care for women and children.

Looking to the future, Peng said the Ten-Year Programme and the Eighth Five-Year Plan for the National Economy and Economic Development drawn up in 1991 state that between 1991 and 2000 China will try to keep annual population growth below 12.5 per thousand, and the figure is expected to drop to less than 10 per thousand by the year 2000. During the 1990s, the population is expected to increase by 151 million, and the number of births per woman will drop from 2.31 in 1990 to 2 by the year 2000, the current level of developed countries.

"It is difficult to say exactly what future plans will be," Peng said. "But according to the demographic experts, if China consistently implements its family planning policy, the mainland population will be 1.5 billion by 2025 and the population growth will come to a standstill between 2040 and 2050. By that time, the population will probably be about 1.6 billion."

"Many Western observers . . . have willingly overlooked the grossest kinds of human violations: forced abortions, forced sterilisations, forced contraception."

China's One-Child Policy Is Repugnant and Unnecessary

Editors of the *Far Eastern Economic Review*

The editors of the *Far Eastern Economic Review* assert that the Communist Party in China is using the one-child-per-family policy to compensate for the party's failure to properly promote development in the country. They see the one-child policy as ill-advised, invasive, and destructive. The Chinese government should instead view its citizens—present and future—as vital resources, the editors maintain, pointing to Taiwan, Hong Kong, and Singapore as examples of heavily populated and successful Chinese enclaves.

As you read, consider the following questions:

1. What results do the editors report from the policy of holding local Chinese jurisdictions responsible for their birthrates?
2. How does China enforce its one-child policy, according to the editors?
3. What lesson do the editors suggest China learn from Taiwan, Hong Kong, and Singapore?

"Free the Masses," an editorial by the editors of the *Far Eastern Economic Review*, July 8, 1993. Reprinted with permission.

Of all the malignant doctrines that have been loosed upon the Chinese people over their long history, few have caused as much mischief as the People's Party's anti-people programme. The communist population control policy of the past 20 years rests on the assumption that China owes its lack of development not to decades of excess and misrule by a one-party policy state but to Chinese mothers and their babies. And because many Western observers share this belief, they have willingly overlooked the grossest kinds of human violations: forced abortions, forced sterilisations, forced contraception.

Far from expressing regret for these barbarisms, China has lately been touting its success. This 11 July—World Population Day 1993—the Chinese government can claim to have reached population reduction targets hitherto thought impossible until the year 2010. The numbers for 1992 show unprecedented drops in the birth rate, with the total fertility rate (the average number of babies a woman bears over a lifetime) plunging to between 1.8 to 1.9, below the standard replacement rate of 2.1. A Westerner quoted in the *Washington Post* hailed the figures as nothing short of "miraculous." But even the United Nations Fund for Population Activities worries about how.

The High Price for Exceeding the One-Child Limit

Although Chinese officials either deny reports of coercion or attribute them to the zealotry of local officials, their policies invite abuse. Official directives mandate that families that choose to have more than one child may be denied permission to build a house, have their electricity and water cut off, lose work preference and so on. Chinese villages report officials who swoop in and drag off women to be sterilised or have their pregnancies terminated. Chinese women who become pregnant while studying abroad have received orders from home to abort or else.

In 1991, a new dimension was added. Henceforth not only would offending parties be punished, but so would local government officials in jurisdictions where births had not been brought down to Peking's satisfaction. In one infamous case, local authorities worried about exceeding the next year's quota forced a young woman into premature labour on New Year's Eve, killing the baby and nearly killing the woman. According to Dr. John Aird, the former head of the China branch of the US Bureau of the Census, the emphasis is "to get the job done by whatever means necessary." The precipitous drop in births has more to do with such intervention than any "miracle." As Peng Peiyun, the director of China's State Family Planning Commission, puts it, "Persuasion may have to be applied many times. . . . We in China consider it to be persuasion and reasoning until she agrees."

Understandably, issues dealing with sexuality and procreation

Absolutely Not Allowed

The following letter was written to "Chi An," a young Chinese woman who was temporarily in the United States with her husband. The letter was written by an official from the Population Control Office of the truck factory where Chi An had worked in China. Chi An herself had functioned as a population control officer for the truck factory, tracking down and aborting women who were pregnant with "illegal" children.

Comrade Chi An:

Your news that you had accidentally become pregnant caught me by surprise. I have made some inquiries about whether the one-child limitation applies to Chinese living abroad. . . .

I am afraid that I do not have good news for you. When you left for America three years ago, the birth control policy in our country was already very strict. The "one-couple, one-child" policy is now even stricter, especially since [Chinese Communist Party Central Committee] Directive Number Seven was announced last year. Party General Secretary Zhao Zhiyang recently ordered officials to redouble their efforts to enforce the technical policy on birth control [mandating IUD insertion after one child, sterilization after two, and abortion for women pregnant without authorization, that is, those who do not have a quota to give birth].

In the last few months, some women pregnant with "illegal" children have been forced to have abortions during the eighth or ninth month of pregnancy, or even at the time of birth. Some women claim that they heard their babies cry but were told later by birth control officials that the infants had been stillborn. Officials have used physical force, dragging or pushing pregnant women to the abortion clinics for the operation. Even in extreme cases like this, higher officials have supported them, saying the birth control policy cannot be violated.

Regardless of where you are living now, you are still officially attached to the Liaoning Truck Factory. If you come back at the end of this year pregnant, even if you are eight or nine months along, you will absolutely not be allowed to have your baby. If you really want this baby, stay in America until the child is born. How the Party will treat you when you come back with a second child I cannot say with certainty. There will be fines and probably other punishments as well. But at least you will have your baby.

Please think carefully about our country's one-child policy and how much you want this baby before making a decision. Don't come back until you do.

Wishing you and your family health and happiness, I am,

Your friend,
Gong Chang
Population Control Office, Liaoning Truck Factory

Quoted in Steven W. Mosher, *A Mother's Ordeal,* 1993.

excite passions when considered as public policy. Legal abortion, for example, continues to be a contentious issue in many parts of the world. But our argument with China is not with abortion or contraception for those who choose it. Our argument is limited to the brutal means employed by the Chinese government and the dubious economic rationale that sanctions such means. Few honest observers would confuse programmes or Western assistance designed simply to offer contraception with the Party's violent intrusion into the womb.

China's Population Is an Asset

The tragic irony is that a China that saw its billion-plus people as assets rather than liabilities would have few peers in might and influence. Tiny Taiwan, Hongkong and Singapore are all monuments to what Chinese can achieve when freed from the statist yoke. These economic tigers rank among the earth's most crowded places, yet fret about low birth rates and labour shortages. In contrast, China watcher Steven Mosher recounts in his book *A Mother's Ordeal* how a Chinese nurse studying in America received orders from home to abort a second pregnancy. "How convenient," she says, "for the authorities to have a prestigious foreign theory—overpopulation—that allows them once again to shift the blame onto the Chinese people." And how shameful the acquiescence of so many of the rest of us.

"The spread of AIDS is only one by-product of a system that has become too 'modern' for its own good."

AIDS and Self-Control

Joseph Sobran

Joseph Sobran, a commentator on social and political issues, is critic-at-large for the *National Review* and contributing editor for the *Human Life Review*. In the following viewpoint, Sobran charges that the modern state is incapable of policing sexual behavior and is thus unable to wipe out sexually transmitted diseases, especially AIDS. He argues instead for the rejuvenation of "the tribe"—the network of immediate social relationships that is capable of limiting misbehavior through subtle pressures and incentives that push people to control themselves responsibly.

As you read, consider the following questions:

1. What, specifically, does Sobran mean by the term "the tribe"?
2. According to the author, how does the tribe regulate sexual behavior?
3. What effect does Sobran believe the state has had on the spread of AIDS?

Excerpted from Joseph Sobran, "AIDS and the Tribe," *The Human Life Review*, Winter 1992. Copyright ©1992 by The Human Life Foundation, Inc. Reprinted with permission.

When Magic Johnson announced that he was HIV-positive, the public reaction followed a familiar pattern. First the basketball star was lachrymosely embraced as a "hero." He had "heightened public awareness" of the AIDS problem, much as Anita Hill was said to have "raised the nation's consciousness" about the problem of sexual harassment merely by accusing Judge Clarence Thomas of having committed it.

But the second phase of the reaction discerned something excessive, mawkish, and simplistic in the first. A few sportswriters (a more conservative breed than most journalists) observed that sexual promiscuity had become the norm among professional basketball players, pro athletes in general—and Magic Johnson in particular. Some were surprised that the AIDS virus hadn't shown up among athletes more often than it already had. Groupies are a regular postgame sight outside athletes' dressing rooms, and some players have been known to end a working day by taking two or three of them back to their homes or hotels.

Johnson himself remorsefully confirmed this. In a long article in *Sports Illustrated* the week after his announcement, he confessed that, besieged by eager women from the beginning of his career, he had always "done my best to accommodate them." From now on, he pledged, he would urge young people to practice "safe sex." This new mission was welcomed with a long, satisfied purr from the media. There was a third phase, hardly noticed. Barely a month after his sensational revelation, Johnson had formed a partnership with the Archdiocese of Los Angeles. He added an important codicil to his earlier promise: he would exhort young people to practice "safe sex, which means no sex."

Perhaps coincidentally, it was at this point that the media's interest in Magic Johnson faded to near zero.

To his credit, Johnson took full responsibility for his own fate. He blamed only himself, and tried movingly to maintain a facade of good cheer. But his endorsement of abstinence was not the message the media were eager to carry for him. . . .

The Media and "Safe Sex"

The media continued to plump for "safe sex," which definitely didn't mean *no* sex. It meant condoms. Somehow, the essence of the sexual revolution had to be salvaged, though hedged by prudent precautions. . . .

Today more than ever, to fornicate is to swim in polluted waters. The risk is incalculable. The safe-sexers are in essence recommending that we play Russian roulette with rubber bullets. They fail on their own narrow terms. More important, they are blind to the real problem. But even conservatives may not be seeing the problem whole.

Laments that family morality has broken down are true enough, but they are only part of the story. It is also true that well-meaning liberals' programs have contributed to the breakdown. But our whole society is becoming thoroughly politicized, and the conservative instinct to call for more police and sterner laws can also be a bogus cure for an extra-political malady.

The Disappearance of the Tribe

A deeper insight was recently offered by the columnist William Raspberry, who noted the quiet disappearance from modern society of "the tribe." By this he meant the extended network of kinship, friendship, and hard-to-define "relatedness" that used to back up the nuclear family. Sociologists have called it *Gemeinschaft*, the society one constantly experiences as "mine.". . .

The word "tribe" conjures up images of primitive societies in which men dance in loincloths and warpaint with upraised spears. It shouldn't. A tribe is a kinship system, and it may be highly sophisticated. Elizabethan England was highly tribal in this sense; who you were depended on whom you were related to, not on things like a Social Security number.

In fact, all societies are more or less tribal. Ours is becoming less so. And there is plenty of reason to believe that this is not progress, but gradual disaster.

The tribe is not a local custom but a dimension of all human life. Being highly political—that is, state-dominated—we have become oblivious to it. Jews are sometimes humorously or derisively referred to as "the Tribe." This implies, correctly, that they have anomalously preserved an extrapolitical kinship system. But it should not imply that there is something wrong with this. It's a sign of health in a sick world.

The Matrix of Morals and Manners

The state makes statutes and formal laws, but the tribe is the matrix of morals and manners, which are the real stuff of social order. Modern society has lost something vital by becoming more political and less tribal, because the state is no substitute for the tribe. The state can only use force or propaganda, of which "safe sex" is a fair specimen. But the tribe has innumerable subtler pressures and incentives that are far more efficacious.

Your tribe consists of those you feel related to in ways you may not even be able to express. The fear of immediate disgrace before your "people"—the people you refer to as "we" without specifying the antecedent of the pronoun—or the loss of their affection, loyalty, and esteem is one of the most powerful controls on misbehavior, and it operates far more constantly and swiftly than the remote prospect of a prison sentence. In fact it usually operates without our thinking about it: it decides what forms of behavior are, for "us," unthinkable.

The family without a tribe to support it is fragile. Most criminals come from broken homes, yes, but also from tribes that have dissolved. This is probably why there are so many black criminals: unlike voluntary immigrants, who often came here in tribal waves, blacks were forcibly uprooted from their kinship systems when brought here as slaves. After emancipation, they began building families and kinship-based communities; but by now the welfare state has destroyed them again. It's ironic that when we picture a tribe, we are likely to imagine a black African tribe, when African-Americans have suffered from systematic detribalization at the hands of benevolent as well as malicious whites.

Reprinted by permission of Chuck Asay and Creators Syndicate.

The modern state is suspicious of and even hostile to the family, which it associates with "privilege" and "accidents of birth" that prevent the kind of bureaucratized equality it seeks to promote. Insofar as it is even aware of the tribe, the state is even more hostile to it. It sees only the negative side of tribal enmities and prejudices, and has no regard for tribal loyalties. Instead of merely supplementing family and tribe, the state has worked actively to supplant them.

But like nature, society has a delicate ecology, and the state, along with the many well-educated state-minded people who drive it, has been indifferent to the "environmental impact" of ostensibly benign social programs. The state's rationalism is at odds with the informality, traditionalism, and fluidity of tribal ways, which are destroyed by the state's coercion and bureaucratic controls. Increasingly, the tribal is a mere residue within politicized society.

Policing Sexual Behavior

The reason this is so serious, for our present purpose, is that the tribe is ideal for policing the very kind of problematic conduct the state is finding itself impotent to affect: above all, the sexual. The state knows nothing of morals or manners; they are not its province, and it can only act stiffly and irrelevantly when it tries to address them. In the eyes of the state, we are isolated individuals, and sex can only be regarded as an affair between individuals. But sex is a supremely *social* concern, and the tribe has always recognized it as such.

It's only natural that sexual freedom should grow along with the state. To the state's social planners, it is a matter of indifference whether a sexual act occurs within marriage, or even whether it is heterosexual. It's also natural that militant homosexuals should be as political as they are: they want to enlist the state against the tribe's morals, which they condemn as "bigotry."

In most societies marriage is a tribal affair, not just a private mutual contract between the two spouses. The presence, witness, and festivities of the tribe are felt to be essential to the wedding ceremony. Sexual unions are a tribal concern for the most basic of reasons: they determine who will be related to whom. And marriage defines these relations firmly. Tribal societies usually frown on sex outside marriage precisely because its natural result is to produce people without real relations or responsibilities, a fact our society hasn't yet noticed. The whole idiom of kinship sounds quaint among us: kin, folks, misbegotten, bastard—such terms in their literal senses have an archaic or exotic ring now. They used to mean something.

Outright coercion, the state's modus operandi, is inappropriate for policing sexual behavior. To that extent the liberals are right. The trouble is that they are rapidly abolishing the only level of society that has always policed sex with fair success. Of course a certain amount of fornication and adultery has always happened "anyway." So has burglary. But the present epidemic is only possible in a society where kinship pressures have been gradually weakened. Tribal societies can shame people into sexually responsible conduct without a policeman in every bedroom, but we have made this kind of sanction almost impossible, and there is no alternative way. . . .

The Spread of AIDS

As the uproar over AIDS shows, the state simply can't cope with sexual irresponsibility. In fact it has promoted it. For the state to demand chastity of us would be hugely presumptuous, even tyrannical, and in any case impracticable. But the family can *expect* it of us, and the tribe can uphold it as a standard of honor, using ties of affection and loyalty more potent than force or violence because they engage our self-respect as no merely external penalties can.

The state is useful for dealing with egregious criminals who are at war with society. But it can't and shouldn't attempt to police our common faults, which include most sexual vices (in the old sense of sins and weakness). The modern statist mentality can't grasp this. It feels that whatever is immoral should be made illegal, and that whatever is legal, or whatever can't be effectively proscribed by law, should be regarded as moral. . . .

The spread of AIDS is only one by-product of a system that has become too "modern" for its own good, in which people have been encouraged to seek intimacy without even establishing real relationships first. In our society, sex *is* the "relationship." Far from being "outdated," the old rules turn out to have had more practical pertinence than anyone could have realized while they were still generally respected. That they are not the kind of rules the state can enforce doesn't mean that the state should disregard them, as the state-minded have done. No wonder those sexual energies only the tribe can police effectively are now running amok, and bringing death rather than life. And a society that has refused to feel shame is finding itself troubled with an unexpected burden of guilt.

Can anything be done? Well, yes. It's too glib to say simply that we can return to the old rules, though they are pretty much the only rules we can ever have in matters of sex. Even the most sensible rules can't stand up to "the fire in the blood" if they are supported by nothing more than long-range calculation. They require, for one thing, an image of virtue to make them cohere and to give them urgency when calculation takes the night off.

The decay of the tribe, moreover, is like any other environmental disaster. It takes time to recover, like a forest after a fire. Those who demand a "cure" for AIDS instantly if not yesterday are displaying the same quick-fix attitude they bring to sex. But the social recovery will be like a reforestation program, if it happens at all. And it won't even begin until we all understand what we have done to the human infrastructure that carries moral traditions.

"*It is people living, not dying, who bring population growth to a stop.*"

AIDS and Population "Control"

Gerard Piel

Gerard Piel, founder and chairman emeritus of *Scientific American* and author of *Only One World*, rejects the "ugliest manifestations" of the AIDS pandemic: the idea that it might serve as a "solution to overpopulation." Citing historical data, Piel predicts that the demographic transition that the industrialized countries are now completing—to low birth, death, and population growth rates and long life expectancy—will also be made by the rest of the world. Piel supports "sustainable development" to bring human numbers and needs into accord with the earth's resources. Failure to stop the AIDS pandemic will only divert resources needed for this demographic transition, he warns, while delay will ultimately result in a larger world population.

As you read, consider the following questions:

1. What ultimate effect on population numbers did the Black Death and World Wars I and II have, according to Piel?
2. In Piel's view, how did the demographic history of Europe contradict Malthus's theory?
3. What effects has industrial revolution had on the demographic statistics of China and India, according to the author?

The now worldwide AIDS pandemic finds its ugliest manifestation in the proposition that AIDS has arrived in time to stop the population explosion. One hears it voiced by otherwise blameless people. Some see AIDS as the solution, in particular, for the "problem" of Africa. There the rate of population growth is highest and poverty deepest. Epidemiologists of the World Health Organization estimate that Africans constitute about 10 million of the 15 million people infected worldwide with the human immunodeficiency virus (HIV) and so fated to die of AIDS.

The Durability of the Species

The AIDS proposition scants history and grossly underestimates the durability of the human species, Africans included. At its present rate of transmission, HIV will infect some 200 million people by 2010. The African share of the casualties might then approach 100 million. That, as a disciple of Thomas Malthus observed of the million Irish who perished in the 1845-50 potato famine, would scarcely be enough.

The Black Death, to which proponents of this cure for population growth hopefully compare the AIDS pandemic, carried off more than half the people of 14th-century Europe. By the middle of the 17th century, the European population had arrived at the point on the growth curve to which it would have increased by that time without deflection by the Black Death.

The paroxysm of violence that seized the industrial world through the three decades from the start of World War I to the end of World War II killed 200 million people. That was more than 10 percent of all the people who lived in those years. Their absence was not remarked in 1970, when the rate of world population growth reached its all-time peak, at around 2 percent.

It was Malthus who made economics the dismal science, but he also made this branch of moral philosophy a science. He rooted economics in what had been the unrelieved experience of humankind from the time of the agricultural revolution and the opening of the first village markets. "Apart from short, exceptional periods," Alfred North Whitehead observed, "the normal structure of society was that of a comparatively affluent minority subsisting on the labors of a teeming population checked by starvation and other discomforts."

The Demographic Transition

At the very time Malthus set out his baleful equations [population grows geometrically while the means to sustain a population grow only arithmetically], however, industrial revolution had begun to make the growth of production outrun population. Within 20 years of Malthus's death, moreover, John Stuart Mill discovered from inspection of baptismal records that the birth rate of England had begun to decline. This discovery did not shake the conviction, which Mill shared with Malthus, that population growth was the "dynamics of political economy," for the population of prospering England was exploding.

The population of all the European countries undergoing industrial revolution was exploding during this period. Now, after this gigantic increase, which multiplied the number of Europeans 20 times over that in 1600 and avalanched them onto all continents, the populations of all the industrial countries are at or approaching zero growth. These lucky 1.25 billion people— counting the Japanese, the first non-Europeans, in their numbers—are completing the so-called demographic transition. From near-zero growth in 1600 at high death rates and high birth rates with life expectancy at 25 years, they are arriving at near-zero growth again but at low death rates and low birth rates and with life expectancy at 75 years.

Joel Pett/*Lexington Herald-Leader*. Reprinted with permission.

Recent history gives every reason to expect that the other three quarters of the world population will make the demographic transition. The leading edge of industrial revolution— mass education, sanitation and primary medicine, and the green revolution—has brought down death rates and lengthened life expectancy throughout the preindustrial world. The rest of humankind has entered the first phase of the demographic transi-

221

tion. Hence the ongoing swelling of the population.

Entrance into the second phase is marked for some few developing countries by decline in their birth rates. These are countries where industrial revolution has proceeded furthest and where its increasing product is most widely shared—small countries like Costa Rica and Sri Lanka and also the biggest countries, India and China.

Whitehead cited India and China as "instances of civilized societies which for a very long period in their later histories maintained themselves with arrested technology. . . . They provided the exact conditions for the importance of the Malthusian Law." By the turn of the 19th century, when Malthus published his *Essay on Population*, they were the world's most populous countries.

AIDS Is Not a Solution for Population Growth

The impact of AIDS on future mortality—and therefore population growth—in developing regions engenders both concern and speculation. Some even contend that AIDS is "solving" the population problem. This cynical view is wrong for two reasons: First, additional premature death is one of the worst things that can happen to individual families and therefore contributes to declining quality of life. Additional deaths add to the problem; they are not a solution to the problem. Second, the socioeconomic distress resulting from the deaths of skilled men and women in their prime working ages, and often holding positions vital to operating their country's basic infrastructure, are far greater than problems resulting from high growth rates, at least in the short term. The dramatic increase in the number of AIDS orphans constitutes a serious social problem. Because AIDS progresses slowly, infected individuals live long enough to have children: therefore, AIDS may not reduce the growth rate significantly if fertility remains high. Demographer John Bongaarts has estimated that by 2000, AIDS will produce an additional 10.5 deaths per 1,000 persons in sub-Saharan Africa in the worst case scenario and an additional 1.7 deaths per 1,000 under the most optimistic scenario.

Wolfgang Lutz, *The Future of World Population*, 1994.

Since the end of World War II, India and China have been engaged in industrial revolution, China leading. With life expectancy lengthening to 60 years in India and to 70 years in China, their huge populations have more than doubled. In both countries, calories per capita now meet the daily requirement, and potable water is available to three quarters of their citizens. India has reduced its child death rate to 142 per 1,000 live births, and China to 42. In India, 27 percent of the population lives in cities, in China, 33 percent. Literacy among the female population is 34 percent in India and 62 percent in China. Contraceptives are in use in 43 and 71 percent of their households, respectively. As these statistics suggest, both nations have entered the second phase of the demographic transition. The fertility rate in India has declined from more than six (infants per female reproductive lifetime) to four; in China it is 2.3, close to the zero growth rate of 2.1

AIDS Diverts Resources

How to hasten the passage of the preindustrial world through the demographic transition was the principal topic before the United Nations Conference on Environment and Development, the Earth Summit, held in Rio de Janeiro in the summer of 1992. The major product of the conference, Agenda 21, is now the agenda of the United Nations. It sets out a program of "sustainable development" to bring human numbers and appetites into accord with the finite resources of the earth before the end of the next century. The AIDS pandemic can only divert physical resources and human energy from this hopeful and urgent enterprise. Delay portends a larger ultimate world population. Industrial revolution has set the terms of a morality different from that implied by the Malthusian equation. It is people living, not dying, who bring population growth to a stop.

Periodical Bibliography

The following articles have been selected to supplement the diverse views presented in this chapter.

John Bongaarts — "Population Policy Options in the Developing World," *Science*, February 11, 1994.

David Brown — "Two Million Orphaned by AIDS," *The Washington Post*, June 11, 1993.

Paul Burkhead — "Stirring the Pot: Immigrant and Refugee Challenges to the United States and the World," *Journal of International Affairs*, Winter 1994.

Carole Collins — "Women as Hidden Casualties of the Cold War," *Ms.*, November/December 1992.

Barbara Culliton — "AIDS Against the Rest of the World," *Nature*, July 4, 1991. Available from 65 Bleecker St., New York, NY 10012.

Paul Demeny — "Policies Seeking a Reduction of High Fertility: A Case for the Demand Side," *Population and Development Review*, June 1992. Available from One Dag Hammarskjöld Plaza, New York, NY 10017.

Garrett Hardin — "Different Paths, Same Aims for Population Control," *USA Today*, April 22, 1992.

S. Kamaluddin — "Malthusian Nightmare," *Far Eastern Economic Review*, May 16, 1991. Available from GPO Box 160, Hong Kong.

William McGurn — "The Politics of People Power," *Human Life Review*, Winter 1994. Available from 150 E. 35th St., New York, NY 10016.

Donald Minkler — "Demographic Trends and Policies in the Quest for Sustainability," *Boston College Environmental Affairs Law Review*, Winter 1994.

Frances Mitsuka — "Islam and Birth Control: Not a Moral Conflict," *The Middle East*, June 1993. Available from I.C. Publications, Box 261, Carlton House, 69 Gt. Queen St., London WC2B 5BN.

S.D. Mumford — "The Vatican and World Population Policy," *The Humanist*, March/April 1993.

Suzanne Sullivan — "Where No Man Has Gone Before," *Off Our Backs*, November 1993. Available from 2423 18th St. NW, Washington, DC 20009.

For Further Discussion

Chapter 1

1. Malthus did not consider contraception a viable "preventive" way to reduce fertility and thus control population. (His religious beliefs precluded this, and he wrote before many modern methods of contraception had been invented.) Discuss the importance of this omission.

2. Engels said that it is a "fact" that "children are like trees, returning abundantly the expenditure laid out on them." Is this the case in modern, industrialized countries? Explain your answer.

3. Engels saw the advance of science resulting in improved food production. Are there limits to increasing food production? If so, what are they?

Chapter 2

1. In all of the viewpoints in this chapter, there is no mention of the possibility of a dramatic increase in mortality rates due to a modern plague such as AIDS or some other natural or manmade catastrophe. Is this a serious omission? Why or why not?

2. The neo-Malthusians neglect the depopulation that a number of developed countries (like Germany) are experiencing, due to fertility rates' being lower than mortality levels. Is this an issue worthy of attention or is it insignificant? Explain your answer.

3. Is it possible that neo-Malthusians and anti-neo-Malthusians differ on their attraction and affinity to the human species? Explain.

Chapter 3

1. Should residents of developed countries make any lifestyle changes to lessen their impact on the environment? Should residents of less developed countries? Explain your answers, including any such suggested changes.

2. Do people from more developed countries have the right to ask people from less developed countries to have fewer children? Why or why not?

3. Speculate on the kinds of scientific advances, if any, that might result in an increased food supply to feed the planet's

expanding population. Rank your speculations in order of probability.

4. How might people from more developed countries differ from those in less developed countries in their definitions of the word "poverty"? What relevance might these differences have in the discussion of population size and growth?

Chapter 4

1. Given the fact that we are all immigrants or the descendants of immigrants—with the exception of American Indians—is it justifiable, from an ethical or moral point of view, to ask for restrictions on immigration into the United States? Why or why not?

2. Is the concept of international borders outdated? Why or why not?

3. Should immigration into the United States be based on the skills a prospective immigrant brings to this country or on whether the prospective immigrant has relatives residing in the United States? Explain your answer.

Chapter 5

1. You have just been appointed minister of U.S. Population Policy by the president of the United States. What would your national population policy consist of? Be specific. What would your international population policy consist of? Again, be specific.

2. The viewpoint by Mohammed Aslam Cheema and William Keeler on the Programme of Action of the Cairo conference has only one sentence on the topic of contraception. Is this important? If so, how would you explain the paucity of discussion on contraception in this viewpoint? If not, why not?

3. What sort of joint population policy might the United States and Mexico develop to deal with the problem of illegal immigration of Mexican nationals into the United States? Be specific.

4. Some thinkers believe that there should be no national boundaries and that people should be able to move at will from one geographical area to another. They see people as citizens of the world who should be able to live wherever they desire. Does this view have any merit? Why or why not?

Organizations to Contact

The editors have compiled the following list of organizations concerned with the issues debated in this book. The descriptions are derived from materials provided by the organizations. All have publications or information available for interested readers. The list was compiled on the date of publication of the present volume; names, addresses, and phone numbers may change. Be aware that many organizations take several weeks or longer to respond to inquiries, so allow as much time as possible.

The Brookings Institution
1775 Massachusetts Ave. NW
Washington, DC 20036
(202) 797-6620

A liberal research and education organization, the Brookings Institution publishes its research on economics and development, government, and foreign policy in the quarterly *Brookings Review*, an *Annual Report*, and a quarterly newsletter.

Carrying Capacity Network (CCN)
1325 G St. NW, Suite 1003
Washington, DC 20005
(202) 879-3044

CCN is concerned about world population issues and disseminates information to other organizations working on issues related to the earth's carrying capacity. It publishes the *Immigration Briefing Book*; the bimonthly *Clearinghouse Bulletin*, which includes environmental legislation updates; and the quarterly *Focus*, which provides in-depth coverage of current environmental issues.

Catholics for a Free Choice (CFFC)
1436 V St. NW, Suite 301
Washington, DC 20009
(202) 986-6093

CFFC is an educational organization of dissenting Roman Catholics that supports the right to legal reproductive health care, especially family planning and abortion. Its publications include the quarterly *Conscience: A Newsjournal of Prochoice Catholic Opinion*, as well as monographs and pamphlets.

Federation for American Immigration Reform (FAIR)
1666 Connecticut Ave. NW, Suite 400
Washington, DC 20009
(202) 328-7004

FAIR works to stop illegal immigration and to limit legal immigration. It publishes the *FAIR Immigration Report*, the quarterly *FAIR Information Exchange*, periodic *FAIR Papers*, and a periodic newsletter.

The Heritage Foundation
214 Massachusetts Ave. NE
Washington, DC 20002
(202) 546-4400

The foundation is a conservative public policy research institute. It publishes position papers on a wide variety of topics through its publications the weekly *Backgrounder*, the quarterly *Policy Review*, and the Heritage Lecture series.

International Planned Parenthood Federation
Western Regional Office
902 Broadway, Tenth Fl.
New York, NY 10010
(212) 995-8800

International Planned Parenthood works throughout the world at the grassroots level to promote family planning. Its publications include a quarterly magazine, *Forum*, as well as occasional studies and position papers.

International Women's Health Coalition (IWHC)
24 E. 21st St.
New York, NY 10010
(212) 979-8500

IWHC supports women's reproductive health in the developing world via innovative health care programs and policy research. It offers educational materials on reproductive health and copublished the "Rio Statement" to represent a feminist position at the 1994 UN Conference on Population and Development held in Cairo, Egypt.

National Audubon Society Population Program
801 Pennsylvania Ave. SE, Suite 301
Washington, DC 20003
(202) 547-9009

The Population Program of the National Audubon Society promotes citizen action and education on the effect of population growth on the environment. The society publishes the bimonthlies *Audubon* and *Audubon Activist*.

Negative Population Growth (NPG)
210 The Plaza
PO Box 1206
Teaneck, NJ 07666
(201) 837-3555

NPG is concerned with population and environmental issues and works to promote a decrease in U.S. and world populations. It publishes a triannual newsletter, *Human Survival*, and various position papers, including *Zero Net Migration*, *Beyond Family Planning*, and *Family Responsibility*.

Planned Parenthood Federation of America
810 Seventh Ave.
New York, NY 10019
(212) 514-7800

Planned Parenthood is America's oldest and largest voluntary reproductive health care organization. Its local centers provide reproductive health care services and educational programs. Its extensive publications include pamphlets and brochures on these topics.

The Population Council
One Dag Hammarskjöld Plaza
New York, NY 10017
(212) 644-1300

The council develops social, biomedical, and health science and technology in developing countries. Its numerous publications include the quarterly *Population Development Review*, the bimonthly *Studies in Family Planning*, and books such as *Resources, Environment, and Population* and *The New Politics of Population*.

Population Crisis Committee
1120 19th St. NW, Suite 550
Washington, DC 20036
(202) 659-1833

The committee provides education on population issues and funds family planning programs in developing countries. It publishes the periodic *Population Briefing Paper*.

The Population Institute
110 Maryland Ave. NE, Suite 207
Washington, DC 20002
(202) 544-3300

The institute informs leaders, journalists, and educators about efforts to balance population with the earth's resources. It publishes the bimonthly newsletter *Popline* and the monograph *Towards the Twenty-First Century*.

Population Reference Bureau
1875 Connecticut Ave. NW, Suite 520
Washington, DC 20009
(202) 483-1100

The bureau gathers, interprets, and disseminates information on population. Its many publications include the quarterly journal *Population Bulletin*, the monthly *Population Today*, and the *Population Handbook*.

The Rockford Institute
934 N. Main St.
Rockford, IL 61103
(815) 964-5819

The institute is a conservative research center that studies the relationship between religion and society, including issues of economics, civil liberties, and family. Its publications include the monthly magazines *Family in America* and *Chronicles: A Magazine of American Culture*.

Sierra Club International Population Program
408 C St. NE
Washington, DC 20002
(202) 547-1141

The Sierra Club's International Population Program works to stabilize world populations at sustainable levels via grassroots organizing and legislative campaigns. The Sierra Club's publishing arm includes Sierra Club Books, the bimonthly magazine *Sierra*, and the periodic *Sierra Club National News Report*.

The Urban Institute
2100 M St. NW
Washington, DC 20037
(202) 833-7200

The institute is a policy research and educational organization concerned with national urban issues, including population and immigration. It publishes the *Policy and Research Report* three times a year, *Policy Bites* and *Update* bimonthly, and various reports, books, and papers.

World Bank
Population and Human Resources Dept.
1818 H St. NW
Washington, DC 20433
(202) 473-1091

The bank's Population and Human Resources Department provides demographic information for world and national populations. It publishes numerous studies, policy papers, and books. For a list of World Bank publications, write Box 7247-8619, Philadelphia, PA 19170-8619.

Worldwatch Institute
1776 Massachusetts Ave. NW
Washington, DC 20036
(202) 452-1999

The institute is an interdisciplinary research organization that works to inform policymakers and the public about global and environmental issues. It publishes the bimonthly *World Watch* magazine, periodic *Worldwatch Papers*, and the annual *State of the World* report.

Zero Population Growth (ZPG)
1400 16th St. NW, Suite 320
Washington, DC 20036
(202) 332-2200

ZPG works to achieve a sustainable balance of population, resources, and the environment both in the United States and worldwide. It monitors and reports on legislative and judicial actions affecting population-related issues. Its publications include the quarterly *ZPG Activist* as well as brochures and pamphlets such as *Planning the Ideal Family, USA by Numbers: A Statistical Portrait of the United States*, and *Selected Resources on Population*.

Bibliography of Books

Virginia Abernethy   *Population Politics: The Choices That Shape Our Future*. New York: Plenum Press, 1993.

Gigi M. Berardi   *World Food, Population, and Development*. Totowa, NJ: Rowman and Allanheld, 1985.

Ester Bosenrup   *Economic and Demographic Relationships in Development*. Baltimore: Johns Hopkins University Press, 1990.

Lester Brown   *Our Demographically Divided World*. Washington: Worldwatch Institute, 1986.

Lester Brown,   *Saving the Planet: How to Shape an Environmentally Sustainable Global Economy*. New York: Norton, 1991.
Christopher Flavin,
and Sandra Postel

Lynne Brydon and   *Women and the Third World*. Cambridge: Edward Elgar, 1989.
Sylvia Chant

Daniel Callahan and   *Ethical Issues of Population Aid*. New York: Irvington Publishers, 1981.
Phillip G. Clark

Ellen Chesler   *Women of Valor*. New York: Simon & Schuster, 1992.

Nazli Choucri   *Multidisciplinary Perspectives on Population and Conflict*. Syracuse, NY: Syracuse University Press, 1984.

David Coleman and   *The State of Population Theory: Forward from Malthus*. New York: Blackwell, 1986.
Roger Schofield

F. Kurt Cylke Jr.   *The Environment*. New York: HarperCollins, 1993.

Ruth Dixon-Mueller   *Population Policy and Women's Rights: Transforming Reproductive Choice*. Westport, CT: Praeger, 1993.

Paul R. Ehrlich and   *The Population Explosion*. New York: Simon & Schuster, 1990.
Anne H. Ehrlich

Robert W. Fox and   *Crowding Out the Future: World Population Growth, U.S. Immigration and Pressures on Natural Resources*. Washington: Federation for American Immigration Reform, 1992.
Ira H. Mehlman

D.V. Glass   *Introduction to Malthus*. London: Watts & Co., 1953.

Robert Goodland,   *Population, Technology, and Lifestyle*. Covelo, CA: Island Press, 1992.
Herman Daly, and
Salah El Serafy

Lindsey Grant	*Elephants in the Volkswagen: Facing the Tough Questions About Our Overcrowded Country.* New York: W.H. Freeman, 1992.
Germaine Greer	*Sex and Destiny: The Politics of Human Fertility.* New York: Harper & Row, 1984.
Pranay Gupte	*The Crowded Earth: People and the Politics of Population.* New York: Norton, 1984.
Garrett Hardin	*Living Within Limits: Ecology, Economics, and Population Taboos.* New York: Oxford University Press, 1993.
Garrett Hardin	*Population, Evolution, and Birth Control.* San Francisco: W.H. Freeman, 1964.
James Harf and Thomas Trout	*The Politics of Global Resources: Population, Food, Energy, and Environment.* Durham, NC: Duke University Press, 1986.
Betsy Hartmann	*Reproductive Rights and Wrongs: The Global Politics of Population Control and Contraceptive Choice.* New York: Harper & Row, 1987.
Mitchell Kellman	*World Hunger: A Neo-Malthusian Perspective.* New York: Praeger, 1986.
Paul Kennedy	*Preparing for the Twenty-First Century.* New York: Random House, 1993.
Klaus M. Leesinger	*All Our People: Population Policy with a Human Face.* Washington: Island Press, 1994.
Priyatosh Maitra	*Population, Technology, and Development: A Critical Analysis.* Brookfield, VT: Gower, 1986.
Bonnie Mass	*Population Target: The Political Economy of Population Control in Latin America.* Toronto: Women's Press, 1976.
Ronald L. Meeks	*Marx and Engels on the Population Bomb.* Berkeley, CA: Ramparts Press, 1971.
Scott W. Menard and Elizabeth W. Moen	*Perspectives on Population: An Introduction to Concepts and Issues.* New York: Oxford University Press, 1987.
Karen L. Michaelson	*And the Poor Get Children: Radical Perspectives on Population Dynamics.* New York: Monthly Review Press, 1981.
Charles B. Nam	*Understanding Population Change.* Itasca, IL: Peacock, 1994.
OECD	*Migration: The Demographic Aspects.* Paris: OECD Publications and Information Center, 1991.

Gillian Phillips	*Power, Population and the Environment: Women Speak.* Toronto: Weed Foundation, 1992.
Gerard Piel	*Only One World: Ours to Make and Keep.* New York: W.H. Freeman, 1992.
Jonas Salk	*World Population and Human Values: A New Reality.* New York: Harper & Row, 1981.
Dominick Salvatore	*World Population Trends and Their Impact on Economic Development.* New York: Greenwood Press, 1988.
Miguel A. Santos	*Managing Planet Earth: Perspectives on Population, Ecology, and the Law.* New York: Bergin & Garvey, 1990.
Gita Sen and Adrianne Germain	*Population Policies Reconsidered: Health, Empowerment, and Rights.* Cambridge, MA: Harvard University Press, 1994.
Julian Simon	*Population and Development in Poor Countries.* Princeton, NJ: Princeton University Press, 1992.
Julian Simon	*Population Matters.* New Brunswick, NJ: Transaction Publications, 1989.
Charles Strangeland	*Pre-Malthusian Doctrines of Population: A Study in the History of Economic Theory.* New York: Sentry Press, 1904.
Michael S. Teitelbaum	*The Fear of Population Decline.* Orlando, FL: Academic Press, 1985.
Henry Tenue	*Growth.* Newbury Park, CA: Sage Publications, 1988.
Irene Tinker	*Population: Dynamics, Ethics, and Policy.* Washington: American Association for the Advancement of Science, 1975.
UNFPA	*Population Perspectives: Statements by World Leaders.* 2nd ed. New York: United Nations Fund for Population Activities, 1985.
Ben Wattenberg	*The Birth Dearth.* New York: Pharos Books, 1987.
W. Weekes-Vagliani	*Women in Development: At the Right Time for the Right Reasons.* Paris: OECD, 1980.
Anthony B. Wolbarst	*Environment in Peril.* Washington: Smithsonian Institution Press, 1991.
Richard Woods	*Future Dimensions of World Food and Population.* Boulder, CO: Westview Press, 1981.
Anthony Zimmerman	*Catholic Viewpoint on Overpopulation.* New York: Hanover House, 1961.

Index

China, 24, 62, 72, 222, 223
  family planning policies of, 181
    are inhumane, 210, 212
    are necessary, 204-208
      con, 209-212
    forced sterilization program, 98-99
    success of, 205
  farm production, 119, 206
  infant mortality, 205-206
  population growth, 205, 207
Clinton, Bill, 99, 115, 163, 178
Cohen, Joel E., 64
conservation, water, 130-32
Cousteau, Jacques-Yves, 90

Daily, Gretchen C., 82
deforestation, 91
DeFreitas, Gregory, 157
developing countries
  agriculture in, 88, 97, 113, 119
  global economy's effect on, 170-72
  labor in, 172-73
  migration from 169-73
  population growth in, 83-84, 181
    policies to prevent, 98-99, 184
    promotes economic growth, 62
  poverty in
    due to unjust economic systems,
      184-86
    effect on children, 112
  relations with First World, 99, 178
  rising incomes in, 73, 74
  water problems in, 128
development, 78, 88, 184, 194
  AIDS threatens, 223
  destroys environment, 109-10, 113
  failures in the 1980s, 170
  inequitable, 184-85
  lack of, causes poverty, 116-17
  strategies needed for, 186-87
  will not reduce South-North
    migration, 169-73
  see also sustainability
disease, 18, 42, 112, 220
  sexually transmitted, 190, 197, 198
  see also AIDS; HIV
diversity, 137
  and immigration issue, 138, 145
  should be limited, 140, 141
drug trade, illegal, 95, 172

economists, 37, 39, 71
  faulty theories of, 38
  on population's role, 62, 97-98, 181
economy
  division of labor, 172
  free market, 94-95
  global
    impact on developing nations,
      170-72, 185
    promotes emigration from Third

World, 172-73
  socialist, 119
education
  immigrants' use of, 152
  is overstated, 160-61
  for women, 189, 194-95
Ehrlich, Anne, 67
Ehrlich, Paul R., 67, 82, 97
energy
  consumption, 91
    by affluent countries, 181
    per capita, 84-85, 87-88
  maximizing generation of, 43-44
  plant, 67-68
Engels, Frederick, 36
England
  checks on population of, 33-35
  economic development of, 27-28,
    34, 74, 220-21
  immigration to, 63, 139, 143
  poverty in, 25, 35, 37
English Poor Laws, 23, 29, 37
environment
  crisis
    is real, 107-10
    myth of, 104-106
  degradation of
    increased population causes, 83,
      84, 113, 180-81
      con, 80-81
    unjust economies and militarism
      cause, 186
  policies to protect
    family planning, 59, 180-81
    market incentives, 88-89, 181
    population control, 108, 181
  water shortages
    conservation can alleviate, 129-32
    population growth causes, 125-28
  see also agriculture; carrying
    capacity (Earth's)
environmentalists, 58, 99, 105
  doom prophesied by, 97, 98
  opposition to water diversion
    projects, 106
  prolife attacks on, 59-60
Essay on the Principle of Population,
  An (Malthus), 23, 29, 222
Ethiopia, 126
Europe
  Third World immigrants to, 169
  water quality in, 126, 128
  zero population growth in, 221

Falkenmark, Malin, 125
families
  definition of
    should be expanded, 187
      con, 193-94
  difficulty of rearing, 32-33, 34
  government hostility toward, 216-17

236

and immigration policies, 166, 172
limiting size of, 37, 38, 100, 182
men should share responsibilities,
189-90
should impose morality, 215-16, 218
see also children
family planning
abortion's role in, 193, 197, 201, 203
China's policy on
is inhumane, 210, 212
need for, 206-207
success of, 205
cultural beliefs against, 206
feminist concerns about
government-supported, 179-80
helps the environment, 59, 180-81
men's responsibility for, 198
must be promoted, 124, 181-82,
199-201
see also birth control; fertility rate;
policies, on population
famine, 25-26, 76, 220
Far Eastern Economic Review, editors
of, 209
female circumcision, 138-39, 179, 187
feminists
agenda of
economic opportunity for women,
100
health care, 180, 184, 186, 189
hurts population control, 177-82
necessary for transforming policy,
183-90
attacks on, 99
oppose fundamentalism, 187, 189
fertility rate, 98, 178
has been declining, 97, 120, 181, 223
should be increased, 18-20
fisheries, 109
Fix, Michael, 155
Flavin, Christopher, 113
Food and Agriculture Organization
(FAO), 79, 119, 123
food supply
grain production, 123, 124, 206
growth in, 119, 123
cannot keep pace with population,
32, 67-68, 88, 113
con, 40, 97, 120
due to scientific advances, 66, 88
limits on, 67-68
shortage of
is real, 122-24
myth of, 118-21
synthesizing, 44-45
using the ocean for, 42-43
see also agriculture
Frank, Judy Knight, 106
Fremlin, Joseph H., 41
fundamentalism, religious, 139, 184,
185, 187, 189, 195

gender relations
equality in, 189-90
see also women
Glass, D.V., 31
Godwin, William, 30, 31-32
government. See policies, on
population
Graham, Frank, Jr., 57
green revolution, 91
has reduced population problem, 97
con, 79, 81, 88
Grigg, Neil S., 131
growth, in population
Biblical passage on, 19
blamed on the poor, 37, 38
checks on, 25-26, 34-35, 42
international agencies should work
to stop, 90-95
con, 96-100
is beneficial, 61-63
is serious problem, 29-35, 83-84, 112
depletes Earth's resources, 64-68, 91
myth of, 36-40, 97
root of most world problems, 57-60
limits on
social, 85-86, 87
technical, 42-47
makes nations poor, 24
makes nations prosperous, 22, 62-63
rate of, 58, 83-84
in China, 205
doubling, 42, 178
geometric, 32, 40
must be brought to zero, 66, 68
U.N. projections on, 65, 84, 91-92,
108
will lead to population shortage,
69-74, 120-21
scientific progress will permit, 41-47
should be encouraged, 17-22
con, 23-28
space travel is impractical solution
to, 48-53
see also carrying capacity (Earth's)

Hardin, Garrett, 44, 48, 87, 136
health care, 182, 195
feminist agenda for, 180, 184, 186-87,
188, 189
for immigrants, 152, 199
nations should provide
reproductive,
197-98, 200-201
HIV, 188, 189, 197, 201, 220
Hon, Katherine, 131
Hong, Evelyn, 188
Hong Kong, 62, 143, 170, 212
housing, 46-47, 63
Huddle, Donald, 147, 159, 160, 161
human rights, 197
abortion violates, 193

Simmons, Alan B., 168
Simon, Julian L., 62-63, 69, 142
Singapore, 62, 170, 212
Smith, Adam, 30
Sobran, Joseph, 213
Social Security, 150, 151, 152, 160
society, 30
  future, with maximum population, 47
  tolerant vs. intolerant, 139-40
  tribal, imposes morality, 215-18
soil depletion, 79, 86, 108
space
  sending Earth's excess population
    into is impractical, 49-53
  travel, 51
    sociology of, 52-53
    time required for, 49-50
Spain, 21-22, 24
Struthers, Sally, 111
Süssmilch, Johann Peter, 17
sustainability, 78, 80, 81, 86, 88
  in resource management, 89
  see also development

taxes
  paid by immigrants, 149, 150-51
    are underestimated, 156, 158, 160
technology
  advances in, 97
    make carrying capacity studies
      invalid, 80-81
    will not permit unlimited growth,
      86-88, 92-93
  agricultural, 76, 77, 79, 80, 88
  cannot solve water shortages, 126
  environmental impact of, 84
Thomas, Cal, 114
Toolan, David S., 96
Townsend, Joseph, 23
trade, 28, 185
  evils caused by, 37-38
  international blocs of, 170, 172

UNESCO, 77, 79
United Nations
  Conference on Environment and
    Development, 89, 92, 99, 180, 223
  family planning policies
    are harmful, 98-100, 184
    should include voluntary
      abortion, 188
      con, 192-93, 201, 203
    should promote reproductive
      rights, 190
  Fund for Population Activities, 91-
    92, 98, 112, 210
    Clinton's restoration of funding
      to, 99, 115
    Reagan's funding cutoff, 58, 178
  International Conference on

Population and Development, 93,
    178, 184, 196
  abortion opponents' stance, 191-95
  projections on population growth,
    65, 84, 91-92, 188
  see also UNESCO
United States
  agricultural production in, 73
  customs of, 144, 145
  politics of, 144-45
  population control policies in, 115-17
  population growth in, 63, 65
  population's impact on Earth
    compared to others, 85
  water conservation in, 130, 131
  see also immigration, into the U.S.

vegetarianism, 42, 67, 86

war, 18, 119, 185, 220
water
  humans are depleting supplies of,
    86, 108
  management of, 131
  quality of, 127-28
  shortages of
    conservation can alleviate, 129-32
    population growth causes, 125-28
  use of, 126, 130-31
Wattenberg, Ben J., 70, 104
welfare. See public assistance
Westoff, Charles F., 177
white population, 138, 143
Widstrand, Carl, 125
Wilson, Pete, 166
women
  discrimination against, 124, 186
  family planning practices
    are central for, 198
    should be encouraged, 182
    should be included in policy
      development, 197-98
    U.N. population programs have
      harmed, 98-99, 184
  fertility rate, 186, 188
  fundamentalists' attack on, 187, 189
  genital mutilation of, 138-39, 179,
    187
  improved economic status for, 100,
    179, 186
  migration of, 186, 199
  role of should be expanded, 195
  sexuality of, 189
  violence against, 185, 186, 187, 189,
    195, 199
World Health Organization, 201, 220
Worldwatch Institute, 122, 129

zero population growth, 66, 68, 119,
  221

240